COMBAT IN BUILT-UP AREAS

Subcourse Number IN0531

United State Army Infantry School
Fort Benning, GA 31905-5593

8 credit hours

Effective Date: December 1992

OVERVIEW

In this subcourse you will learn the principles governing military operations in urbanized terrain, specifically how to wage combat in built-up areas.

There are no prerequisites for this subcourse.

Unless otherwise stated, the masculine gender of singular pronouns is used to refer to both men and women.

TERMINAL LEARNING OBJECTIVE:

ACTION: You will identify the principles of combat in built-up areas.

CONDITION: You will be given information from FM 90-10-1.

STANDARD: To demonstrate competency of this task, you must achieve a minimum of 70 percent on the subcourse examination.

REFERENCES: The material contained in this subcourse was derived from the following publication:

FM 90-10-1

Table of Contents

LESSON 1

PRINCIPLES OF COMBAT IN BUILT-UP AREAS

OVERVIEW

LESSON DESCRIPTION:

In this lesson you will learn the principles guiding combat in built-up areas and military operations on urbanized terrain (MOUT). You will learn about the offensive and defensive operations of potential adversaries, our own concept of the offense and defense in an urban environment with examples of battalion task force, company, and platoon attacks on defended built-up areas. You will also learn the characteristics of built-up areas, and defensive operations at the battalion, company, and platoon levels.

TERMINAL LEARNING OBJECTIVE:

ACTION: Identify the principles of combat in built-up areas.

CONDITION: You will be given information from FM 90-10-1.

STANDARD: The principles of combat in built-up areas will be identified in accordance with FM 90-10-1.

REFERENCES The material contained in this lesson was derived from the

INTRODUCTION

The increased population and accelerated growth of cities have made the problems of combat in built-up areas an urgency for the U.S. Army. This type of combat cannot be avoided. The distribution of smaller, built-up areas within the urban complex make isolation by encirclement increasingly difficult. Military operations on urbanized terrain (MOUT) can now be defined as the future battlefield in Europe and Asia with brigade and higher-level commanders focusing on these operations. At the tactical level, the battalion commander and his subordinates must focus on the actual combat in built-up areas. This subcourse provides the infantry battalion commander and his subordinates a source for tactics, techniques, and procedures for fighting in built-up areas.

PART A - INTRODUCTION TO COMBAT IN BUILT-UP AREAS

1. <u>Background</u>.

Friendly and enemy doctrine reflect the fact that more attention must be given to urban combat. Expanding urban development affects military operations as the terrain is altered. Although the current doctrine still applies, the increasing focus on low intensity conflict (LIC), urban terrorism, and civil disorder emphasizes combat in built-up areas is unavoidable.

    a. <u>AirLand Battle</u>. AirLand Battle doctrine describes the Army's approach to generating and applying combat power at the operational and tactical levels. It is based on securing or retaining the initiative and exercising it aggressively to accomplish the mission. The four basic AirLand Battle tenets of initiative, agility, depth, and synchronization are constant. During combat in built-up areas, the principles of AirLand Battle doctrine still apply -- only the terrain over which combat operations will be conducted has changed.

    b. <u>Cities</u>. Cities are the centers of finance, politics, transportation, communication, industry, and culture. Therefore, they have often been scenes of important battles (Figure 1-1).

        (1) Operations in built-up areas are conducted to capitalize on the strategic and tactical advantages of cities and to deny those advantages to the enemy. Often, the side which controls a city has a psychological advantage which is usually enough to determine the outcome of larger conflicts.

        (2) Even in insurgencies, combat occurs in cities. In developing nations, control of only a few cities is often the key to control of national resources.

Thus, urban guerrilla war is quickly replacing rural guerrilla war as the most common form of insurgency. The city riots of the 1960s and the guerrilla and terrorist operations in Santo Domingo, Caracas, Belfast, Managua, and Beirut indicate the many situations which can result in combat operations in built-up areas.

(3) Built-up areas also affect military operations because of the way they alter the terrain. In the past 40 years, cities have expanded, losing their well-defined boundaries as they extend into the countryside. New road systems have opened areas to make them passable. Highways, canals, and railroads have been built to connect population centers. Industries have grown along those connectors creating "strip areas." Rural areas, although retaining much of their farm-like character, are connected to the towns by a network of secondary roads (Figure 1-2).

CITY	YEAR	CITY	YEAR
RIGA	1917	*SEOUL	1950
MADRID	1936	BUDAPEST	1956
WARSAW	1939	*BEIRUT	1958
ROTTERDAM	1940	*SANTO DOMINGO	1965
MOSCOW	1942	*SAIGON	1968
STALINGRAD	1942	*KONTUM	1968
LENINGRAD	1942	*HUE	1968
WARSAW	1943	BELFAST	1972
*PALERMO	1944	MONTEVIDEO	1972
*BREST	1944	QUANGTRI CITY	1972
WARSAW	1944	AN LOC	1972
*AACHEN	1944	XUAN LOC	1975
ORTONA	1944	SAIGON	1975
*CHERBOURG	1944	BEIRUT	1975-1978
BRESLAU	1945	MANAGUA	1978
*WEISSENFELS	1945	ZAHLE	1981
BERLIN	1945	TYRE	1982
*MANILA	1945	*BEIRUT	1983
*SAN MANUAL	1945	*PANAMA CITY	1989-1990
		*COLON	1989-1990

*DIRECT US TROOP INVOLVEMENT

Figure 1-1. Cities contested during 20th century conflicts.

(4) These trends have occurred in most parts of the world, but they are the most dramatic in Western Europe. European cities tend to grow together to form one vast built-up area. Entire regions assume an unbroken built-up character, as is the case in the Ruhr and Rhein Main complex. Such growth patterns block and dominate the historic armor avenues of approach, and decrease the amount of open maneuver area available to an attacker. It is estimated a typical brigade sector, will include 25 small towns, most of which would lie in the more open avenues of approach (Figure 1-3).

(5) Extensive urbanization provides conditions the defending force can exploit. Used with mobile forces on the adjacent terrain, antitank forces defending from built-up areas can dominate avenues of approach, greatly improving the overall strength of the defense (Figure 1-4).

4

(6) Forces operating in such areas may have elements in open terrain, villages, towns, or small and large cities. Each of these areas calls for different tactics, task organization, fire support, and combat service support (CSS).

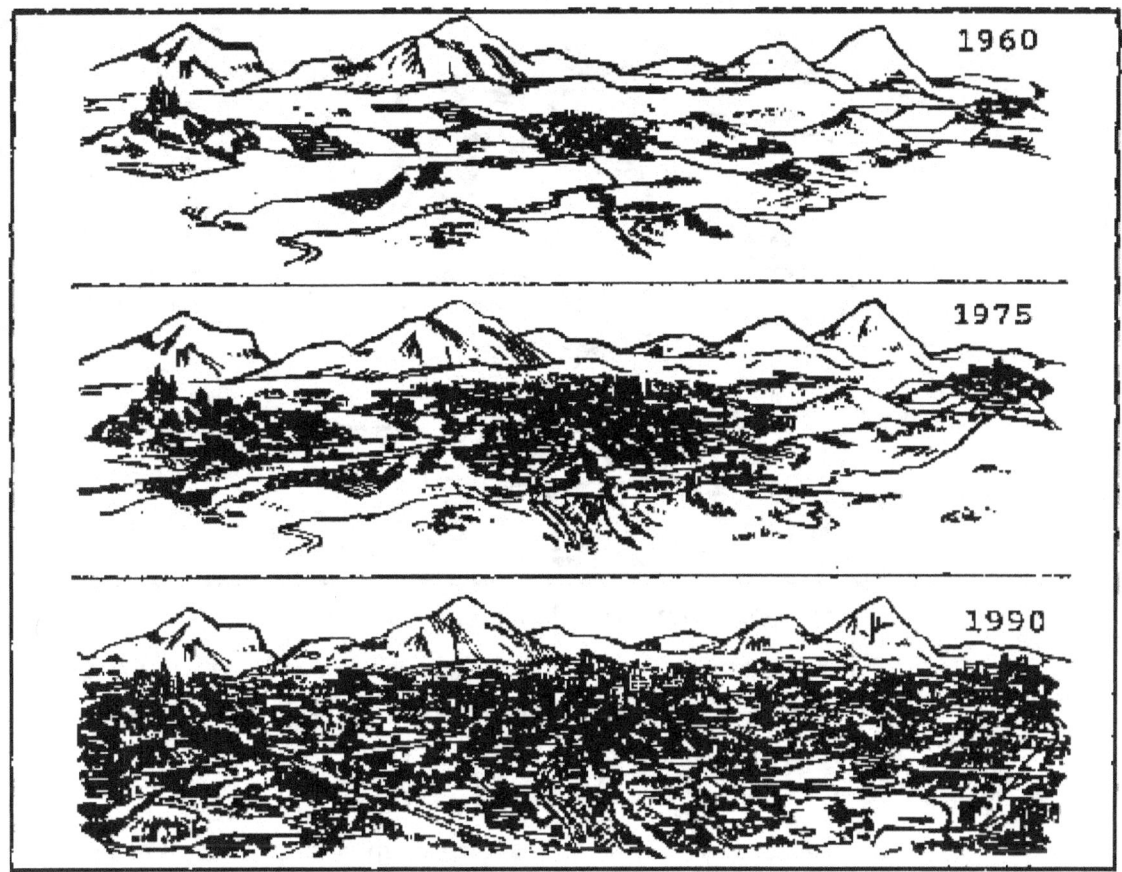

Figure 1-2. Urban terrain sprawl

c. The Threat in Built-up Areas. The Commonwealth of Independent States and other nations using former Soviet doctrine, devote much of their training to urban combat exercises. Indications are, they too believe such combat would be unavoidable in future conflicts. During the late 1980s, they published hundreds of articles on combat in built-up areas.

(1) The stated preferred form of attacking a city is from the march to quickly neutralize the city. Should that attack fail, the units would be organized for an attack by storm, attaching armor, artillery, and engineers to their motorized rifle battalions. They would probably have assaulted built-up areas with strong forces, because the loss of men and equipment was considered less important than the loss of time.

Figure 1-3. Urban areas blocking maneuver areas

(2) A list of success requirements for offensive operations in built-up areas have been developed by the former soviet planners. These requirements were:

- Concealing preparation of assault groups.

- Using surprise to seize enemy strongpoints at the city's edge.

- Rapidly exploiting initial success by the immediate follow-up of preparatory fires.

- Using heavy weapons in a direct-fire role by task-organized assault groups.

(3) The threat of combat in built-up areas cannot be limited to former Soviet doctrine. Throughout many Third World countries, the possibility of combat in built-up areas exists through acts of insurgents, guerrillas, and terrorists.

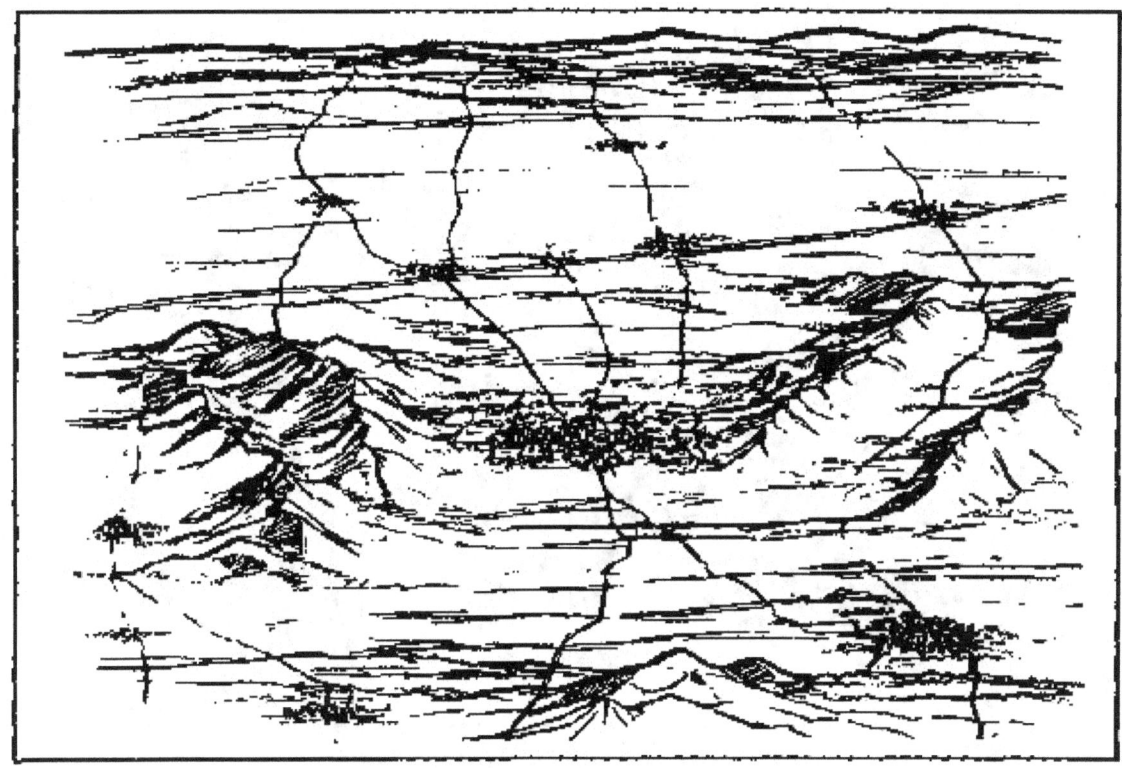

Figure 1-4. Available fields of fire

2. <u>Characteristics and Categories of Built-up Areas.</u>

One of the first requirements for conducting operations in built-up areas is to understand the common characteristics and categories of such areas.

    a. <u>Characteristics</u>. Built-up areas consist mainly of man-made features such as buildings. Buildings provide cover and concealment, limit fields of observation and fire, and block movement of troops, especially mechanized troops. Thick-walled buildings provide ready-made, fortified positions. Thin-walled buildings with fields of observation and fire may also be important.

        (1) Streets are usually avenues of approach. However, forces moving along streets are often canalized by the buildings and have little space for off-road maneuver. Thus, obstacles on streets in towns are usually more effective than those on roads in open terrain since they are more difficult to bypass.

        (2) Subterranean systems found in some built-up areas are easily overlooked but can be important to the outcome of operations. They include subways, sewers, cellars, and utility systems (Figure 1-5).

7

Figure 1-5. Underground systems

b. <u>Categories</u>. Built-up areas are classified into four categories:

- Villages (population of 3,000 or less).

- Strip areas (urban areas built along roads connecting towns or cities).

- Towns or small cities (population up to 100,000 and not part of a major urban complex).

- Large cities with associated urban sprawl (population in the millions, covering hundreds of square kilometers).

Each area affects operations differently. Villages and strip areas are commonly encountered by companies and battalions. Towns and small cities involve operations of entire brigades or divisions. Large cities and major urban complexes involve units up to corps size and above.

3. <u>Special Considerations</u>.

Several considerations are addressed herein concerning combat in built-up areas.

a. <u>Battles in Built-up Areas</u>. Battles in built-up areas usually occur when one or more of the following conditions are present:

- A city is between two natural obstacles and there is no bypass.

- The seizure of a city contributes to the attainment of an overall objective.

- The city is in the path of a general advance and cannot be surrounded or bypassed.

- Political or humanitarian concerns require the seizure or retention of a city.

8

b. <u>Target Engagement</u>. In the city, the ranges of observation and fields of fire are reduced by structures as well as by the dust and smoke of battle. Targets are usually briefly exposed at ranges of 100 meters or less. As a result, combat in built-up areas consists mostly of close, violent combat. Infantry troops will use mostly light antitank weapons, automatic rifles, and hand grenades. Opportunities for using antitank guided missiles (ATGMs) are rare because of the short ranges involved and the many obstructions interfering with missile flight.

c. <u>Small-unit Battles</u>. Units fighting in built-up areas often become isolated, making combat a series of small-unit battles. Soldiers and small-unit leaders must have the initiative, skill, and courage to accomplish their missions while isolated from their parent units. A skilled, well-trained defender has tactical advantages over the attacker in this type of combat. He occupies strong positions, whereas the attacker must be exposed in order to advance. Greatly reduced line-of-sight ranges, built-in obstacles, and compartmented terrain require the commitment of more troops for a given frontage. The troop density for both an attack and defense in built-up areas can be as much as three to five times greater than for an attack or defense in open terrain. Individual soldiers must be trained and psychologically ready for this type of operation.

d. <u>Munitions and Special Equipment</u>. Forces engaged in fighting in built-up areas use large quantities of munitions because of the need for reconnaissance by fire, which is due to short ranges and limited visibility. Light antitank weapons (LAWs), rifle and machine gun ammunition, 40-mm grenades, hand grenades, explosives, and flame weapons are high-usage items in this type of fighting. Units committed to combat in built-up areas also must have special equipment such as grappling hooks, rope, snaplinks, collapsible pole ladders, rope ladders, construction materials, axes, and sandbags. When possible, those items should be either stockpiled or brought forward on-call, so they are easily available to the troops.

e. <u>Communications</u>. Another characteristic of combat in built-up areas is degraded radio communications caused by the mass of buildings and a high concentration of electrical power lines. This includes the new series of radios. Many buildings are constructed so radio waves will not pass through them. Combined with the difficulty of observation, this can hinder control. Urban operations require centralized planning and decentralized execution. You must trust your subordinates' initiative and skill, which can only occur through training. The state of your unit's training is a vital, decisive factor in the execution of operations in built-up areas.

f. <u>Stress</u>. A related problem of combat in built-up areas is stress. Continuous close combat, intense pressure, high casualties, fleeting targets, and concealed enemy fire produce psychological strain and physical fatigue for the soldier. Such stress requires consideration for the soldiers' and small-unit leaders' morale and the unit's esprit de corps. Reduce stress by rotating units committed to heavy combat for long periods.

g. <u>Restrictions</u>. The law of war prohibits unnecessary injury to noncombatants and needless damage to property. This may restrict the commander's use of certain weapons and tactics. Although a disadvantage at the time, this restriction may be necessary to preserve a nation's cultural institutions and to gain the support of its people. Units must be highly disciplined so the law of land warfare and the rules of engagement are obeyed.

(1) Combat in built-up areas has historically presented soldiers with the opportunity for looting which alienates the civilian population. When soldiers loot, they are tempted to discard needed equipment so they can carry their stolen goods, causing a loss of combat efficiency.

(2) Looting can cause a breakdown of discipline, reduce alertness, increase vulnerability, and delay the progress of the unit. You must strictly enforce orders against looting and expeditiously dispose of violations against the Uniform Code of Military Justice (UCMJ).

PART B - INTELLIGENCE PREPARATION OF THE BATTLEFIELD

Intelligence preparation of the battlefield (IPB) is a key element of operations conducted in built-up areas -- intelligence is an important part of every combat decision. To succeed as fighters in built-up areas, you must know the nature of built-up areas and analyze its effect on both enemy and friendly forces. This part of the lesson consists of information concerning the development of an IPB for any built-up area.

1. Regional Urban Characteristics.

Cities of the world are characterized by density of construction and population, street patterns, compartmentalization, and the presence of utility systems. The difference in built-up areas are in size, level of development, and style.

a. Specific Characteristics of Urban Areas. A summary of regional urban characteristics follows.

(1) Middle East and North Africa. All nations in the region can be reached by sea and urbanization rates are high. This region has long, hot, dry summers and mild winters, making life outside cities difficult. In spite of its vast deserts, greater urban congestion has resulted. Ancient cities have expanded into the current metropolises and many new cities have been created because of the petroleum industry (mainly in the Persian Gulf).

(2) Latin America. Most urban centers can be reached by sea with many capitals serving as ports. This is a region with a mainly tropical climate. Its architecture has a strong Spanish influence characterized by broad avenues radiating outward from a central plaza with a large church and town hall. Upper and middle class sections combine with urban centers, while the lower class sections are located further out.

(3) Far East. Except for Mongolia, all nations in this region can be reached

by sea. Urbanization is dense, especially in coastal cities where modern commercial centers are surrounded by vast industrial developments and residential centers.

(4) <u>South Asia</u>. This region has a great European influence with wide busy streets which are overcrowded. Urban centers may be composed mainly of poorer native sections with few or no public service and alleys no more than a yard wide.

(5) <u>Southeast Asia</u>. This region also has strong European influences with all capitals and major cities serving as seaports. Urban centers contain both the older, high-density native quarters with temples or religious shrines, and modern sections with boulevards, parks, and warehouses.

(6) <u>Sub-Sahara Africa</u>. In contrast to other regions, this region cannot be accessed by sea and has impassable terrain. Except for a few kingdoms, towns did not exist before the arrival of the Europeans. As a result, urban areas are relatively modern and without an "old quarters," although many do have "shanty towns."

b. <u>Characteristics of Urban Areas</u>. A typical urban area consists of the city core, commercial ribbon, core periphery, residential sprawl, outlying industrial areas, and outlying high-rise areas. Each of the model's regions has distinctive characteristics. Most urban areas resemble the generalized model shown in Figure 1-6.

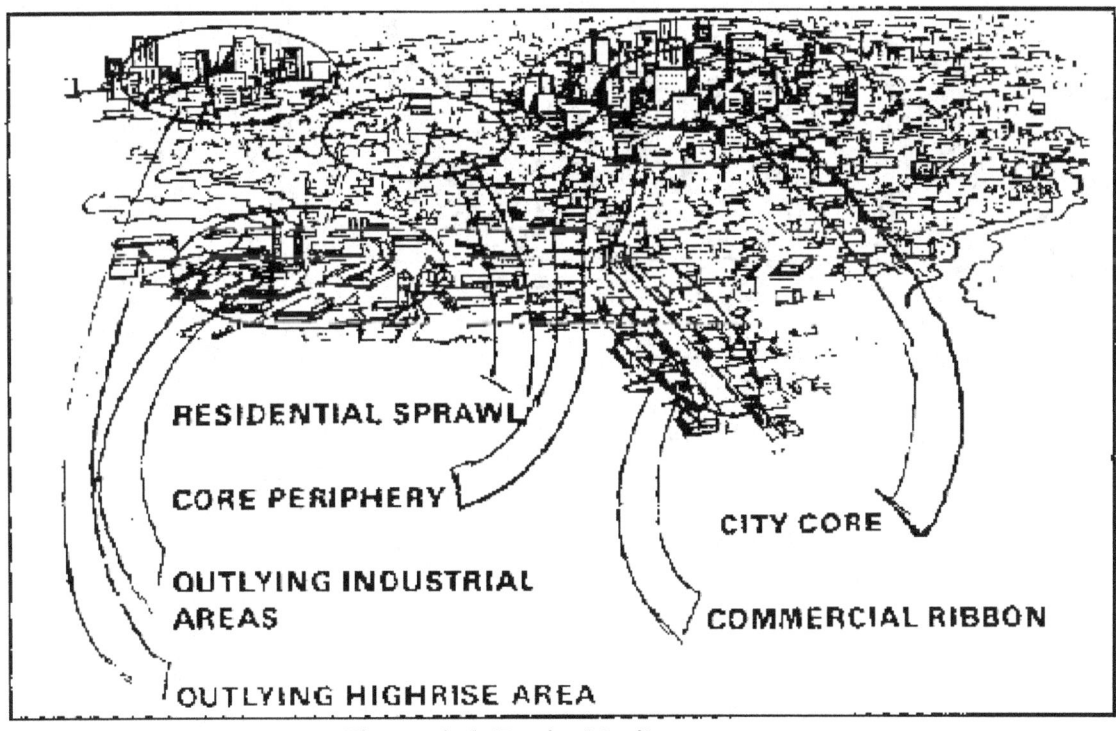

Figure 1-6. Typical built-up area

(1) In most cities, the core has undergone more recent development than the core periphery. As a result the two regions are often quite different.

11

Typical city cores of today are made up of high-rise buildings, which vary greatly in height. Modern planning for built-up areas allows for more open spaces between buildings than in old city cores or in core peripheries. Outlying high-rise areas are dominated by this open construction style more than city cores (Figures 1-7 and 1-8).

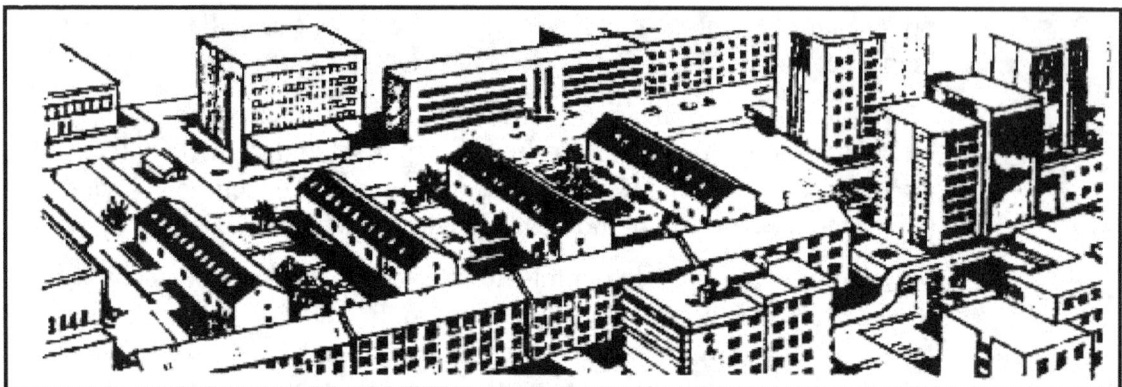

Figure 1-7. City core

Figure 1-8. Outlying high-rise area

(2) Commercial ribbons are rows of stores, shops, and restaurants built along both sides of major streets through built-up areas. Usually, such streets are 25 meters wide or more. The buildings are uniformly two to three stories tall --about one story taller than the dwellings on the streets behind them (Figure 1-9).

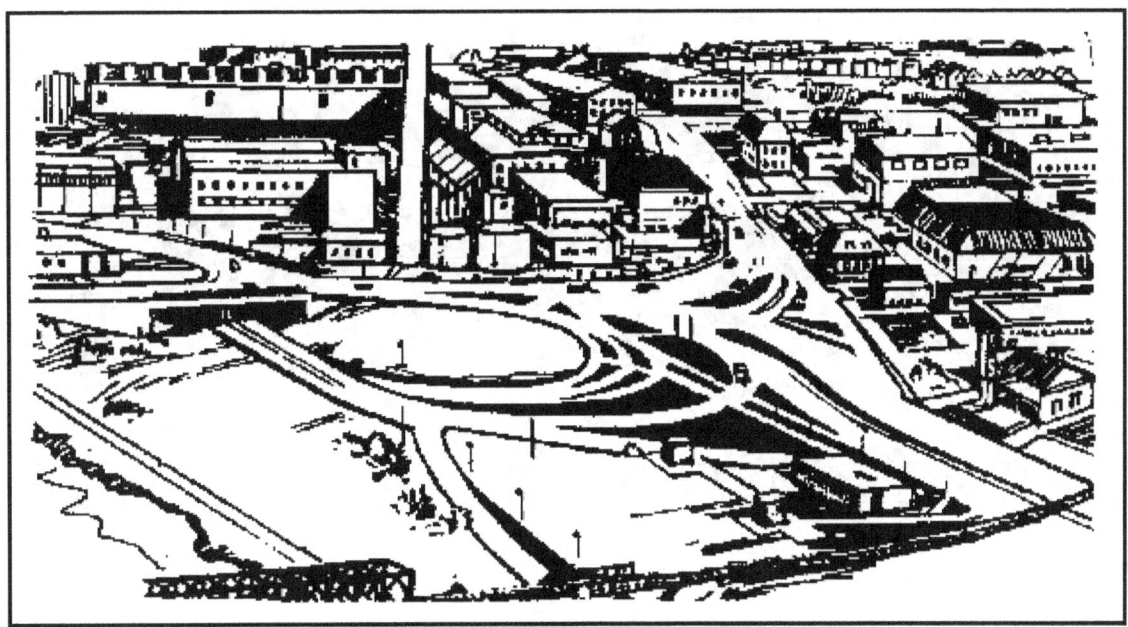

Figure 1-9. Commercial ribbons

(3) The core periphery consists of streets 10 to 20 meters wide with continuous fronts of brick or concrete buildings. The building heights are fairly uniform -- two or three stories in small towns, 5 to 10 stories in large cities (Figure 1-10).

Figure 1-10. Core periphery

(4) Residential sprawl and outlying industrial areas consist of low buildings one to three stories tall. Buildings are detached and arranged in irregular patterns along the streets with many open areas (Figures 1-11 and 1-12).

13

Figure 1-11. Residential sprawl

Figure 1-12. Outlying industrial areas

2. <u>Analysis of Buildings</u>.

An analysis of buildings provides essential information in developing the concept of combat operations in built-up areas.

    a. <u>Types of Construction</u>. The two basic types of building construction are mass (or frameless) and framed.

        (1) <u>Mass-construction Buildings</u>. Mass-construction buildings are those in which the outside walls support the weight of the building and its contents. The older mass-construction buildings are usually made of thick brick or stone walls. Mass-construction buildings normally have thicker walls and fewer windows than framed buildings. The windows must be aligned vertically so the walls can support the weight of the building. Additional support especially in wide buildings, comes from using load-bearing interior walls, strongpoints (called pilasters) on the exterior walls, cast-iron interior columns, and arches or braces over the windows and doors (Figure

14

1-13). Modern types of mass-construction buildings are wall-and-slab structures such as many modern apartments and hotels, and "tilt-up" structures, commonly used for industry or storage. Mass-construction buildings are built in many ways as follow:

- The walls can be built in place using brick, block, or poured-in-place concrete.

- The walls can be prefabricated and "tilt-up" or reinforced-concrete panels.

- The walls can be prefabricated and assembled like a number of boxes.

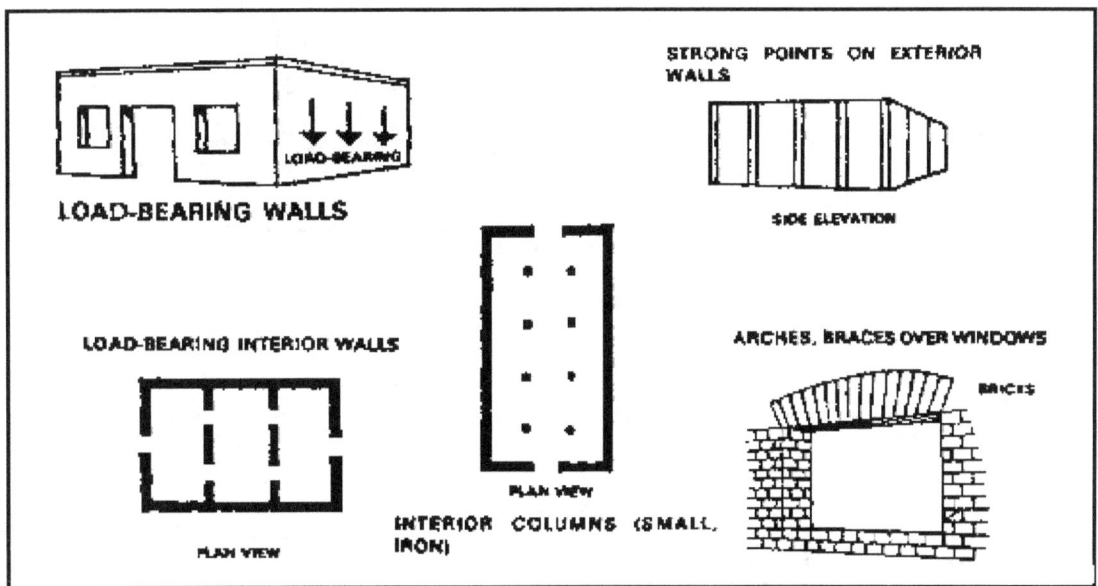

Figure 1-13. Mass-construction building

(a) <u>Brick Buildings</u>. Brick buildings are the most common and most important of the mass-construction buildings. In Europe, brick buildings are commonly covered with a stucco veneer so the bricks do not show (Figure 1-14).

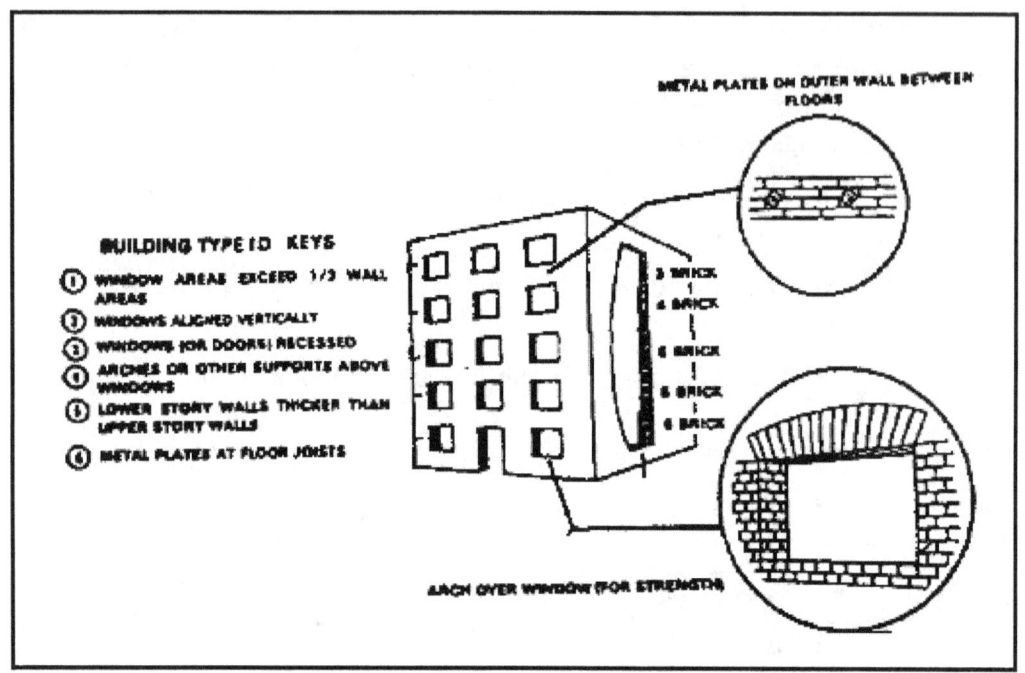

Figure 1-14. Brick buildings

One of the most common uses of brick buildings is the small commercial store. These brick stores are found in all built-up areas, but most commonly in the core periphery (Figure 1-15).

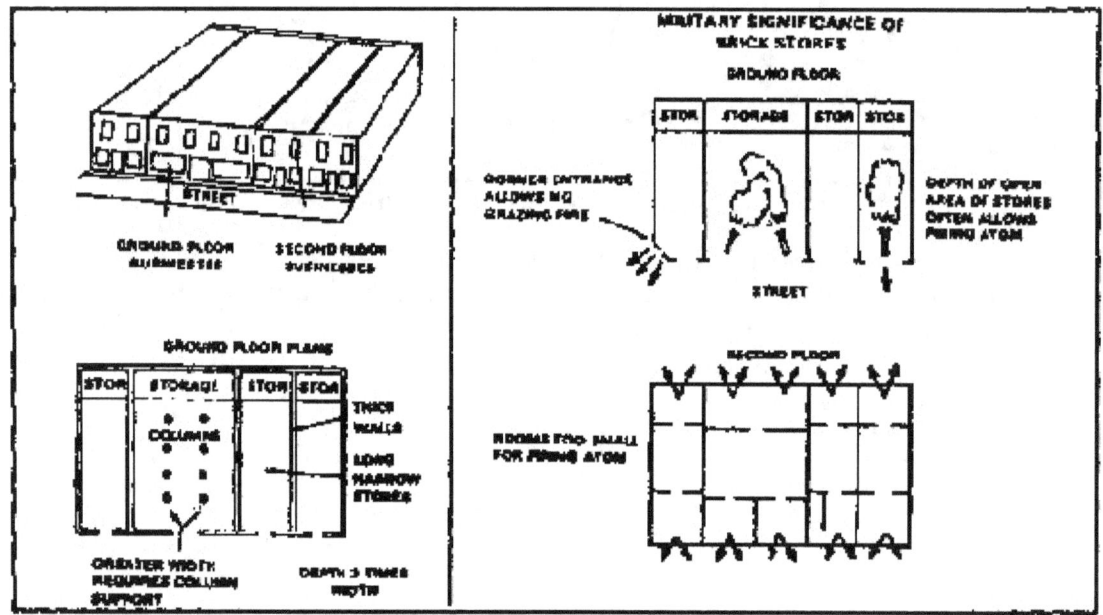

Figure 1-15. Brick store

(b) Warehouses. Another common mass-construction building in industrial areas and along commercial ribbons is the warehouse. It is built of poured-in-place concrete reinforced with steel bars or of prefabricated walls that are "tilt-up." The walls of warehouses provide good cover although the roof is vulnerable. The

16

warehouses' large open bays permit firing of antitank guided missiles (ATGMs) and, because they are normally found in outlying areas, often afford adequate fields of fire for ATGMs. These buildings are built on slabs, which can normally support the weight of vehicles and can provide excellent cover and concealment for tanks (Figure 1-16).

(c) <u>Box-wall Buildings</u>. Another mass-construction building is the box-wall principle type. It is made from prefabricated concrete panels, which are made up of six to eight-inch-thick reinforced concrete. The outside wall is often glass. The box-wall principle building provides good cover, except at the glass wall.

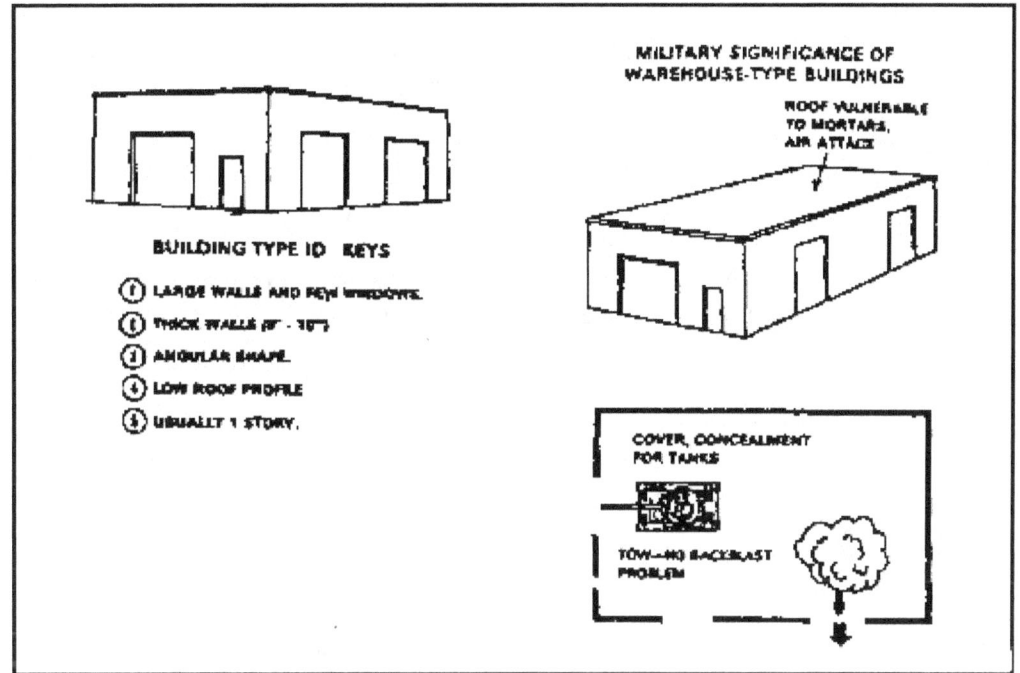

Figure 1-16. Warehouse

The rooms are normally too small for ATGMs to be fired. A good circulation pattern exists from room to room and from floor to floor. These buildings are commonly used as hotels or apartments and are located in residential and outlying areas (Figure 1-17).

17

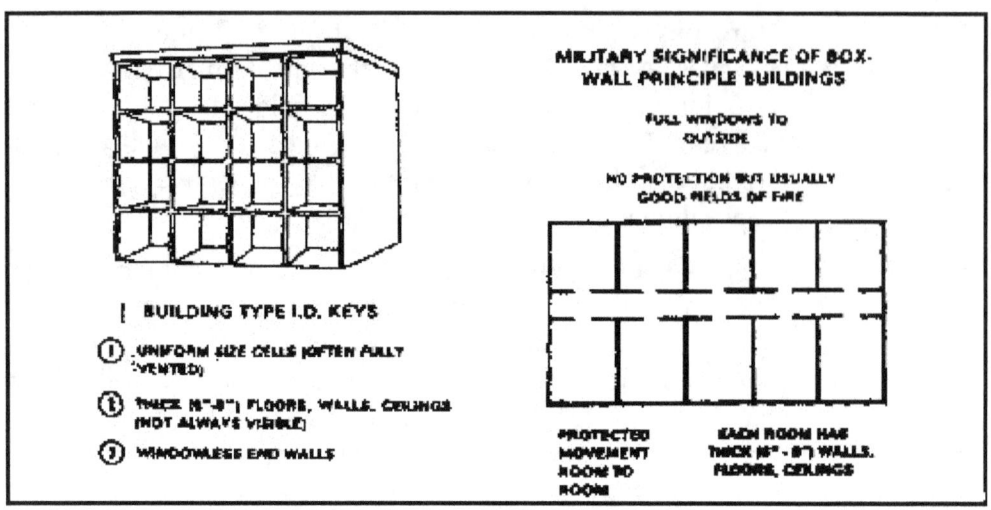

Figure 1-17. Box-wall principle building

(d) <u>Public Gathering Places</u>. Public gathering places (churches, theaters) are mass-construction buildings with large, open interiors. The walls provide good cover, but the roof does not. The interior walls are not load-bearing, and are normally easy to breach or remove. These buildings have adequate interior space for firing ATGMs. They are often located next to parks or other open areas and, therefore, have fields of fire long enough for ATGMs. Public gathering places are most common in core, core periphery, residential, and outlying high-rise areas (Figure 1-18).

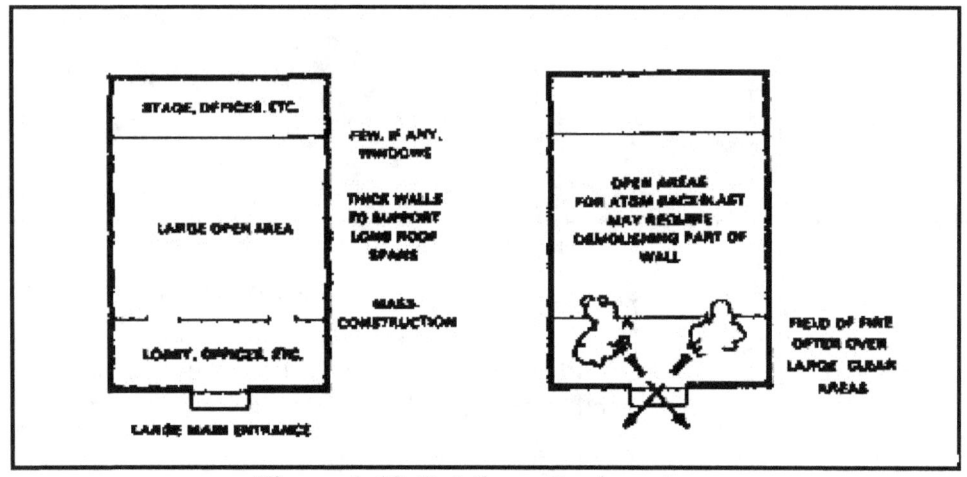

Figure 1-18. Public gathering place

(2) <u>Frame Construction</u>. Framed buildings are supported by a skeleton of columns and beams, and are usually taller than frameless buildings. The exterior walls are not load-bearing and are referred to as either, heavy-clad or light-clad buildings. Heavy-clad walls were common when framed buildings were first introduced. Their walls are made of brick and block, which are sometimes almost as thick as frameless brick walls, although not as protective. Light-clad walls are more modern and may be constructed mostly of glass (Figure 1-19).

18

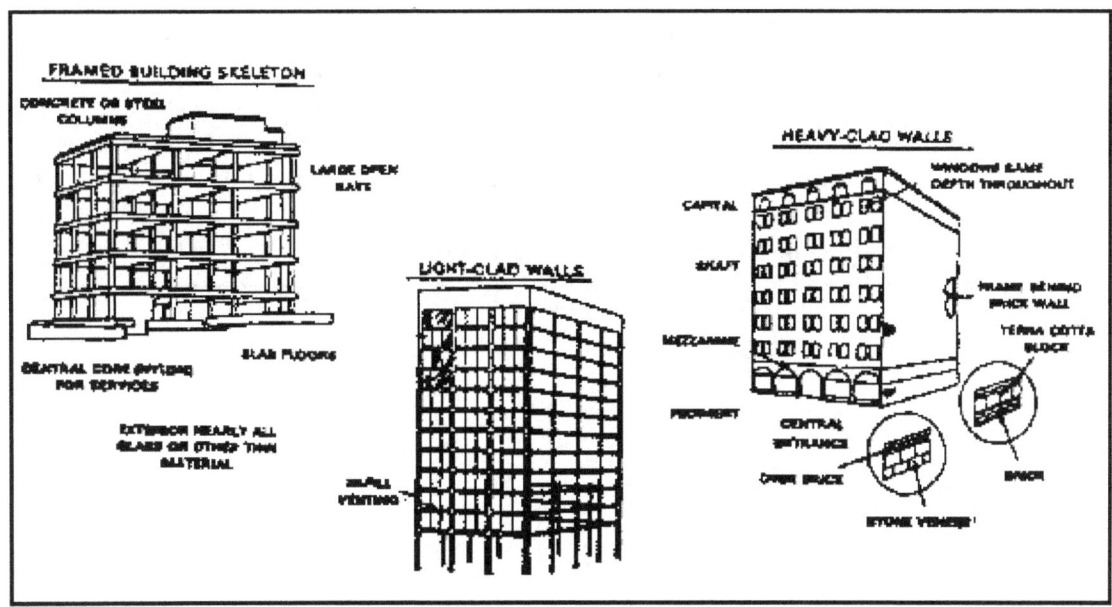

Figure 1-19. Framed buildings

(a) <u>Heavy Clad</u>. Heavy-clad framed buildings are found in core and core periphery areas. They can be recognized by a classic style or architecture in which each building is designed with three sections -- the pediment, shaft, and capital. Unlike the brick building, the walls are the same thickness on all floors, and the windows are set at the same depth throughout. Often the frame members (the columns) can be seen, especially at the ground floor. The cladding, consisting of layers of terra cotta blocks, brick, and stone veneer, does not provide as good a cover as the walls of brick buildings. It protects against small-arms fire and light shrapnel, but does not provide much protection against heavy weapons (Figure 1-20).

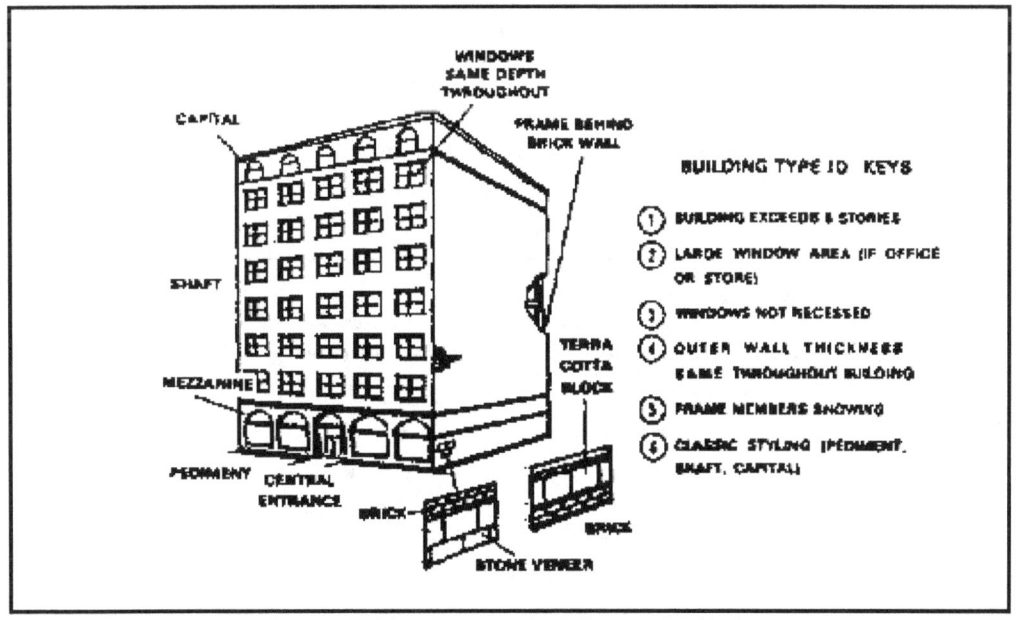

Figure 1-20. Heavy-clad frame building

19

The floor plans of these buildings depend upon their functions. Office buildings normally have small offices surrounding an interior hall. These offices have the same dimensions as the distance between columns (some large offices are as large as two times the distance between columns). These rooms are too small to permit firing of ATGMs but do provide some cover for snipers or machine gunners (Figure 1-21).

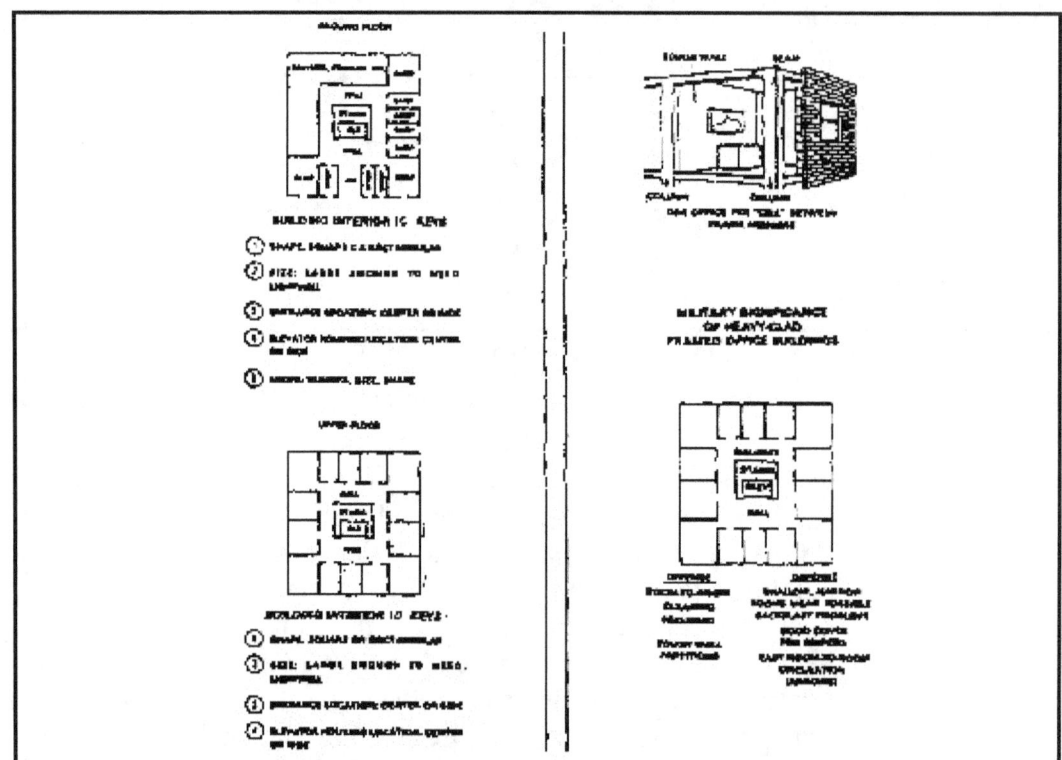

Figure 1-21. Floor plan of heavy-clad framed office building with office and military details

Department stores normally have large open interiors. Such areas permit firing ATGMs (if there are adequate fields of fire). Often a mezzanine level with a large backblast area permits firing down onto tanks. Steel fire doors often exist between sections of the store (Figure 1-22).

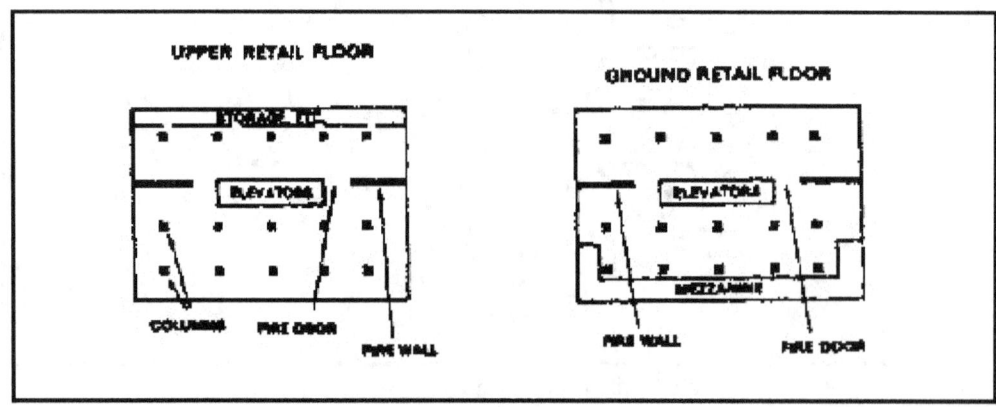

Figure 1-22. Heavy-clad framed department store

The steel fire doors are activated by heat. Once closed, they are difficult to breach or force open, but they effectively divide the store into sections (Figure 1-23).

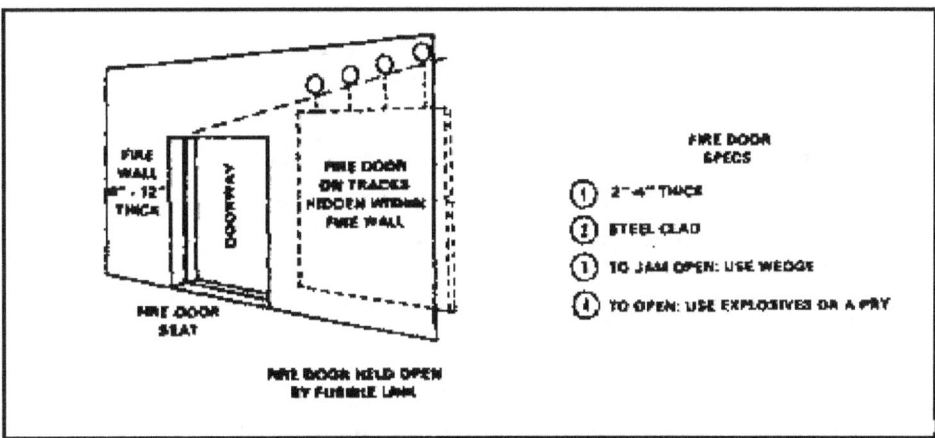

Figure 1-23. Fire wall and fire door

Another type of heavy-clad, framed building is used as a high-rise factory (Figure 1-24). Such buildings can normally be easily recognized because the concrete beams and columns are visible from the outside. They are usually located in older industrial areas. The large windows and open interior favor the use of ATGMs. Because the floors are often made to support heavy machinery, this building provides good overhead cover.

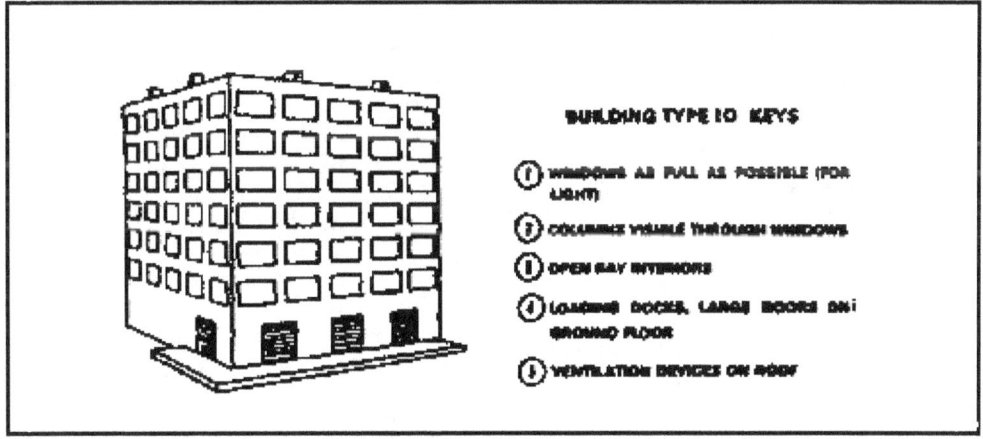

Figure 1-24. High-rise factory

(b) Light Clad. Most framed buildings built since World War II are light-clad buildings. They are found in both core and outlying high-rise regions. Their walls consist of a thin layer of brick, lightweight concrete, or glass. Such materials provide minimal protection against any weapon. However, the floors of the buildings are much heavier, and provide moderate overhead cover (Figure 1-25).

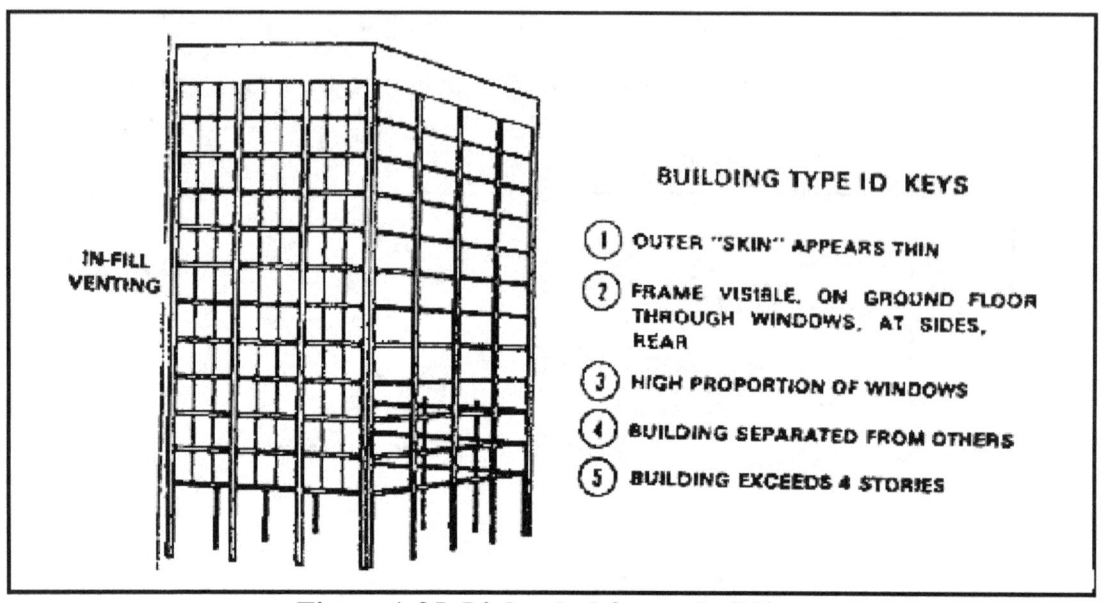

Figure 1-25. Light-clad frame building

The rooms in light-clad frame buildings are much bigger than those in heavy-clads. This feature along with the' fact the buildings usually stand detached from other buildings, favors employment of ATGMs. The interior partitions are thin and light, and are easy to breach (Figure 1-26).

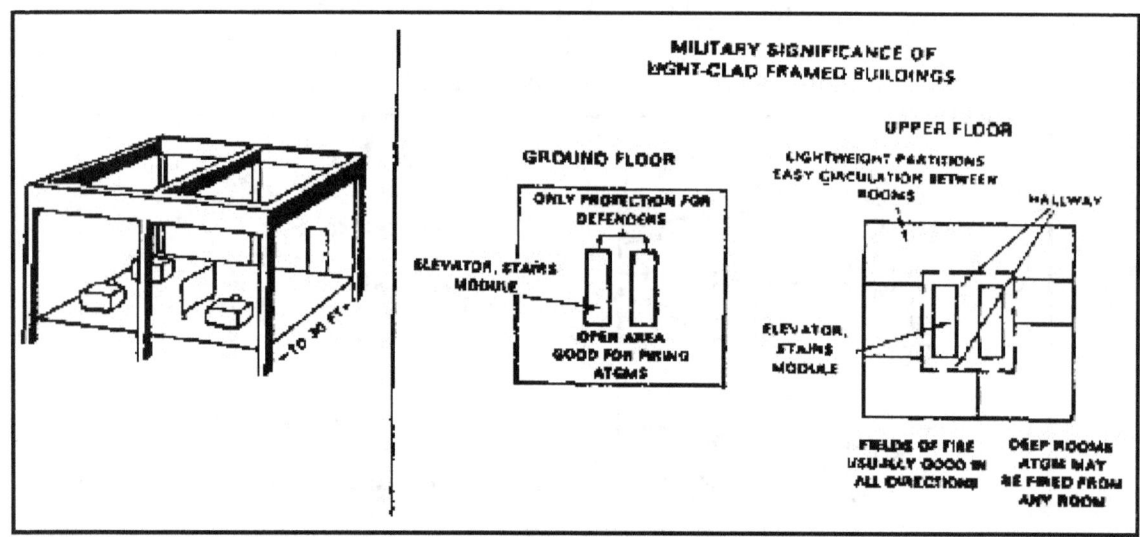

Figure 1-26. Rooms in light-clad frame structure

(c) <u>Garage</u>. Another type of framed building is the garage, which is often found in cities and has no cladding. The garage is one of the few buildings in an urban area in which all floors support vehicles. It provides a means to elevate vehicle-mounted, tube-launched, optically-tracked, wire-guided (missiles) (TOWs), and the open interiors permit firing of ATGMs. Garages are normally high enough to provide a 360-degree field of fire for antiaircraft weapons. For example, a Stinger could hide under the top floor of the garage, come out to engage an aircraft and then take cover again (Figure 1-27).

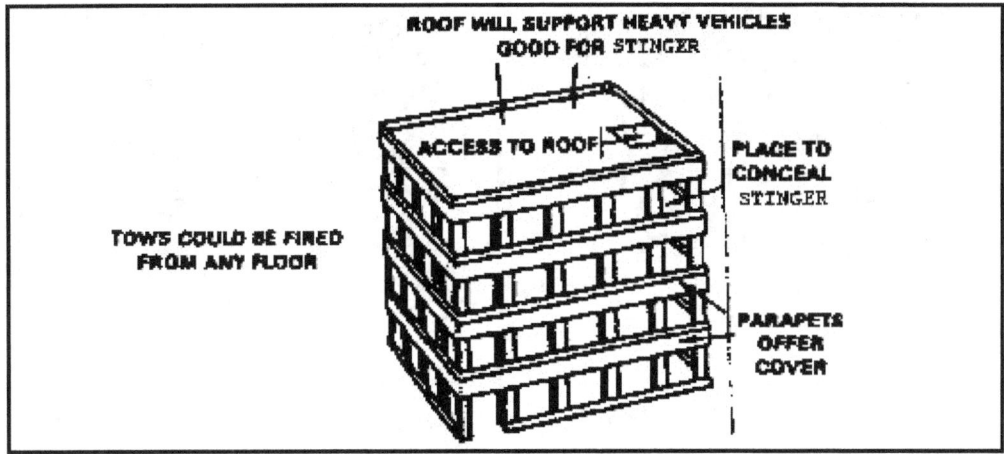

Figure 1-27. Garage

b. Floor Plans. Floor plans in buildings follow predictable patterns. One of the factors that determines floor plans is building shape (Figure 1-28). The basic principle governing building shape is that rooms normally have access to outside light. This principle helps to analyze and determine the floor plans of large buildings.

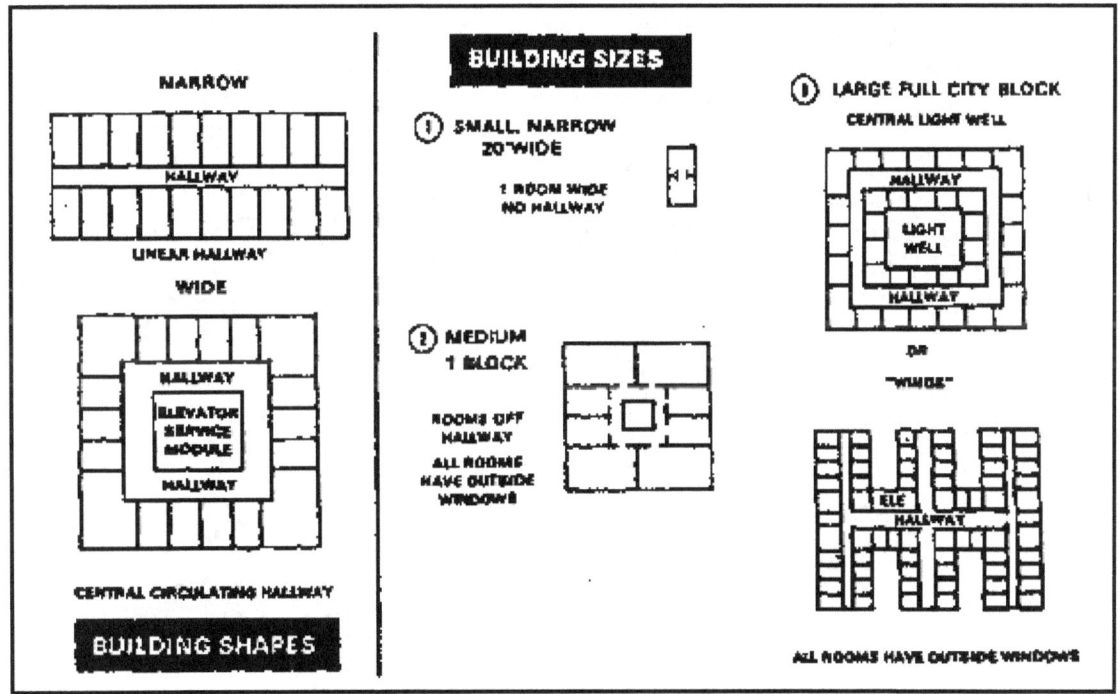

Figure 1-28. Building shapes and sizes

c. Residential Areas. The two basic types of houses in the western world are located in and around cities and in rural areas. City houses are normally mass-construction brick buildings while rural buildings in the continental U.S. are commonly made of wood. In Germany, wood is extremely scarce and rural buildings are normally constructed of concrete blocks (Figure 1-29).

23

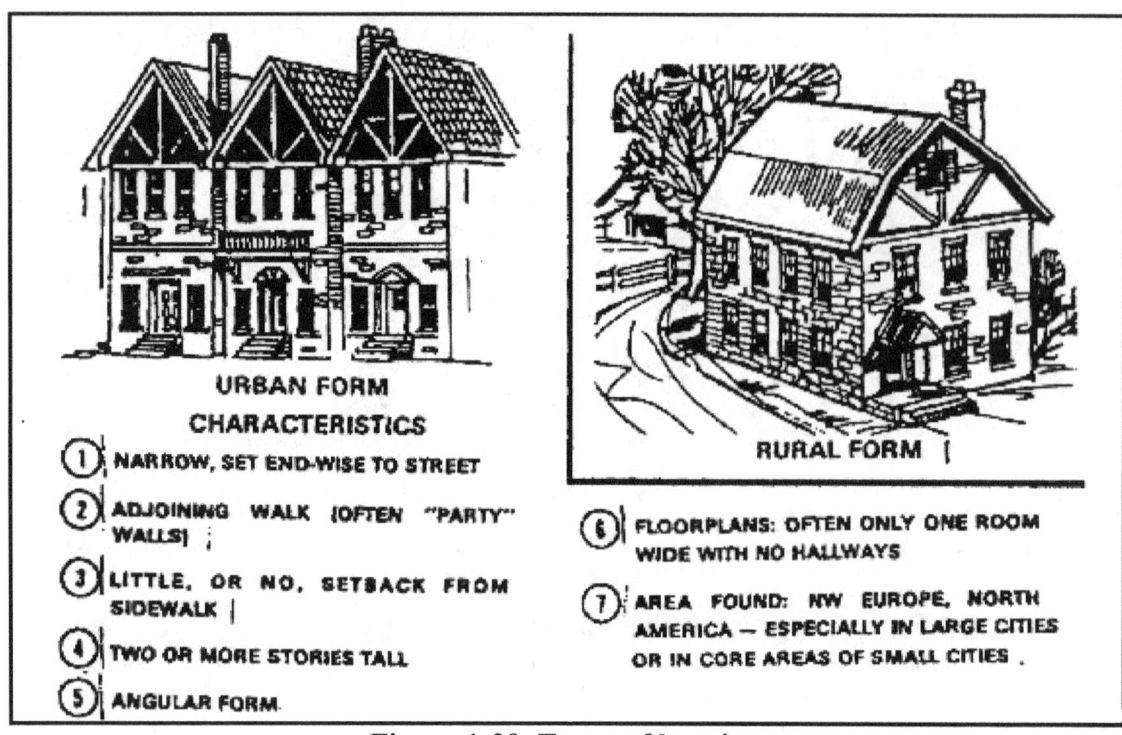

Figure 1-29. Types of housing

(1) Another common type of building structure in Europe is called the Hof-style apartment building (Figure 1-30).

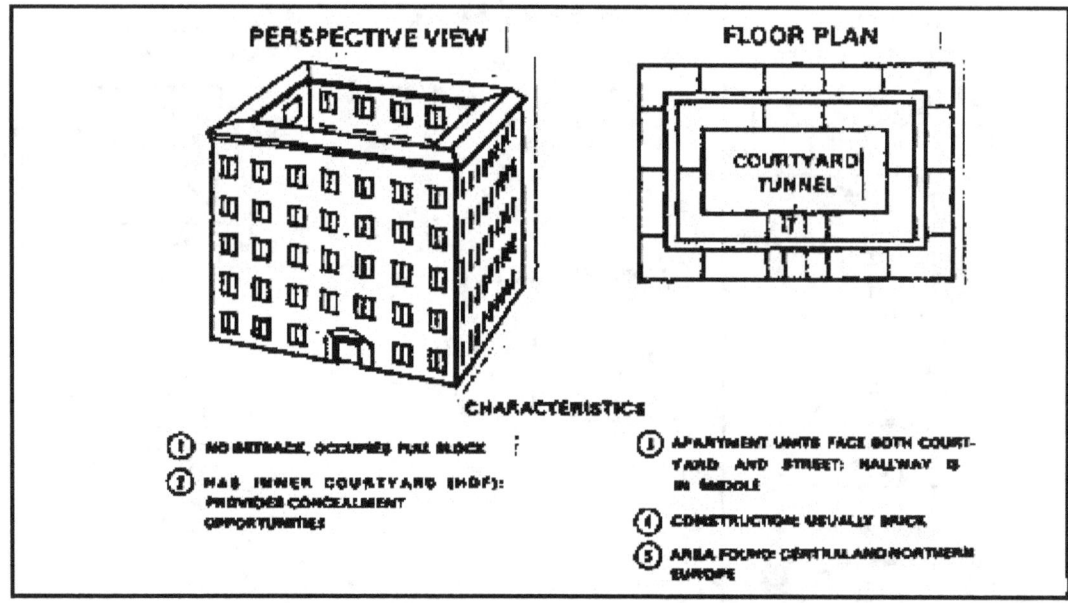

Figure 1-30. Hof-style apartment building

(2) In the mideast and tropical regions the most common housing is the enclosed courtyard. Houses are added one to another with little regard to the street pattern. The result is a crooked narrow maze which is harder to move through or fire in than dense European areas (Figure 1-31).

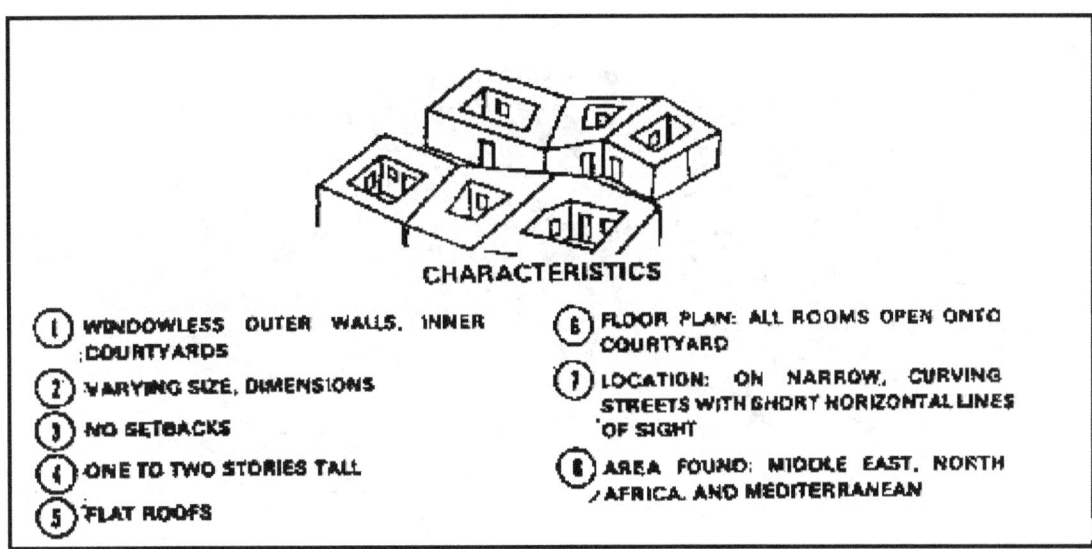

Figure 1-31. Enclosed courtyard

c. <u>Characteristics of Buildings</u>. Certain characteristics of both mass-constructed and frame-style buildings can be helpful in analyzing a built-up area (see Figure 1-32).

TYPE OF CONSTRUCTION	BUILDING MATERIAL	HEIGHT (STORIES)	AVERAGE WALL THICKNESS (cm)
Mass	Stone	1 to 10	75
Mass	Brick	1 to 3	22
Mass	Brick	3 to 6	38
Mass	Concrete Block	1 to 5	20
Mass	Concrete Wall and Slab	1 to 10	22 to 38
Mass	Concrete "Tilt-ups"	1 to 3	18
Framed	Wood	1 to 5	3
Framed	Steel (Heavy Cladding)	3 to 50	30
Framed	Concrete/Steel (Light Clading)	3 to 100	2 to 8

Figure 1-32. Characteristics of buildings

d. <u>Distribution of Building Types</u>. Certain types of buildings dominate certain parts of a city which establishes patterns within a city. Analysis of the distribution and nature of these patterns has a direct bearing on military planning and weapon selection (Figure 1-33).

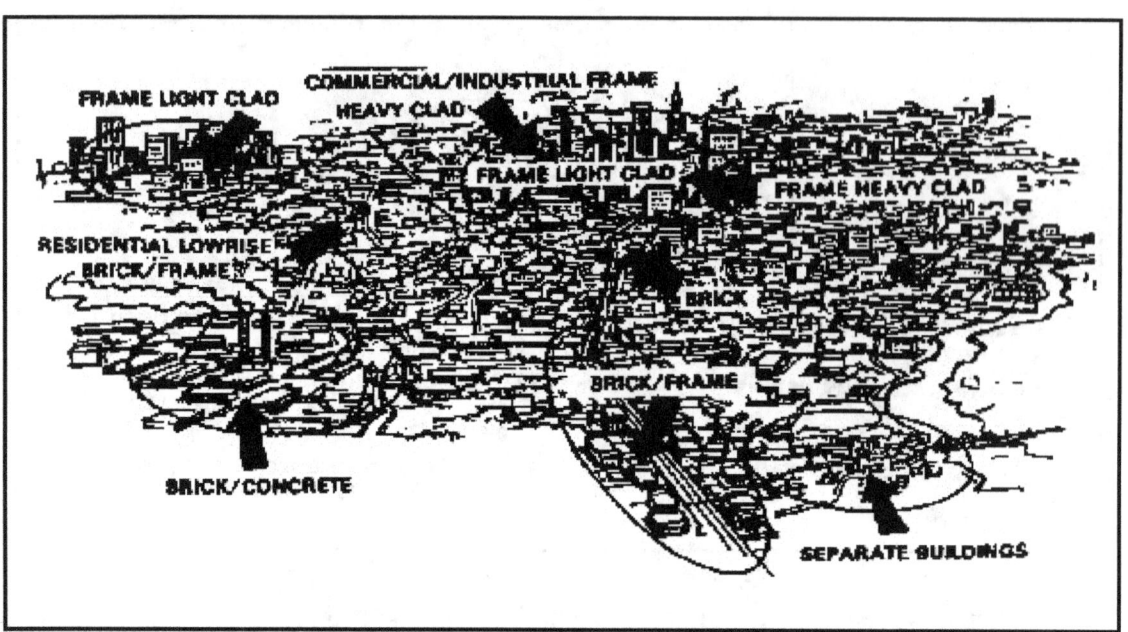

Figure 1-33. Distribution of building types

(1) <u>Mass Construction</u>. Mass-construction buildings are the most common structures in built-up areas forming about two-thirds of all building types. Brick structures account for nearly 60 percent of all buildings especially in Europe.

(2) <u>Core Area</u>. Steel and concrete framed multistory buildings have an importance far beyond their one-third contribution to total ground floor area. They occupy core areas -- a city's most valuable land -- where, as centers of economic and political power, they have a high potential military significance.

(3) <u>Open Space</u>. Open space accounts for about 15 percent of an average city's area. Many open spaces are grass-covered and are for parks, athletic fields and golf courses; some are broad, paved areas. The largest open spaces are associated with suburban housing developments where large tracts of land are recreation areas.

(4) <u>Streets</u>. Streets serving areas consisting of mostly one type of building normally have a common pattern. In downtown areas for example, high land values result in narrow streets. Street widths are grouped into three major classes: seven to 15 meters, located in medieval sections of European cities; 15 to 25 meters, located in newer planned sections of most cities, and 45 to 50 meters, located along broad boulevards or set far apart on large parcels of land. As you can see in Figure 1-34, when a street is narrow, observing or firing into windows of a building across the street can be difficult because the observer is forced to look along the building rather than into its windows. When the street is wider the observer has a better chance to look and fire into the window openings.

26

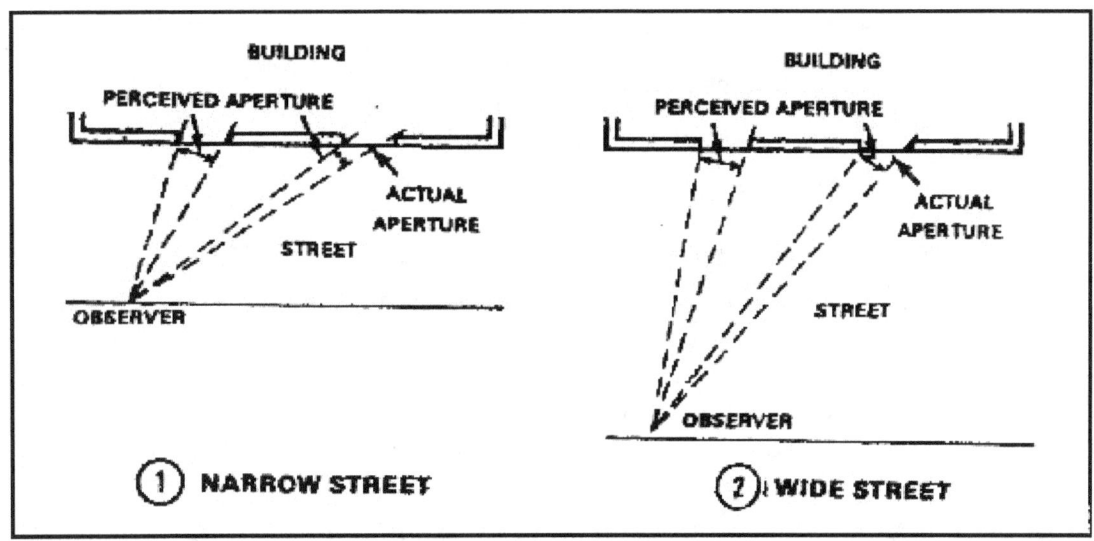

Figure 1-34. Line-of-sight distances and angles of obliquity

3. Terrain and Weather Analysis.

Terrain analysis for the battle in a built-up area differs significantly from that of open country, whereas a weather analysis does not. Although special considerations peculiar to the urban environment must be considered, a weather analysis for urban combat is mostly the same as for other operations.

 a. Built-up Area Considerations of the IPB. Several special considerations have implications in a terrain analysis and must be considered when developing the tactical plan for combat. Special terrain products must be developed to include specialized overlays, maps, and plans augmented by vertical or handheld imagery. The depiction of NO-GO, SLOW-GO, key terrain, obstacles, and avenues of approach/mobility corridors must focus on the terrain analysis.

 (1) Military maps, normally the basic tactical terrain analysis tools, do not provide sufficient detail for a terrain analysis in built-up areas. Due to growth, towns and cities are constantly adding new structures and demolishing existing ones. Therefore, any map of a built-up area, including city maps or plans published by the city, state, or national government, will be inaccurate and obsolete.

 (2) The nature of combat can radically alter the terrain in a built-up area in a short period. Incidental or intentional demolition of structures can change the topography of an area and destroy reference points, create obstacles to mobility, and provide additional defensive positions for defenders.

 (3) Maps and diagrams of the following are of key importance during urban operations:

- Sewer systems.
- Subway systems.
- Underground water systems.

27

- Elevated railways.
- Mass transit routes.
- Fuel/gas supply and storage facilities.
- Electric power stations and emergency systems.
- Mass communications facilities (radio, telephone).

Sewer and subway systems provide covered infiltration and small-unit approach routes. Elevated railways and mass transit routes provide mobility between city sectors and point to locations where obstacles might be expected. Utility facilities are key targets for insurgents, guerrillas, and terrorists and their destruction can hinder the capabilities of a defending force.

(4) Certain public buildings must be identified during the terrain-analysis phase of an IPB. Hospitals, clinics, and surgical facilities are critical because the laws of war prohibit their attack when not being used for military purposes other than medical support. As command and control breaks down during urban operations, hospitals become an important source of medical support to combat forces. The locations of civil defense air raid shelters and food supplies are critical in dealing with civilian affairs. The same is true during insurgency, guerilla, or terrorist actions.

(5) Stadiums, parks, sports fields, and school playgrounds are of high interest during both conventional and unconventional operations in built-up areas. They provide civilian holding areas, interrogation centers, insurgent segregation areas, and prisoner of war holding facilities. These open areas also provide helicopter landing sites. These areas provide logistic support areas and offer air resupply possibilities because they are often centrally located within a city or city district.

(6) Construction sites and commercial operations are of interest such as lumberyards, brickyards, steelyards, and railroad maintenance yards. They serve as primary sources of obstacle and barrier construction materials when rubble is not present or is insufficient. They can also provide engineers with materials to strengthen existing rubble obstacles or with materials for antitank hedgehogs or crib-type roadblocks.

(7) Roads, streams, and bridges provide high-speed avenues of movement. They also provide supporting engineer units locations to analyze as demolition targets and to estimate requirements for explosives.

(8) Public baths, swimming facilities, and cisterns are useful in providing bathing facilities. These facilities also provide an alternate water source when public utilities break down.

(9) A close liaison and working relationship should be developed with local government officials and military forces. In addition to information on items of special interest, they may provide information on the

population, size, and density of the built-up area; fire fighting capabilities; the location of hazardous materials; police and security capabilities; civil evacuation plans; and key public buildings. They may also provide English translators if needed.

b. Military Aspects of Urban Terrain. Urban terrain analysis is based on the five military aspects of terrain in respect to individual buildings and street layouts. The restrictive nature of urban terrain causes concern with minimum rather than maximum weapon ranges.

(1) Observation and Fields of Fire.

(a) Dense Random Construction. Weapon ranges and observation distances seldom extend more than 100 meters. Narrow streets limit tank turret traverse and do not allow for minimum ATGM ranges. Buildings and narrow streets restrict the deployment of heavy direct-fire weapons. Short observation distances and fields of fire require assigning small sectors to defending units.

(b) Closed-orderly Block. Observation and fields of fire extend up to 350 meters and are sufficient for heavy direct-fire weapons and ATGMs in most areas. Streets and open areas permit establishing normal supporting fires. Indirect fire observation is limited by numerous tall buildings and smoke. Flanking fires can normally be established along straight sections and in other open spaces. Attacking forces require small narrow attack zones and high troop density.

(c) Dispersed Residential Area. Winding streets often reduce weapon ranges to less than 250 meters, but straight street sections usually extend weapon ranges. Buildings, hedges, bushes, walls, and other obstructions limit the effectiveness of small-arms, ATGMs, and heavy direct-fire weapons. The defender can establish mutually supporting fires while the attacker cannot.

(d) High-rise Areas. Both offensive and defensive operations may establish mutually supporting fires between buildings. Maximum weapon ranges are achieved by positioning weapons in the upper stories of buildings.

(e) Industrial/transportation Areas. These areas are often situated on the outskirts of cities. Open areas provide excellent observation and fields of fire over the entire area and facilitate close air support (CAS) and indirect fires employment. Smoke from burning fuel storage could hinder accurate fire direction.

(2) Cover and Concealment.

(a) Dense Random Construction. Buildings provide many concealed infantry positions and isolated armored vehicle positions. Thick masonry, stone, and brick walls offer protection from direct fire. Adequate overhead protection is found only in basements

29

since most roofs, ceilings, and floors are constructed of wood or plaster. Underground systems offer protection and often permit movement between battle positions.

(b) Closed-orderly Block. Heavy construction provides protection against direct and indirect fires. However buildings selected for shelter must be evaluated for their ability to withstand collapse. Underground systems are extensive and provide storage areas, protection, and mobility. Those underground systems not used must not be blocked by either obstacles or maneuver elements. Advancing along open streets should be avoided if possible.

(c) Dispersed Residential Areas. Walls, fences, hedges, and houses provide limited cover and concealment. Overhead protection varies, but basement positions usually provide sufficient overhead cover. Construction often permits the concealment of and provides limited cover for armored vehicles.

(d) High-rise Areas. High-rise structures provide protection from indirect fires but, only limited protection from direct fires. Cover and concealment are often not available unless adjacent buildings are secured. Attacking forces must employ heavy covering fire, smoke, and rapid movement from one building to another.

(e) Industrial/transportation Areas. Little cover and concealment is available in these areas due to the construction and the dispersed nature of the buildings. Some concealment is offered by buildings but shed-type buildings should be avoided.

(3) Obstacles.

(a) Dense Random Construction. Narrow streets with buildings constructed directly on the street facilitate the construction or creation of obstacles. Demolition of structures creates instant rubble obstacles.

(b) Close-orderly Block. Wider streets and heavy construction make rubble less of an obstacle. Obstacles are difficult to construct. Once constructed, obstacles are difficult to reduce or bypass because they are easily controlled by fire.

(c) Dispersed Residential Areas. Rubble is not a significant obstacle. Most obstacles in the streets are easily bypassed, but they do reduce mobility.

(d) High-rise Areas. Mines between buildings are the most effective obstacles. Rubble is not a factor unless major structures are destroyed.

(e) Industrial/transportation Areas. Railyards, elevated railways, and roadways, ramps, loading docks, numerous high-tension lines, canals, overpasses, pipelines, and overhead obstructions such as cranes create significant obstacles to movement. Armored vehicles should avoid railyards if possible. Railroad tracks quickly damage vehicles and the open yards provide excellent defensive fields of fire. Rubble is normally easily bypassed.

(4) <u>Key Terrain Examples</u>. The following are examples of key terrain:

- Subway systems.

- Sewer systems.

- Underground water systems.

- Utility (gas and electric) generation, holding, and transmission facilities.

- Telephone exchanges.

- Radio and television stations.

- Rail and transit service connecting points.

- Stadiums, parks, sports fields, and schoolyards.

- Tall buildings (rooftops).

(5) <u>Avenues of Approach</u>.

(a) The battalion is the most effective force of any size which can be employed under urban conditions. Therefore avenues of approach are analyzed only for battalion and smaller-unit operations.

(b) Avenues of approach are dictated by the urban pattern and the actual mission, and cover unusually narrow frontages. When possible, multiple avenues are employed to permit flanking and rear-area attacks in support of the main effort. (See Figure 1-35 for the widths of avenues of approach in the five basic types of urban terrain.).

TYPES OF URBAN TERRAIN	WIDTHS OF AVENUES OF APPROACH
Dense, random construction	150-200 meters
Closed-orderly block	200-300 meters
Dispersed residential areas	300-400 meters
High-rise areas	300-500 meters
Industrial/transportation areas	400-600 meters

Figure 1-35. Widths of avenues of approach

c. <u>Development of Overlays</u>. The modified combined obstacle overlay (MCOO)

31

shows the patterns of construction (for example, high-rise, dispersed residential, etc.) in the area and depicts known obstacles and avenues of approach/mobility corridors. The avenue of approach/mobility corridor overlay shows urban underground systems and should be prepared when appropriate.

(1) An MCOO is prepared using maps of the built-up area or photo maps of the city. If maps are not available, imagery of the built-up area should be annotated with the information.

(2) An avenue of approach/military corridor overlay for urban underground systems is required in areas where the underground systems (sewer, water, subway, gas, steam, or telephone) have pipes, tunnels, or culverts large enough for an individual to crawl through. The overlay should show the size of the tunnels, pipes, and culverts and their approximate orientation. Color-coding helps to distinguish systems of various types and sizes. Subsurface avenues of approach/mobility corridors are listed in order of priority based on the likelihood of use.

d. Special Weather Considerations. Some weather effects peculiar to an urban environment are discussed in the following paragraphs.

(1) Rain or melting snow often floods basements and subway systems. This is especially true when automatic pumping facilities that normally handle rising water levels are deprived of power. Rain also makes storm and other sewer systems hazardous or impassable. Chemical agents are washed into underground systems by precipitation. As a result, these systems contain agent concentrations much higher than surface areas and become contaminated "hot spots." These effects become more pronounced as agents are absorbed by brick or unsealed concrete sewer walls.

(2) Many major cities are located along canals or rivers which often creates a potential for fog in the low-lying areas. Industrial/transportation areas are the most affected by fog due to their proximity to waterways.

(3) Air inversion layers are common over cities especially cities located in low-lying "bowls" or in river valleys. Inversion layers trap dust and other pollutants reducing visibility, and often creating a greenhouse effect which causes a rise in ground and air temperature.

(4) The heating of buildings during the winter, and the reflection and absorption of summer heat makes built-up areas warmer than surrounding open areas during both summer and winter. This difference can be as great as 10 to 20 degrees, and can add to the already high logistics requirements of urban combat.

(5) Windchill is not as pronounced in built-up areas. However, the configuration of streets, especially in closed-orderly block and high-rise areas, can cause wind canalization. This increases the effects of the wind on streets paralleling the wind direction, while cross-streets remain relatively well protected.

(6) Light data (day, night, reduced visibility, etc.) have special significance

32

during urban operations. Night and periods of reduced visibility favor surprise, infiltration, detailed reconnaissance, attacks across open areas, seizure of defended strongpoints, and reduction of defended obstacles. However, the difficulties of night navigation in restrictive terrain, without reference points and near the enemy, forces reliance on simple maneuver plans with easily recognizable objectives.

4. Threat Offensive Operations.

Although the doctrine established by the former Warsaw Pact nations emphasized bypassing built-up areas, their commanders recognized the need to prepare for combat in these areas. Since virtually every ideology antagonistic to U.S. interests was trained and equipped by the former Soviet bloc to a large extent, the continued study of Soviet doctrine will be exceedingly valid for the foreseeable future. Threat doctrine states that formations attacking across developed regions should expect to encounter at least one large built-up area every 40 to 60 km, as well as many villages and strip areas restricting or blocking avenues of approach. The decision to attack built-up areas could be based on tactical, strategic, or political considerations and would normally be made at Army level or above. Threat forces would attack urban areas to accomplish the following:

- To seize political, industrial, logistical, and communications facilities.

- To destroy defending forces within a built-up area.

- To gain passage through a built-up area that cannot be bypassed.

a. Types of Attacks. Threat doctrine prescribes two types of attacks for seizing a built-up area: the surprise attack (also called an attack from the march) and the deliberate attack.

(1) Surprise Attack. A surprise attack is the preferred form of seizing a built-up area. It is a fast, bold movement from the line of march by a strong forward detachment to seize an undefended or lightly defended built-up area. A successful surprise attack would avoid a costly and long street-by-street, house-to-house battle, and would permit the attacking force to move through the city without losing momentum. The surprise attack often seeks to capture intact key facilities such as bridges, railroads, airfields, industrial complexes, and utilities.

(a) The forward detachment is normally a reinforced motorized rifle battalion of a motorized rifle division given the surprise attack mission. The forward detachment normally bypasses defending troops on the built-up area's approaches. If light resistance is encountered, the forward detachment seizes the most important objectives (buildings or bridges) and key streets, splitting the area into isolated pockets of resistance so they can be destroyed piecemeal. The attacking force leaves stay-behind elements in positions they have cleared to keep the withdrawing forces from reestablishing a defense and reoccupying positions through the area.

33

(b) If the surprise attack fails, the forward detachment tries to seize a foothold in the outskirts or an adjacent key terrain feature and waits for the main body to arrive.

(c) Airborne or heliborne forces support ground forward detachments by sealing off flanks or the rear of the objective area. These forces could also be employed as a forward detachment to be used directly in or around the built-up area. A forward detachment operating outside the range of forward artillery would normally receive intensive reconnaissance and CAS from high-performance aircraft and helicopters.

(2) Deliberate Attack. A deliberate attack is conducted when the surprise attack fails or when the built-up area is well defended. This attack would involve a larger force, require more preparation, and have more artillery, mortar, and rocket support than a surprise attack.

(a) Isolation of the objective city is accomplished by denying reinforcement and resupply of city defenders and by blocking escape routes. The size and composition of the force tasked with isolating an objective city are determined by the area's size, shape, and adjacent terrain. A motorized rifle regiment might have two motorized rifle battalions to isolate the city. An exit could be intentionally permitted to lure defenders out of the city and into open terrain where they could be attacked. After isolating the city, other units conducts a siege while the isolation force breaks contact and continues its advance. If his timetable permits, the attacking commander conducts a siege to avoid a costly direct assault (Figure 1-36).

(b) Reconnaissance is continuous during all phases of the deliberate attack. Infiltrators disguised as refugees, or other reconnaissance units, can operate in a built-up area for as long as six days before an assault. Reconnaissance information can be supplemented by studying city maps and plans, and by obtaining current information from local residents. Reconnaissance teams might conduct raids to capture prisoners and documents, or to destroy power systems and other key facilities. Soviet troops would have conducted extensive reconnaissance to learn of the following:

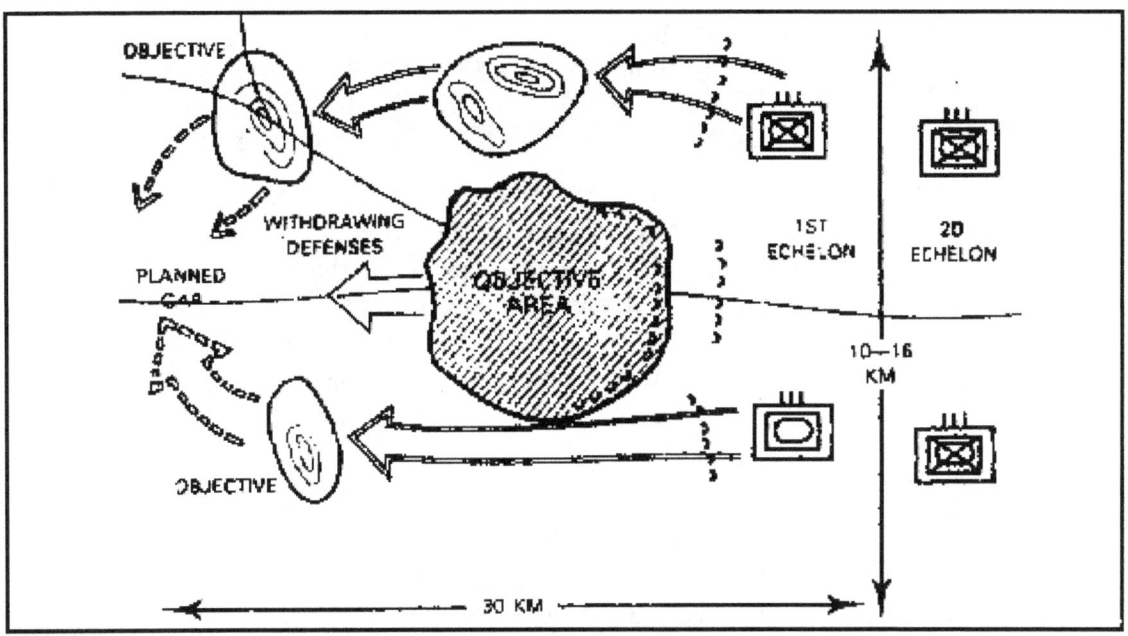

Figure 1-36. Isolation of the objective city

- Defensive dispositions.

- Covered approaches.

- Locations and strengths of defensive strongpoints on the city's outer edge.

- Main routes through the area.

- Key buildings dominating the built-up area.

- Underground passages.

(c) An intense preassault bombardment with howitzers, rockets, mortars, and high-performance aircraft would precede the deliberate attack. Priority of fires would be allocated to the main attack to destroy defensive positions on the city's edge. Artillery attached to assaulting units normally would not participate in the bombardment but would be reserved for direct fire support. Other goals of the bombardment are to destroy communications facilities, heavy weapons positions, command posts, tall structures, troop emplacements, and reserves.

Incapacitating or nonpersistent, lethal chemicals could be employed during the bombardment to inflict casualties while preventing the destruction of key facilities.

Smoke is usually employed during artillery preparations to suppress the defender while attacking forces negotiate obstacles on the approaches and within the objective area.

Any employment of nuclear weapons probably would have occurred during the bombardment if the city's facilities were not

35

needed to support future operations. Nuclear weapons could have been employed on the city's edge to rupture outer defenses to permit a rapid assault into the city's center, or they might have been used within the city's center to destroy defending reserves.

(d) Threat forces would attack to secure a foothold and key objectives during or immediately following the bombardment. One or two battalions might attack each kilometer of the city's circumference. Attacking units would be employed on the most favorable avenues of approach. Simultaneous attacks on the flanks and in the rear would capture specific objectives and fragment the defenses. However, frontal assaults would be conducted only when a city cannot be flanked.

b. Organization. A motorized rifle division (MRD), organized according to Soviet doctrine, usually has one motorized rifle regiment (MRR) conduct the main attack of a built-up area. Within this MRR there are three reinforced motorized rifle battalions (MRBs) called assault detachments, which are the basic enemy units in city warfare.

(1) One reinforced assault detachment is designated as the main attack force. This battalion is reinforced by attaching a tank company, a battery of self-propelled artillery for direct fire, an antitank gun battery, an engineer platoon, and an NBC reconnaissance company. An additional artillery battalion might be placed in direct support for indirect fire in the battalion's zone.

(2) Motorized rifle companies, designated as groups, are organized within the MRB. When conducting the main attack, motorized rifle companies are reinforced with a tank platoon, artillery battery, chemical and flamethrower units, and an engineer squad. Often the battalion antitank gun platoon is attached to the motorized rifle company performing the main attack. Elements of units attached to motorized rifle companies often are further attached down to platoon level, giving each platoon at least one tank or artillery gun. These attachments allow independent operations by platoons in seizing their objectives. These attachments could be made down to squad level.

(3) The second echelon MRRs and MRBs are organized the same as the main attack elements (first echelon). This arrangement allows for replacement of the first echelon without changing attachments during the battle.

c. Supporting Elements. Units conducting the main attack are reinforced with a variety of supporting elements.

(1) Tanks. Tanks supporting motorized rifle companies may be employed by platoons in sections or singly with a motorized rifle squad. A rifle squad moves with each tank and provides close security, relying on the tank for protection and fire support. The lead tank normally fires at lower

36

windows and doors of buildings while following tanks fire into upper floors on both sides of the street. Tanks also support the attack by firing on suspected positions, destroying barricades, and engaging opposing armor.

(2) Artillery. Russian forces recognized the difficulty of centralized fire control and the decreased effectiveness of indirect fire in cities. For these reasons over half of their artillery may be attached and employed in a direct-fire role. The artillery commander is normally located with the motorized rifle battalion commander.

> (a) Direct fire is used to create breaches in buildings, walls, and barricades. Guns displace forward alternately under cover of heavy fire from other guns, tanks, and motorized rifle units. Within the city, self-propelled artillery weapons are often employed as assault weapons and are attached to infantry platoons and squads.

> (b) Division artillery groups under division centralized control are used in a counterfire role. Massed fire from these batteries of heavy artillery is used against large buildings or fortified positions. Other missions for the division artillery group include interdiction and destruction of the defender's supply installations, headquarters, and communications centers.

(3) Antiaircraft Artillery. Doctrine of former soviet employs antiaircraft weapons to protect artillery emplacements, exposed signal installations, and ammunition dumps (mobile CPs normally move into buildings offering protection). The M1986, ZSU 23-4, 2S6, ZSU 57-2, ZU, and ZPU multiple machine guns are also used to suppress the defending force's weapons on the upper stories of buildings. The lighter antiaircraft weapons are often mounted on rooftops. Employment of air support is usually for reconnaissance, fire adjustment, and air defense.

(4) Close Air Support. CAS from fighters is usually aimed at preventing the movement of reserves or reinforcement of the defenders in a town.

(5) Mortars. Mortars cover the defender's routes of movement such as street intersections and alleys. They are emplaced close to their targets, behind walls or inside buildings with destroyed roofs. From these concealed positions, mortars can promptly provide effective fire support for assault groups.

(6) Engineers. Engineers are attached to motorized rifle companies and given one of the following missions:

> Breach obstacles on approaches to the built-up area.

> Clear passages through rubble and barricades.

> Block or clear underground passages.

> Clear or lay mines as required.

(7) Flamethrower Units. These units are attached to block or clear both

aboveground and underground passages.

d. Conduct of the Attack. The conduct of the attack involves the engineer element and the first- and second-echelon assault groups. There are several options as to their employment depending upon the availability of fire support.

(1) During or immediately after preparatory fires, engineers move forward under the cover of smoke with explosives to neutralize barriers and to breach minefields on routes into the city. First-echelon assault groups attack to secure a foothold two or three blocks deep on the city's edge. After securing the initial foothold and rupturing the outer defenses, the first echelon may continue to attack or the second echelon may pass through the foothold and attack along designated streets from one objective to another.

(2) The attack within the city is characterized by bold, rapid movements to secure assigned objectives. Buildings along the route are not systematically searched or cleared unless resistance was strong. Bypassed defenders aren't left to be eliminated by the follow-on echelons or reserve. If the leading echelon is stopped or slowed, the follow-on echelons or reserve may be committed to continue to the objective.

(3) Detected weaknesses in defenses are exploited by mounted attacks. Infantry mounted on tanks, fighting vehicles, or trucks move along streets to their assigned objectives.

(4) In the assault of an objective, the assaulting forces tries to isolate the position by fire or by securing adjacent buildings. Isolation is stressed to prevent defenders from escaping to a rearward position and to deny reinforcement. Attached artillery and tanks are used to suppress defensive fires and to breach walls for assaulting infantry.

(5) Advances along streets are avoided to reduce exposure to effective fire. Doctrine of the former Soviet's stresses the use of covered routes such as available subways, tunnels, and sewers. Artillery and tanks may create covered routes by blasting through intervening building walls. Once the assault of the objective began, supporting fires shift to upper stories and to adjacent buildings. Assaulting infantry clear in sequence, the ground floor, basement, stairways, and each higher floor. Once secured, the position is prepared to repel counter-attacks.

(6) After securing battalion objectives and neutralizing defensive opposition, assault forces move beyond the city to minimize the risk of nuclear or chemical attack while massed in the city. Detailed clearance operations are normally passed to following units or to security formations.

e. Night Attack. Night operations are conducted by the former Soviets in built-up areas to accomplish the following:

Bypass outlying villages being used by the defenders.

Seize initial objectives on the city's edge which could be reached only by an attack across open ground.

Attack across open areas (parks, streets) within cities.

Seize strongpoints.

Reduce street obstacles which are well protected by mines and covered by fires.

Exploit successes of daylight operations by keeping pressure on the defense.

(1) With extensive night training and by use of night vision equipment the former Soviets could be effective in night operations. Their forces were equipped with night viewers, night driving and aiming devices, and sniperscopes. Their doctrine stresses habitually attacking during reduced visibility.

(2) Night attacks are normally preceded by detailed reconnaissance. Reconnaissance units attempt to infiltrate the objectives to obtain detailed information and to guide assault forces. The difficulty of night navigation in cities and the proximity of defending forces favor a simple maneuver plan with close, easily recognized objectives.

(3) Motorized rifle assault forces normally attack in one echelon with units deployed on line. Surprise is achieved by withholding fire support until after the infantry assault has been detected. Once the attack is discovered, direct-support artillery illuminates the objective. Attached tanks and artillery then join assault forces and suppress the defenses with direct fires.

When surprise cannot be achieved, night assaults may be preceded by direct fire against strongly defended buildings. Direct support artillery and mortars attempt to seal off the objective area with indirect fire. Illumination guides forces, illuminates objectives, and blinds the defender. After securing objectives, assault forces consolidate to repel counterattacks.

5. Threat Defensive Operations.

While recognizing the need to defend built-up areas, Warsaw Pact doctrine stresses the need to establish a defense well forward in order to engage and defeat the attacker on the approaches and flanks of the built-up area. The forces of the former Soviet would revert to defense of a built-up area only under the following conditions:

- Attacking forces break through forward defenses.

- The area is of political, strategic, or economic importance.

- The area is a seaport or other critical communications or transportation complex.

a. Types of Defenses. Doctrine of the former Soviet prescribes the MRB to defend as part of a regimental-size unit. Strongpoints constitute each defensive position. Fires are coordinated between strongpoints. Communication trenches are prepared between and within positions. Ambushes are set up in the gaps between defensive positions. Structures impeding effective fire are demolished.

b. Organization. MRB defenses are generally organized into two echelons to provide greater depth and reserves. Company strongpoints are prepared for perimeter defense and form the basis for the battalion defensive position. The reserve is located in a separate strongpoint.

(1) The rear service areas are selected to capitalize on the concealment and cover afforded by the built-up area. Dummy strongpoints are constructed to deceive the enemy, and positions for securing and defending the entrances to and exits from underground structures and routes are established. Security positions are prepared forward of first-echelon defensive positions.

(2) Within a built-up area, a company may defend several buildings with mutually supporting fires or a single large building. Each platoon defends one or two buildings or one or two floors of a single building. Strongpoints are normally prepared in solidly constructed buildings, at intersections, at entrances to public parks and squares, or adjacent to bridges.

c. Missions. The MRB defends as part of a regimental-size unit on a main or secondary avenue of approach. The battalion can be in the first or second echelon, or in the reserve.

(1) On the main avenue of approach (first echelon), the MRB takes the following actions:

- Receives the main attack.
- Inflicts decisive damage on the attacking forces to prevent a breakthrough.

(2) When in the second echelon, or, on a secondary avenue of approach, the MRB:

- Prevents flanking and rear-area attacks.
- Holds defended sites.
- Prevents further advances by an attacking force that has penetrated the built-up area.
- Conducts counterattacks to restore first-echelon positions.

(3) The reserve MRB:

- Reinforces or replaces the first-echelon battalion.
- Covers breaches caused by chemical and nuclear weapons.
- Holds deep sites whose retention is vital to the overall defense.
- Extinguishes or contains fires threatening friendly forces.
- Conducts rear area security.

6. Threat Evaluation and Integration.

The threat evaluation process for urban combat uses a three-step process: develop a threat data base, determine enemy capabilities, and develop a doctrinal template file as threat evaluation for open terrain. However, direct the focus of the evaluation effort toward battalion-size and smaller operations as units of this size are considered the most effective for urban operations. Threat integration for the urban battle is accomplished through the development of situation, event, and decision support templates.

7. Counterinsurgency, Counterguerrilla, and Counterterrorist Operations. During urban counterinsurgency, counterguerilla, and counterterrorist operations, your threat evaluation is similar to that for low-intensity conflict.

a. Population status overlays are prepared for the objective city showing potential neighborhoods or districts where a hostile population could be encountered. Also prepared are overlays showing insurgent/terrorist safe houses, headquarters, known operating areas, contact points, and weapons supply sources. Your overlays will include buildings which are known, or could become, explosives, ammunition, or weapons storage sites.

b. Underground routes are of primary concern when considering insurgent and terrorist avenues of approach and lines of communications. Sewers, subways, tunnels, cisterns, and basements provide mobility, concealment, cover, and storage sites for insurgents and terrorists. Elevated railways, pedestrian overpasses, rooftops, fire escapes, balconies, and access ladders provide mobility and concealment and can serve as relatively good fighting or sniper positions.

c. Although doctrinal templates are not developed for urban insurgency and terrorist operations, pattern analysis will reveal how the insurgent or terrorist group operates and what its primary targets are. Once the group's method of operation is determined, you can develop insurgent trap maps. These maps should pinpoint likely sabotage targets, kidnap or assassination targets, ambush points, and bombing targets. When developing these maps, consider the following as primary insurgent and terrorist targets:

- Electric power generation and transmission facilities.
- Gas production and holding facilities.
- Water and sewer pumping and treatment plants.
- Telephone exchanges and facilities.
- Radio and television stations.

PART C - OFFENSIVE OPERATIONS

Good cover and concealment in a built-up area gives its defenders the advantage -- attackers must fight from the outside into a well-defended position. While a decision to attack a major built-up area usually rests at a level higher than battalion, commanders at all levels must be prepared to fight in such areas. A commander may attack a built-up area to achieve the following advantages:

- To secure and control critical features (bridges, road nets).
- To return the area to friendly control for political reasons.
- To contain an enemy force.
- Because it cannot be bypassed.

Avoid attacks on built-up areas when the following conditions are present:

- Seizure of the area is not required to support future operations and bypassing is tactically feasible.
- Sufficient force is not available to seize and clear the area.
- The area has been declared an "open city" to prevent civilian casualties or to preserve cultural or historical sites.

1. Types of Offensive Operations.

Offensive operations in built-up areas are based an offensive doctrine and are implemented based on mission, enemy, troops, terrain, and time available (METT-T) factors. At battalion level, the offense takes the form of either a hasty or deliberate attack. The hasty or deliberate attack is characterized by as much planning, reconnaissance, and coordination as time and the situation permit.

a. Hasty Attack. Conduct a hasty attack when retaining momentum is crucial. It is feasible when the enemy has not fortified his positions, permitting the attacking force to overwhelm the defense without protracted combat.

Three tasks are common to a hasty attack: finding a weak point or gap in enemy defenses; fixing forward enemy elements; and quickly moving through or around the weak point or gap to key or decisive terrain. Those tasks cannot always be executed in the same order. You must exploit opportunities as they appear. For example, leading units of a battalion may be engaged with forward enemy elements when it becomes apparent a weak point exists in the defensive position. In another case, a reconnaissance force may discover a gap and then be ordered to seize the terrain controlling the gap to prevent enemy reinforcement. Speed is always essential -- if momentum is lost, the hasty attack will fail.

(1) Because the built-up area is itself an obstacle, you conduct a hasty attack in such an area differently than in open terrain. Incomplete intelligence and the concealment available in built-up areas may require the maneuver unit to move through, rather than around, the friendly unit fixing the enemy in place. Control and coordination become most important to reduce congestion at the edge of the area.

(2) Follow-up, on-order missions, or fragmentary orders may be given to a force conducting a hasty attack so it can react to a contingency once its objective is secured.

b. Deliberate Attack. A deliberate attack is a fully synchronized operation employing all available assets against the enemy defense. It is required when enemy positions are well prepared, when the built-up area is large or severely congested, or when the element of surprise has been lost.

Normally, there are three steps in the deliberate attack of a built-up area: isolate the area (objective), secure a foothold, and clear the area. However, the deliberate attack must be preceded by thorough and aggressive reconnaissance to identify avenues of approach, obstacles, and strongpoints.

STEP 1: Isolating the area involves seizing terrain dominating the area so the enemy cannot supply or reinforce its defenders. You can take this step at the same time as the foothold and clearance steps. If isolating the area is the first step, there should be no pause before the following steps that would give the defender time to react (Figure 1-37).

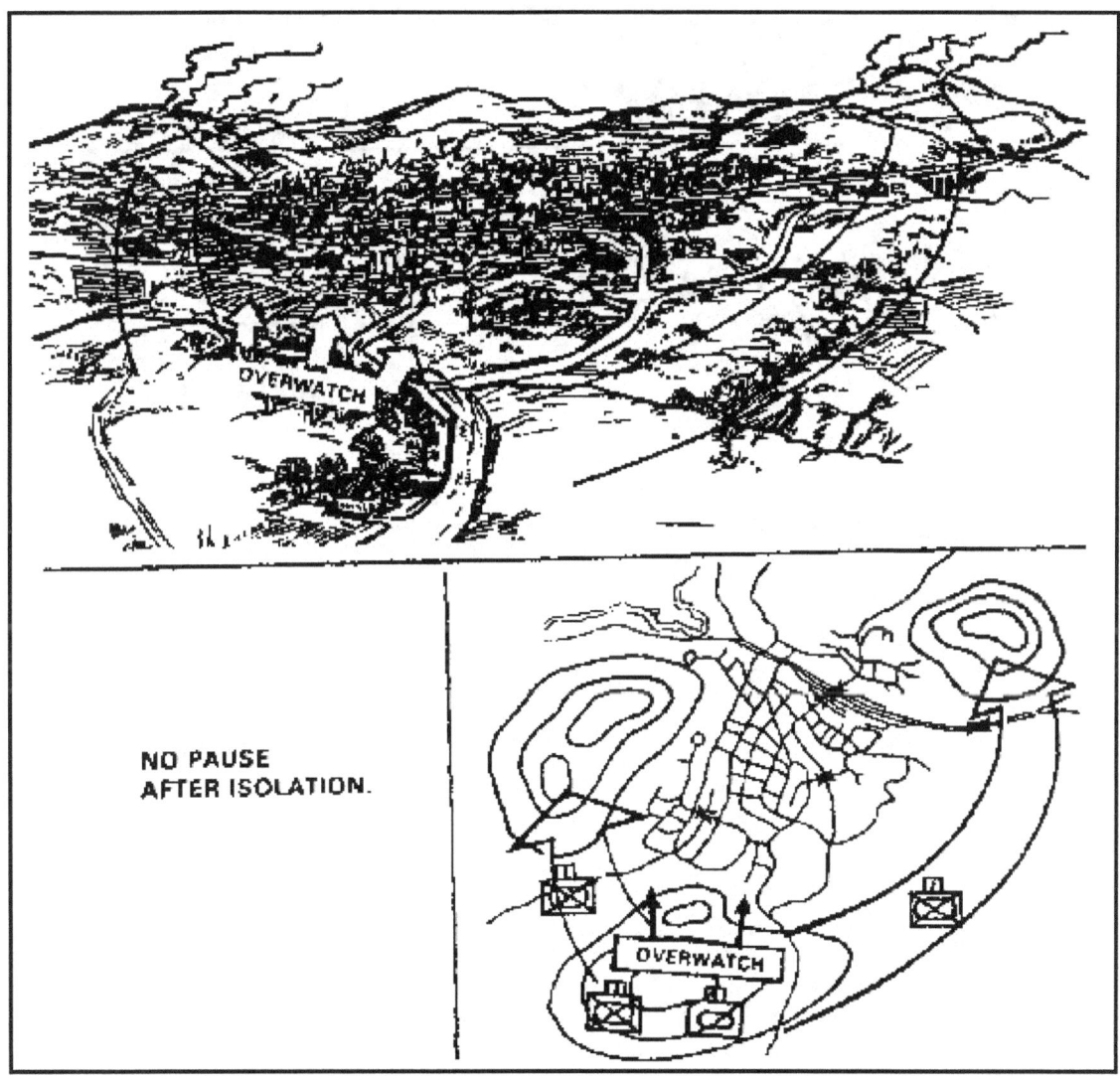

Figure 1-37. Isolation by a battalion task force

STEP 2: Seizing a foothold involves seizing an intermediate objective that provides cover from enemy fire and a place for attacking troops to enter the built-up area. A foothold is normally one to two city blocks and is an intermediate

43

objective of a company. As the company attacks to secure the foothold, it should be supported by suppressive fire and smoke (Figure 1-38).

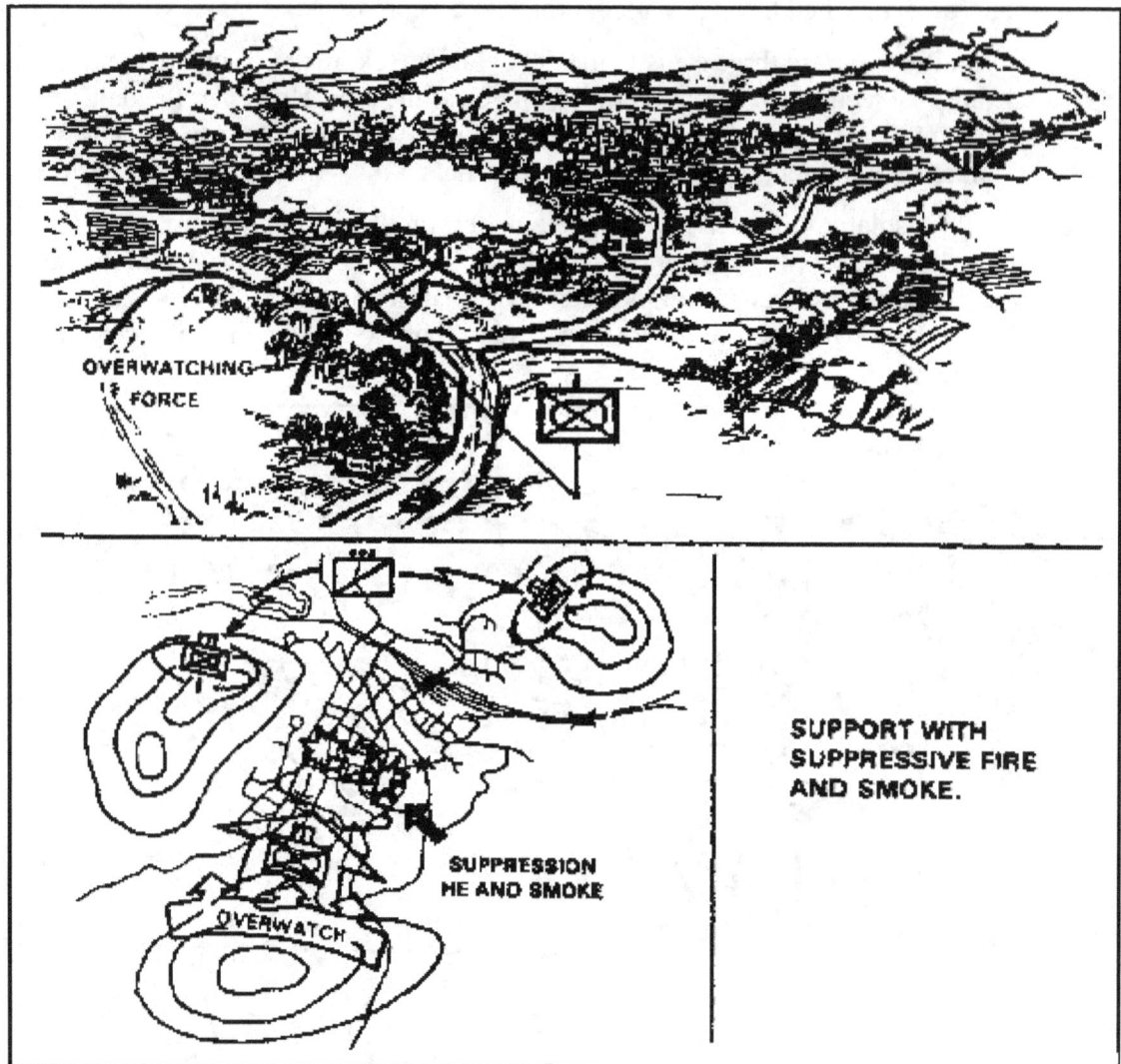

Figure 1-38. Battalion foothold

STEP 3: Clearing the area involves considering METT-T factors before determining to what extent the built-up area must be cleared. You may decide to clear only those parts necessary for the success of your mission if --.

- An objective must be seized quickly.

- Enemy resistance is light or fragmented.

- The buildings in the area are of light construction with large open areas between them. In that case, you would clear only those buildings along the approach to your objectives or only those buildings necessary for security (Figure 1-39).

Figure 1-39. Clearning buildings along the route of attack

On the other hand, a unit may have a mission to systematically clear an area of all enemy, or it may assume that mission in the face of strong, organized resistance or in areas having strongly built buildings close together. Therefore, one or two companies may attack on a narrow front against the enemy's weakest sector. They move slowly through the area, clearing systematically from room to room and building to building. The other company supports the clearing units and is prepared to assume their mission (Figure 1-40).

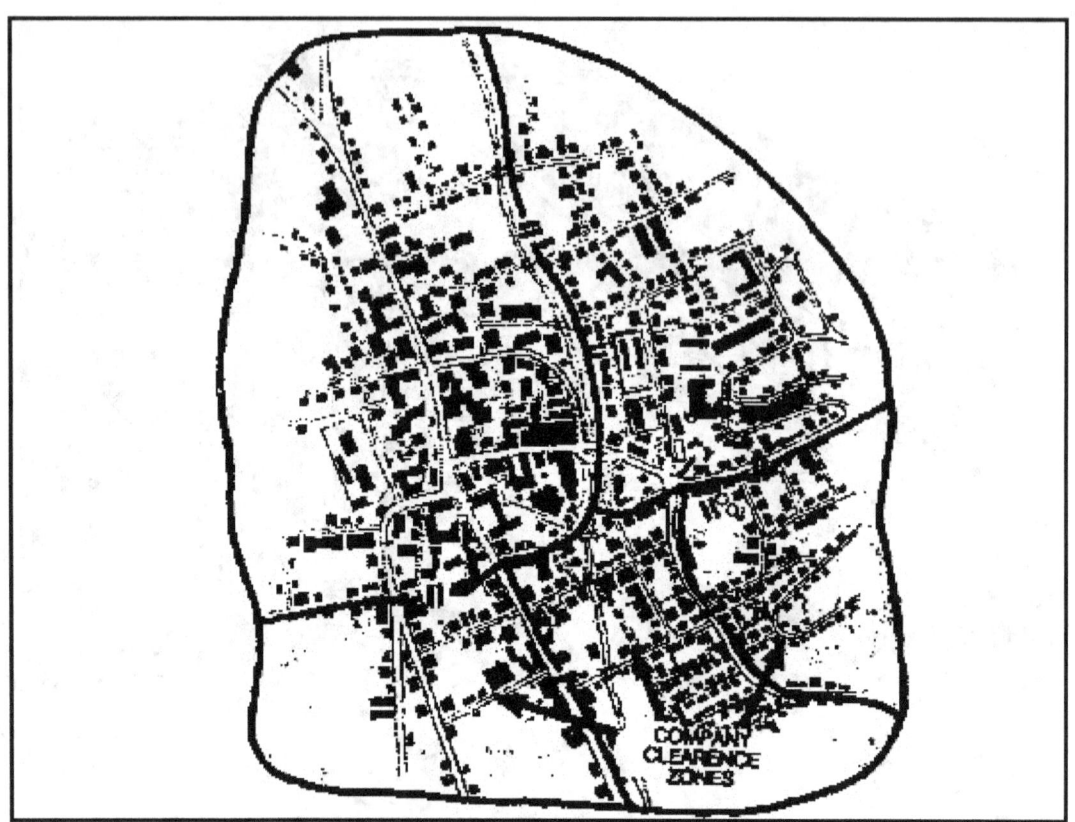

Figure 1-40. Systematic clearance within assigned sectors

2. <u>Planning an Attack</u>.

An attack plan against a well-defended built-up area must be based on METT-T factors. As in any attack, the plan must have a scheme of maneuver and fire support plan which is closely integrated and developed to implement the commander's concept. The attack plan must also cover the details of security, combat service support, and communications.

a. <u>Scheme of Maneuver</u>. In an attack on a large built-up area, a battalion would probably participate as part of an attacking brigade. In that case, the battalion may have to isolate the objective or seize a foothold. If the objective is a smaller, built-up area, a battalion or company may accomplish the entire mission independently, assigning subordinate tasks to its companies or platoons. In either case, the maneuver platoons are assigned the entry and clearance tasks.

(1) <u>The Foothold</u>. When attacking to seize a foothold, the battalion normally assigns a forward company the first block of buildings as its first objective. When an objective extends to a street, only the near side of the street is included. The company's final objective may be buildings at the far edge of the built-up area or key terrain on the far side. Key buildings or groups of buildings also may be assigned as intermediate objectives. Buildings along the route of attack should be identified by numbers to simplify assigning objectives and reporting (Figure 1-41).

46

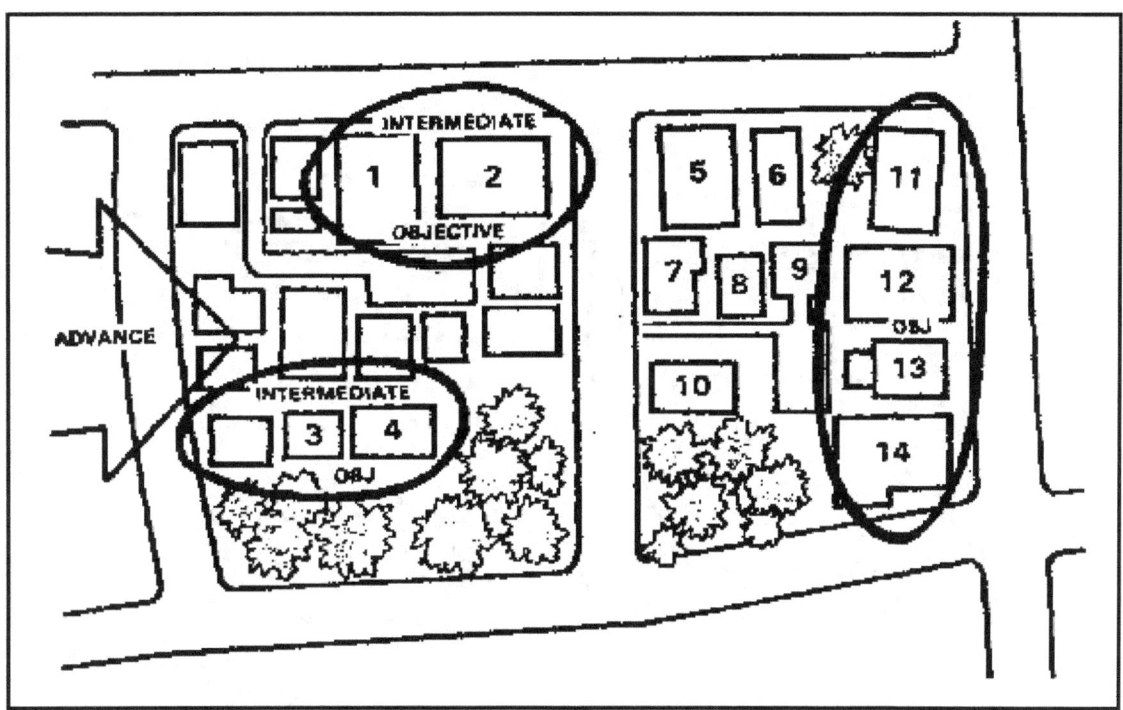

Figure 1-41. Control measures and example of a numbering system

(2) <u>Clearing</u>. When the unit is involved in clearing, bypassing buildings increases the risk of attack from the rear or flank. Thus, the clearing unit must enter, search, and clear each building in its zone of action (limit of advance [LOA]). A single building may be an objective for a rifle squad or, if the building is large, for a rifle platoon or even a company. When the commander's concept is based on speed or when conducting a hasty attack, a battalion may be directed not to clear its entire zone.

(3) <u>Phase Lines</u>. Use phase lines to report progress or to control the advance of attacking units. Principal streets, rivers, and railroad lines are suitable phase lines which should be on the near side of the street or open area. In systematic clearing, a unit may have the mission to clear its zone of action up to a phase line. In that case, the unit commander chooses his own objectives when assigning missions to his subunits.

(4) <u>Boundaries (Limit of Advance)</u>. Battalion and company boundaries are usually set within blocks so a street is included in a company zone. Boundaries must be placed to ensure both sides of a street are included in the zone of one unit (Figure 1-42).

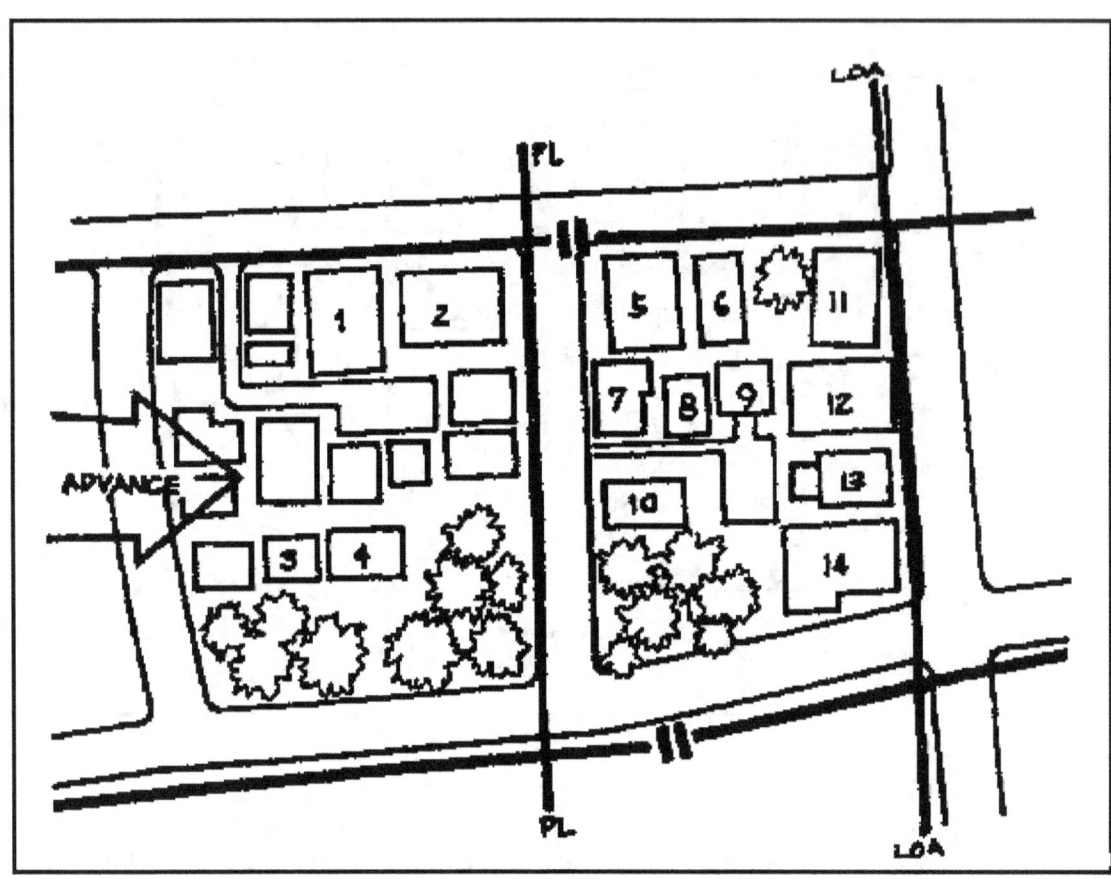

Figure 1-42. Zone and boundaries

(5) <u>Checkpoints</u>. Plan to locate checkpoints and contact points at street corners, buildings, railway crossings, bridges, or any other easily identifiable feature. Checkpoints aid in reporting locations and controlling movement. Contact points are used to designate specific points where units make physical contact.

(6) <u>Attack Position</u>. An attack position may be occupied by forward units for last-minute preparation and coordination. The attack position is often behind or inside the last large building before crossing the line of departure (LD). The LD should be the near side of either a street or rail line.

(7) <u>Front</u>. A unit's assigned frontage for the attack of a built-up area depends on the size of buildings and the resistance anticipated. A company normally attacks on a one- to two-block front, and a battalion on a two- to four-block front, based on city blocks averaging 175 meters in width.

(8) <u>Obscurants</u>. The first phase of the attack should be conducted when visibility is poor. Exploit poor visibility to cross open areas, to gain access to rooftops, to infiltrate enemy areas, and to gain a foothold. If the attack must be made when visibility is good, use smoke to conceal your movement.

(9) <u>Formations</u>. The formation used in an attack depends on the width and depth of the zone to be cleared, the character of the area, enemy resistance,

and the formation adopted by the next higher command.

(10) <u>Reserves</u>. The reserve should be mobile and prepared for commitment. Because of the available cover in built-up areas, the reserve can stay close to forward units. Battalion reserves normally follow one to two blocks to the rear of the lead company. If a company reserve is available, it follows within the same block so it can immediately influence the attack. A unit with a reserve mission may be called upon to perform one or more of the following tasks:

- Attacking from another direction.

- Exploiting an enemy weakness or friendly success.

- Clearing bypassed enemy positions.

- Securing the rear or a flank.

- Maintaining contact with adjacent units.

- Supporting or counterattacking by fire.

(11) <u>Scouts</u>. The reconnaissance platoon is normally employed to screen the battalion's flanks and rear. Its capability for reconnaissance and security is somewhat reduced in built-up areas. Scouts can also help isolate a village or small town. They must be prepared to dismount and enter buildings for reconnaissance or for setting up observation posts (OPs). Infantry platoons and squads conduct reconnaissance patrols and man OPs to supplement the scout platoon effort.

(12) <u>Engineers</u>. Forward companies may have engineers attached for providing immediate support. Engineers equipped with the M728 combat engineer vehicle (CEV) can quickly clear rubble and other obstructions using the blade or the 165-mm demolition gun. Other tasks given the engineers include:

- Preparing and using explosives to breach walls and obstacles.

- Finding and helping to remove mines.

- Destroying fortifications to a maximum range of 925 meters with the demolition gun.

- Clearing barricades and rubble to ease movement.

- Cratering roads and other countermobility measures.

(13) <u>Security</u>. Security in a built up area presents special problems. All troops must be alert to an enemy who may appear from the flanks, from above, or from underground passages (Figure 1-43).

Figure 1-43. Enemy firing from flank

b. <u>Fire Support Plan</u>. The fire support plan may require extensive air and artillery bombardment to precede the ground attack on a built-up area. This supporting fire suppresses the defender's fire, restricts his movements, and possibly destroys his position. However, use of indirect fire in built-up areas with heavily clad construction creates rubble. This can be used effectively for cover, but may also restrict the movements of attacking troops. For that reason, an artillery preparation should be short and violent. Assaulting troops must closely follow the artillery fire to exploit its effect on the defenders. While the enemy is suppressed by the supporting fire, maneuver units move near the final coordination line (FCL). As the attacking force assaults the objective, fires are lifted or shifted to block enemy withdrawal or to prevent the enemy from reinforcing their position.

Prior coordination must be made to determine the techniques and procedures to use for communication, target identification, and shifting of fires. The fire support plan can include the integration of tanks, infantry weapons, artillery, CEVs, and dismounted fires. Fire support can be categorized into indirect and direct fires.

(1) <u>Indirect Fires</u>. Indirect fire is employed in its normal role of support to the maneuver units.

(a) Indirect artillery fire is planned to isolate objectives, to prevent reinforcement and resupply, to neutralize known and suspected command and observation posts, and to suppress enemy defenders. Due to the restricted nature of urban terrain, most indirect artillery fires will be high-angle.

(b) Mortars are the most responsive indirect-fire weapons. They can hit targets of opportunity at the close ranges typical of combat

50

in built-up areas. Forward observers move with the forward units to adjust fire on targets as requested by the supported troops.

(2) Direct Fires. The direct-fire system is the most effective fire support in built-up areas. Once a target can be located in a building, one or two direct-fire rounds can accomplish what entire salvos of indirect-fire artillery cannot. Direct fire support is key to success in fighting in built-up areas. Most direct fire support is provided by armor but can also be provided by howitzers and CEVs. Tanks, howitzers, and CEVs can create rubble and building and street damage restricting movement for the attacking force.

(a) Tanks support by fire when lead units are seizing a foothold. During the attack of a built-up area, tanks overwatch the infantry's initial assault until an entry into the area has been secured. Tanks must be supported by infantry-organic weapons to suppress enemy strongpoints and by ATGMs while they move into overwatch positions. Employ tanks to take advantage of the long range of their main armament. This can usually be achieved with tanks employed outside the built-up area, where they remain for the duration of the attack to cover high-speed armor avenues of approach. This is especially true during the isolation phase.

(b) In house-to-house and street fighting, tanks move down the streets protected by the infantry and in turn support the infantry by firing their main guns and machine guns into enemy positions or OPs. Tanks are the most effective weapon for heavy fire against structures and may be used to clear rubble with dozer blades (Figure 1-44).

Figure 1-44. Tank in direct fire supported by infantry

(c) Large-caliber artillery rounds shot by direct fire are effective for

51

destroying targets in buildings. If available, self-propelled 155-mm howitzers can use direct fire to destroy or neutralize bunkers, heavy fortifications, or enemy positions in reinforced concrete buildings (Figure 1-45). Artillery guns employed in a direct-fire role must be positioned close to the infantry to provide security against an enemy ground attack.

(d) Tanks are vulnerable in built-up areas where streets and alleys provide ready-made fire lanes for defenders. Motorized traffic is greatly restricted, canalized, and vulnerable to ambush and close-range fire. Tanks are at a further disadvantage because their main guns cannot be depressed sufficiently to fire into basements or be elevated to fire into upper floors of buildings at close range (Figure 1-46).

Figure 1-45. Artillery in a direct fire role

Figure 1-46. Tank dead space

(e) In movement down narrow streets, or down wider streets with narrow paths through debris, infantry should move ahead of the tanks, clearing the buildings on each side. The movement of personnel across open areas must be planned with a specific destination in mind. Suppression of enemy positions and smoke to cover infantry movement should also be included in the plan. When needed, tanks move up to places secured by the infantry to hit suitable targets. When that area is cleared, the infantry again moves forward to clear the next area. Due to the restricted movement and limited observation of buttoned-up tanks, infantry must clear the route in advance of the tanks. The tanks and infantry should use the traveling overwatch movement technique. Infantrymen can communicate with the tank crews by using arm-and-hand signals and radio.

(f) For movement down wider streets infantry platoons normally have a section of attached tanks with one tank on each side of the street -- tanks should not be employed singly. Other tanks of the attached tank platoon should move behind the infantry and fire at targets in the upper stories of distant buildings. In wide boulevards you can employ a tank platoon secured by one or more infantry platoons. The infantry can secure the forward movement of the lead tanks, while the rearward tanks overwatch the movement of the lead units.

(g) If an infantry unit must travel streets too narrow for this type of tank support, it uses tanks in single file for support. The tanks move and fire to cover each other's approach while the infantry provides ATGM fire from buildings.

(h) Where feasible, tanks may drive inside buildings or behind walls for protection from enemy antitank missile fire. Buildings should first be cleared by the infantry. Check ground floors to ensure they will support the tank and there is no basement into which the tank could fall and become trapped. When moving, all bridges and overpasses should be checked for mines and booby traps, and for load capacity. Specific infantry elements should be assigned to protect specific tanks.

(i) Direct-fire systems organic to infantry battalions -- mainly ATGMs, recoilless rifles (in some units), and LAWs -- are initially employed to support the seizure of a foothold. Then, if necessary they are brought forward to fight enemy armor within the town. Positioning of antitank weapons in buildings must allow for enough space for backblasts. Antitank weapons are not as effective as tank rounds for neutralizing targets behind walls. They neutralize a target only if the target is located directly behind the point of impact. ATGMs are at a greater disadvantage because of their 65-meter arming distances which limits employment in close-range engagements like those in built-up areas.

3. Example of a Battalion Task Force Attack of a Built-up Area.

Because companies or company teams may become isolated during the operation, some support elements are attached. As shown in this example, Team B and Company C are forward units tasked with clearing the village. Each has engineers attached. Tanks are used to hit hardened targets protected by buildings or rubble. They may also be used to blow an entry point in buildings when the normal entrances are covered by enemy fire. The CEV is used for similar tasks against tough buildings and to clear rubble. All of these actions could be modified for use by any type of infantry unit.

a. Situation. Bonnland, the objective area, sits astride a major road and must be seized so friendly forces can use the road to continue the attack. It is dominated by high ground on either hide. Bonnland and the surrounding terrain are defended by enemy motorized rifle troops in platoon strongpoints. The task force (TF) is organized as follows:

TEAM A	TF CONTROL
A/1-72 Mech (-)	Scouts
3/A/1-1 Armor	Hvy Mort Plt
1 AT Sec	E Co (-)
1 Stinger Tm	Stinger, Sec (-)
	A/14 Engr (-)
	CEV

TEAM B

B/1-72 Mech (-)

54

2/A/1-1 Armor
2/2/A/14 Armor
1 AT Sec
1 Stinger Tm

COMPANY C

C/1-72 Mech (-)
3/2/A/14 Armor
1 AT Sec
1 Stinger Tm

TEAM CLAW

A/1-1 Armor (-)
3/A/1-72 Mech (-)
3/B/1-72 Mech (-)
1/E/1/1-72 Mech and 1
Stinger Tm

b. Deliberate Attack. The TF commander plans to conduct a deliberate attack of the village. The attack has three steps:

(1) STEP 1: Isolating the Village. To isolate the village, the TF commander orders Team A and Team CLAW to seize the high ground on either side of the village (Figure 1-47).

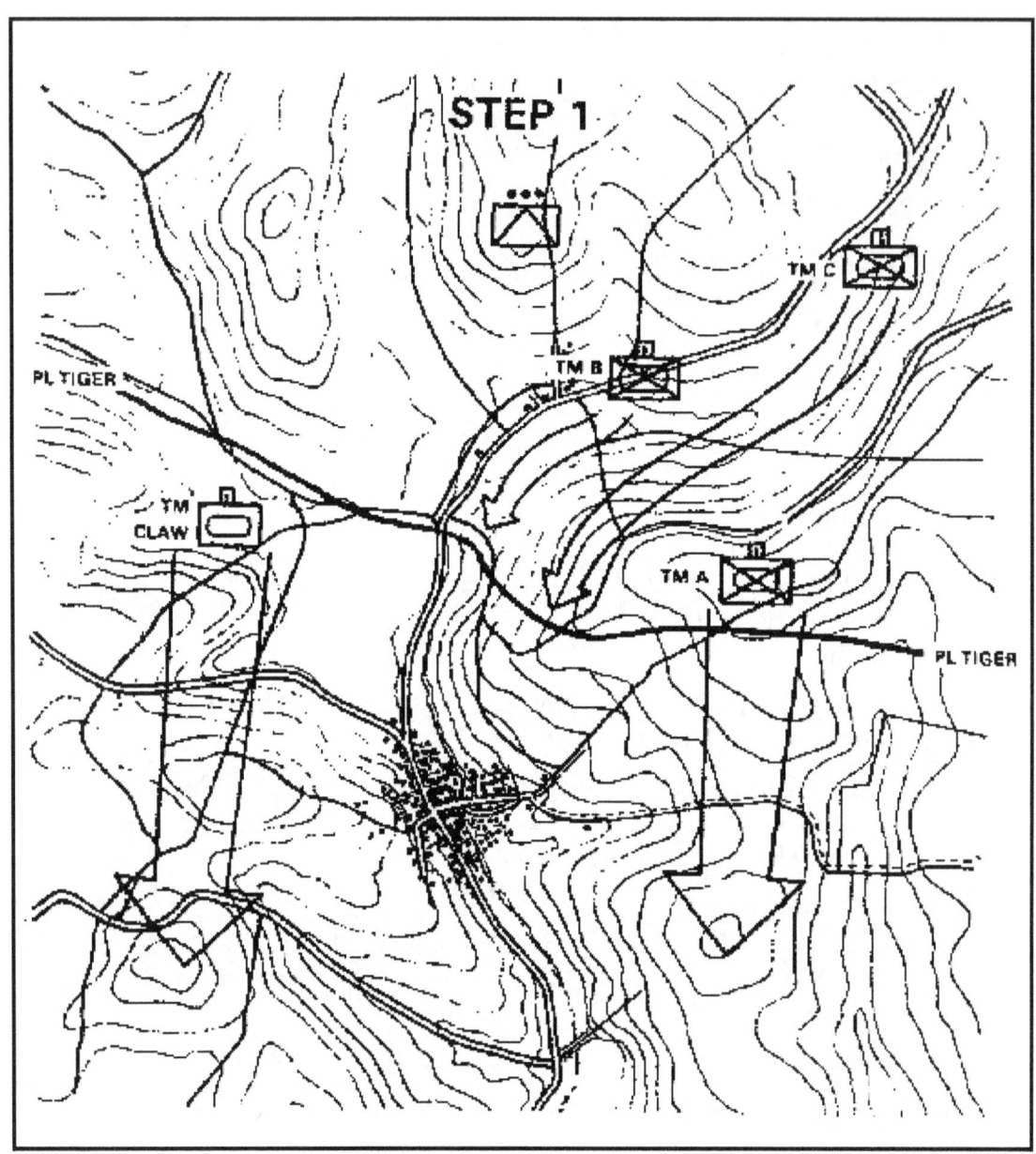

Figure 1-47. Isolation of the village

(2) Step 2: Seizing the Foothold. The scout platoon helps isolate the village by screening between the two forward teams. With Team B and the antitank company (-) overwatching, Company C attacks to seize the foothold. The TF mortars and supporting artillery fire smoke to conceal C Company's approach (Figure 1-48).

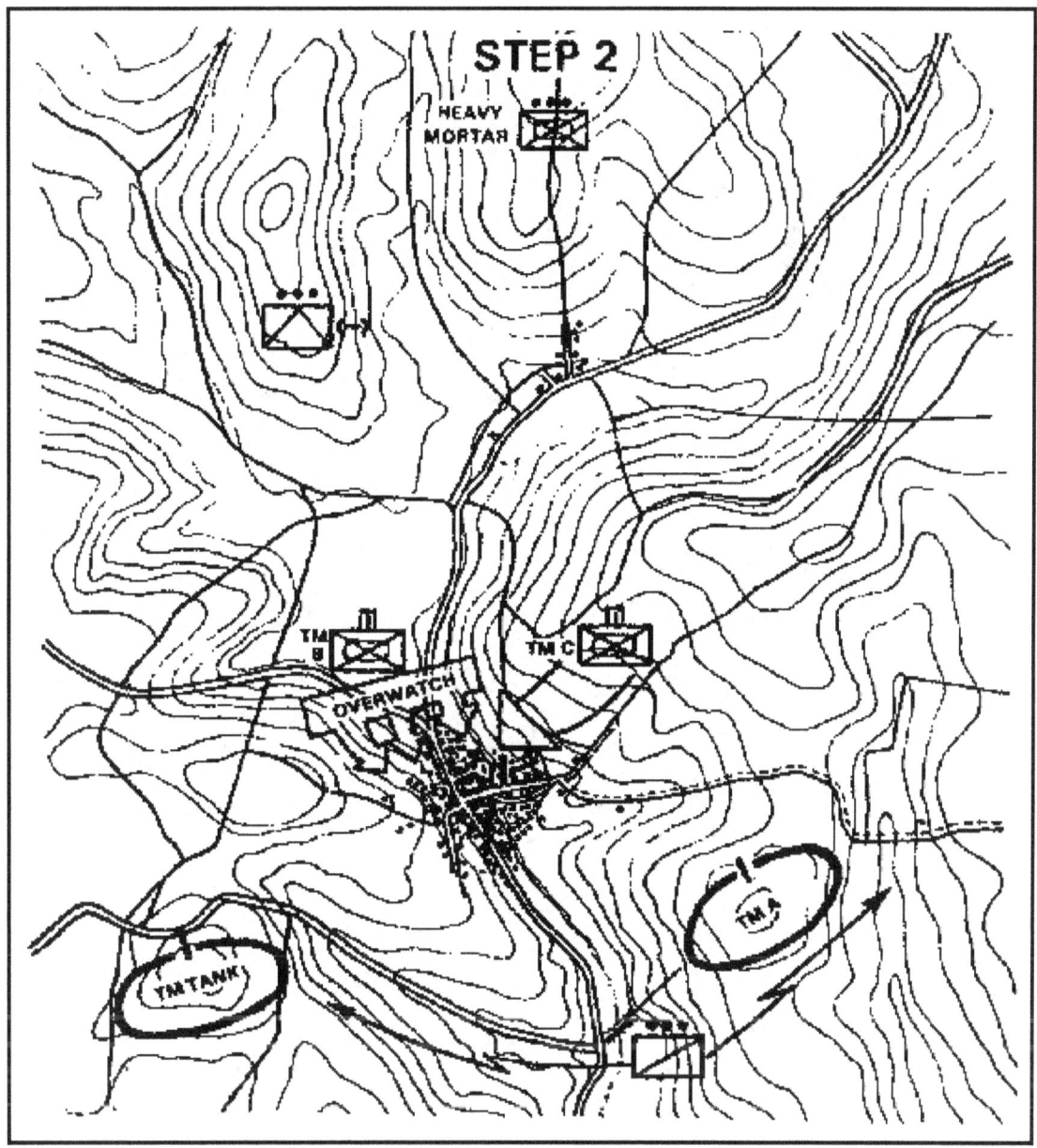

Figure 1-48. Company C attacks to seize the foothold

(3) STEP 3: Clearing the Buildings. When they have secured the foothold, Team B moves forward to join Company C in the foothold. The antitank company (-) continues to overwatch. The village is divided into two company zones. Each company clears its respective zone, building by building (Figure 1-49).

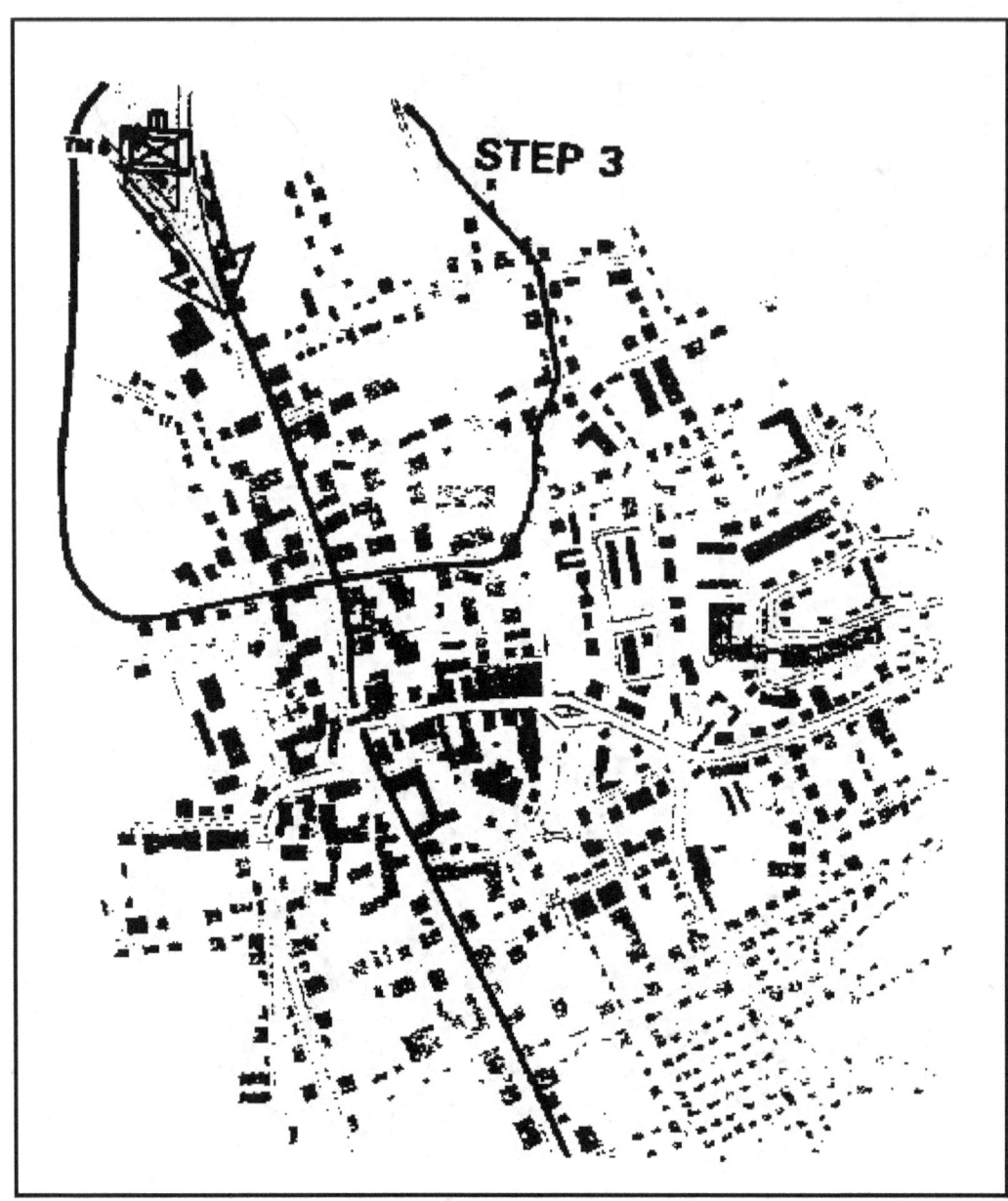

Figure 1-49. Clearing zones

c. <u>Hasty Attack Against an Outpost</u>. A TF in a movement to contact to Bonnland encounters an outpost in a small group of buildings. This situation does not call for a deliberate attack on the built-up area, but the outpost should be eliminated so following units may move along the route (Figure 1-50).

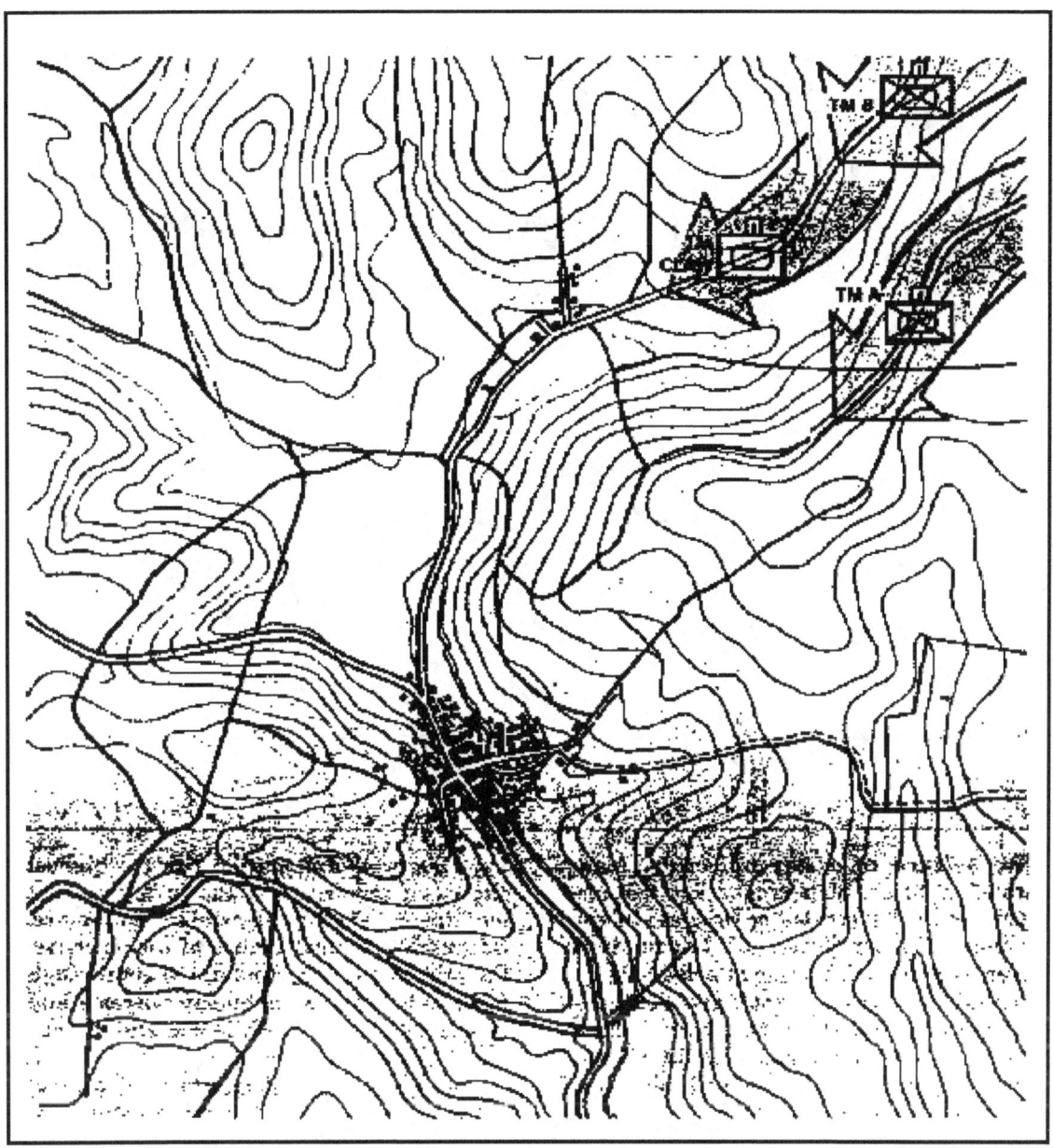

Figure 1-50. Movement formation

(1) The TF commander, must maintain the momentum of his TF and commit only enough combat power to neutralize the outpost. He orders the lead team (Team Tank) on the west axis to bypass the outpost and to continue moving.

(2) Likewise, Team A on the other axis continues its movement. Team B, the trailing team on the west axis, is ordered to clear the outpost and then to catch up with the rest of the TF. The team ordered to clear the outpost should have priority of fire. It may have additional TOWs attached from the antitank company to help isolate and neutralize the outpost (Figure 1-51).

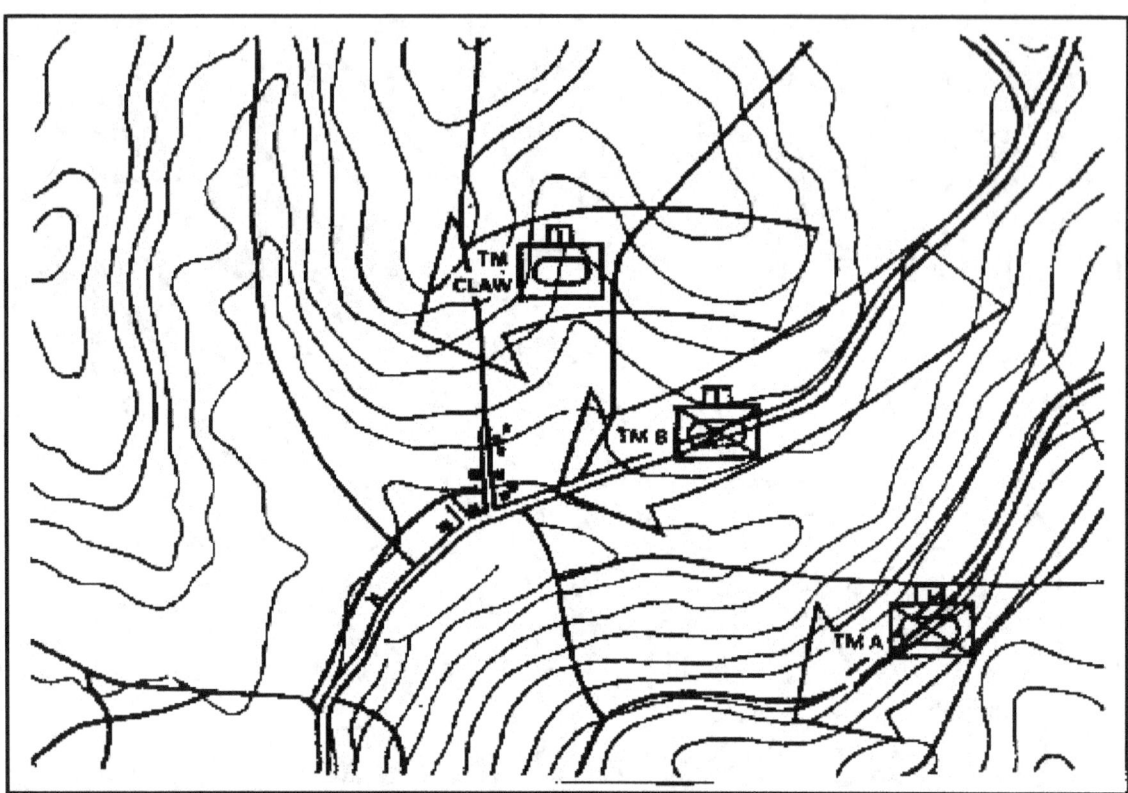

Figure 1-51. Hasty attack to clear the built-up outpost

d. <u>Seizure of a Key Objective</u>. Many built-up areas are built around key features such as road junctions or bridges. In this example, the key feature is a bridge over a river. A normal deliberate attack would not succeed here because it would give the enemy enough time to destroy the bridge. Instead, the commander must plan a rapid advance through the built-up area, leaving the task of clearing to following units.

(1) This type of operation has the highest chance of success when the enemy has not had time to set up a well-established defense. Because of the importance of the objective, the prime considerations are to get through the area fast before the enemy can react and to seize the objective while it is still intact.

(2) The TF should avoid contact with the enemy. If enemy resistance is encountered it should be bypassed. Time-consuming combat must be avoided so the TF can arrive at the bridge as quietly as possible.

(3) The TF commander organizes his TF for movement on two axes to allow for more flexibility in reacting to enemy contact. The lead unit on each axis reconnoiters as it moves. Lead units must find enemy positions, fix them by fire, and quickly bypass them.

(4) The units move mounted toward the built-up area. On reaching the edge of the built-up area, troops stay mounted until they meet enemy resistance so as not to slow the advance. Platoons are dropped off to assume blocking positions and to secure the TF advance.

60

(5) Once the objective is seized, the TF establishes a perimeter defense. The companies clear buildings and expand the size of the perimeter until it is large enough to secure the bridge against enemy action. Attached engineers examine the bridge and clear it of any explosives (Figure 1-52).

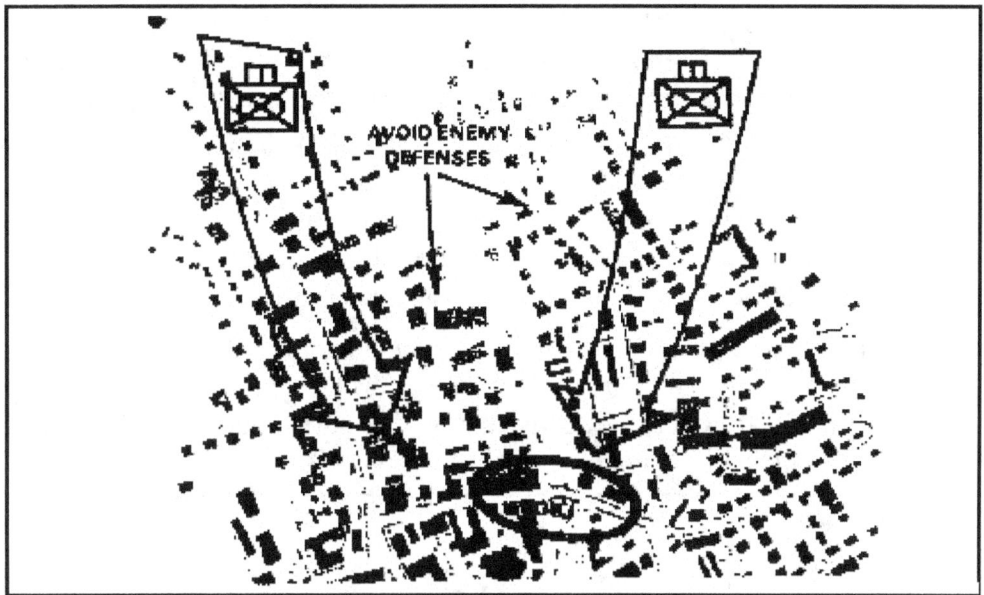

Figure 1-52. Seizure of a key objective

e. Infiltration. This example describes the actions of an infantry battalion conducting an infiltration with engineers attached. With some modification, it could also apply to a dismounted mechanized infantry battalion.

(1) The outskirts of a town may not be strongly defended. Its defenders may have only a series of antitank positions, security elements on the principal approach, or positions blocking the approaches to key features in the town. The strongpoints and reserves are deeper in the city.

(2) A battalion may be able to seize a part of the town by infiltrating platoons and companies between those enemy positions on the outskirts. Moving by stealth on secondary streets, by using the cover and concealment of back alleys and buildings, the battalion may be able to seize key street junctions or terrain features, to isolate enemy positions, and to help following units pass into the built-up area. Such an infiltration should be performed when visibility is poor and no civilians are in the area.

(3) The battalion is best organized into two infiltration companies with engineers attached to each and a reserve company with engineers attached. Each company should have an infiltration lane from 500 to 1,500 meters wide.

(4) The infiltrating companies advance on foot, with stealth, using available cover and concealment. Mortar and artillery fire can be used to divert the enemy's attention and cover the sound of infiltrating troops.

61

(5) TOWs are positioned to cover likely avenues of approach for enemy armored vehicles. The reconnaissance screens the battalion's more vulnerable flanks.

(6) As the companies move into the built-up area, they secure their own flanks. Security elements may be dropped off along the route to warn of a flank attack. Engineers assist in breaching or bypassing minefields or obstacles encountered. Enemy positions are avoided but reported.

(7) The infiltrating companies proceed until they reach their objective. At that time, they consolidate, reorganize, and arrange for mutual support. They patrol to their front and flanks, and establish contact with each other. The company commander may establish a limit of advance to reduce chances of enemy contact or to ensure safety from friendly forces.

(8) If the infiltration places the enemy in an untenable position and he must withdraw, the rest of the battalion is brought forward for the next phase of the operation. If theenemy does not withdraw, the battalion must clear the built-up area before the next phase of the operation (Figure 1-53).

Figure 1-53. Infiltration

f. Securing a Route. A mechanized infantry battalion may have to clear buildings to secure a route through a city. How quickly the battalion can clear the buildings depends on the enemy resistance and the size and number of the buildings. In outlying areas, forward units proceed by bounds from road junction to road

62

junction. Other platoons provide flank security by moving down parallel streets and by probing to the flanks.

(1) Depending on the required speed and enemy situations, the infantry may either move mounted or dismounted. The platoons move down the widest streets, avoiding narrow streets. Each squad overwatches the squad to its front, keeping watch on the opposite side of the street. The overwatching carrier teams are secured by dismounted troops. Except for those troops, the rest of the infantry may stay mounted until required to dismount by enemy fire or to attack an enemy-held building.

(2) When contact with the enemy is made, the tanks support as usual. Supporting fire fixes and isolates enemy positions which dismounted troops maneuver to attack.

(3) Phase lines can be used to control the rate of the company's advance and other action. For example, at each phase line the forward companies might reestablish contact, reorganize, and continue clearing (Figure 1-54).

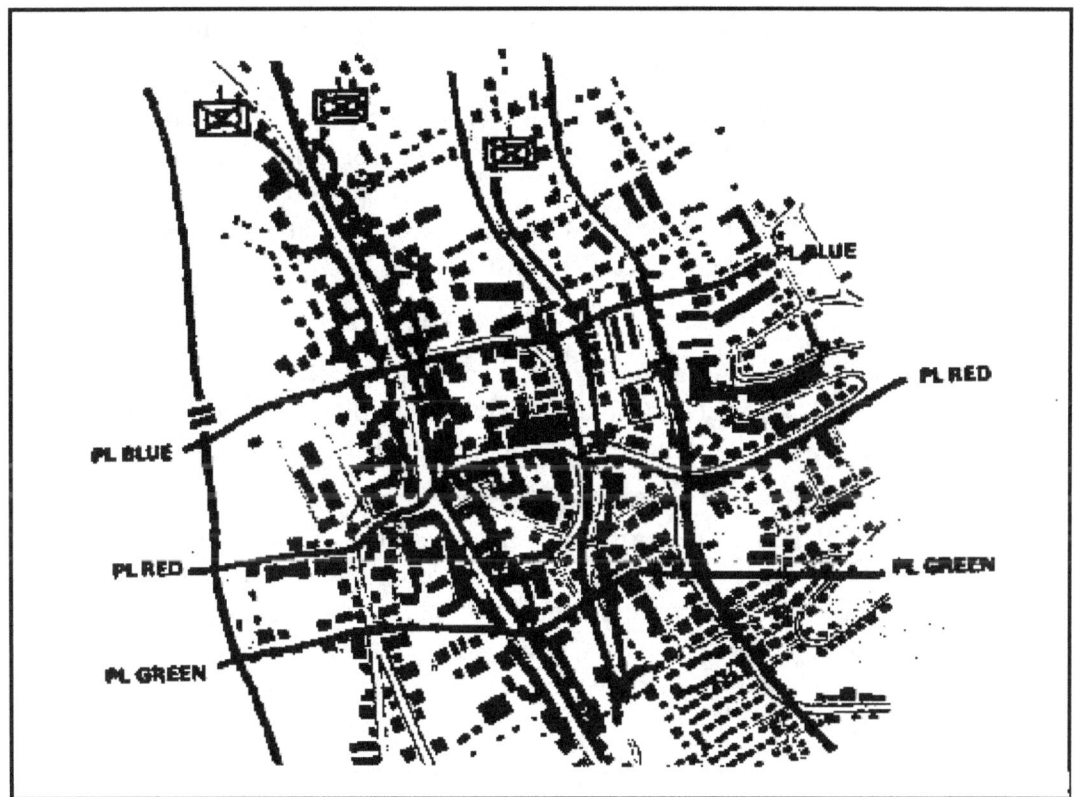

Figure 1-54. Clearing along a route

4. Company Team Attack on a Built-up Area.

The following are techniques which might be employed by a company. These may be independent operations but are normally part of a battalion operation.

a. Attack on a Block. To attack a block in a built-up area, a company should be reinforced with tanks and engineers. The operation can be accomplished either by an infantry unit or, by a dismounted mechanized infantry unit using its carrier-mounted machine guns for fire support.

(1) This operation is characterized by platoon attack supported by both direct and indirect fires. Success depends on isolating the enemy positions (which often become platoon objectives), suppressing enemy weapons, seizing a foothold in the block, and clearing the block's buildings room by room.

(a) Task organization of the company varies because of the nature of the built-up area. For example a nonmechanized infantry company fighting on the outskirts of a city might organize as follows:

- Two rifle platoons reinforced with engineers -- to assault.

- One rifle platoon -- reserve.

- One tank platoon -- in support of the assaulting rifle platoons.

(b) In a core or core periphery area, that same company might be organized as follows:

- Two rifle platoons, each with engineers and tanks, under the platoon leader's operational control (OPCON) -- to assault. (The engineers and tanks are placed under the platoon leader's OPCON due to the independent, isolated combat to be expected in those areas.).

- One platoon -- in reserve.

- All available direct- and indirect-fire weapons should be used to isolate objective buildings. Direct fire down streets and indirect fire in open areas between buildings helps in the objective isolation.

(2) Tanks, machine guns, and other direct-fire support weapons fire on the objective from covered positions. These weapons should not be fired for prolonged periods from one position. The gunners should use a series of positions and displace from one to another to gain better fields of fire and to avoid being targeted by the enemy. Direct-fire support tasks are assigned as follows:

Machine guns fire along streets and into windows, doors, and so forth.

TOWs and Dragons fire at enemy tanks and other armored vehicles.

Tanks fire at targets protected by walls and make entrances in buildings (Figure 1-55).

Riflemen engage targets of opportunity.

(3) Before an assault, the company commander should employ smoke to

conceal the assaulting platoons. He secures their flanks with direct-fire weapons and by employment of the reserve if necessary.

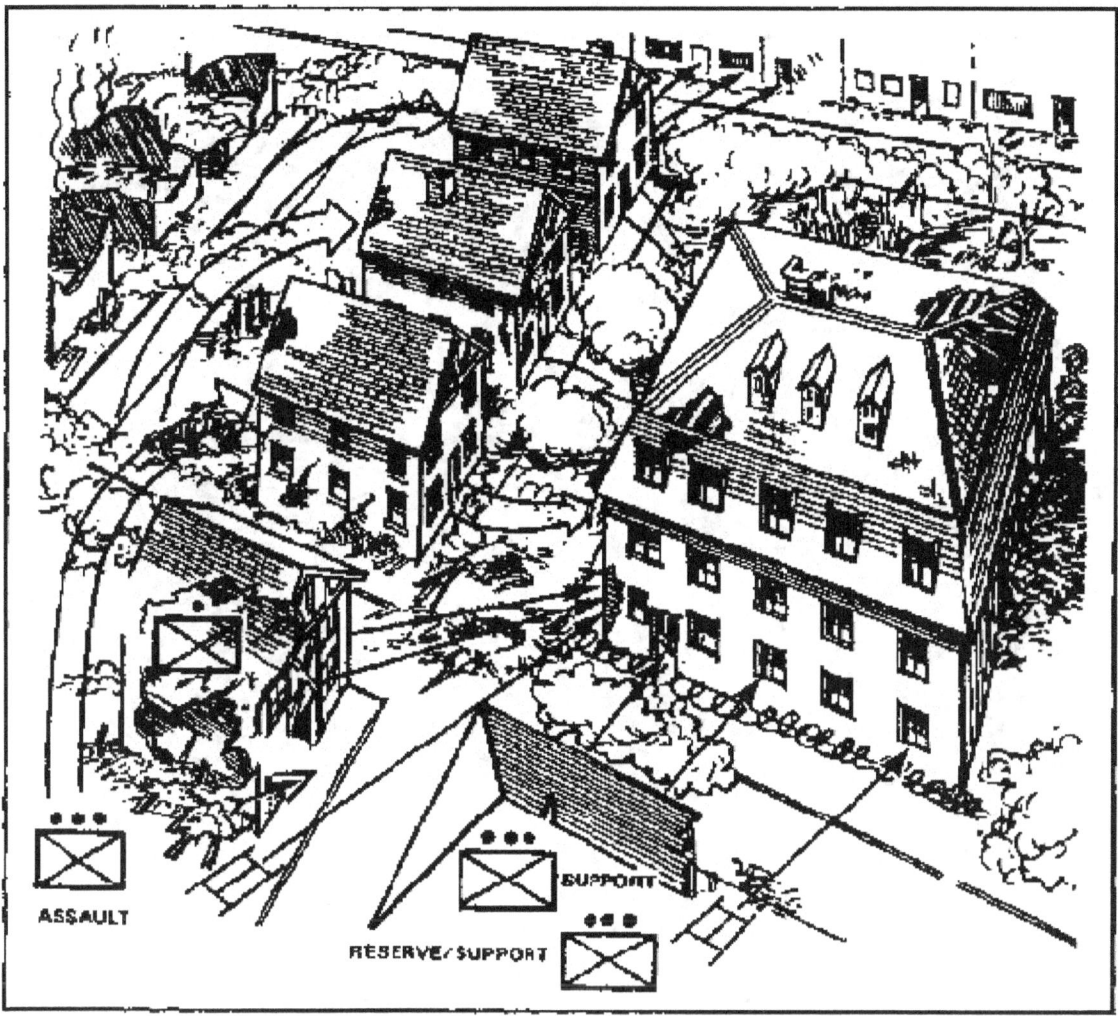

Figure 1-55. Company attack of a strongpoint

(a) Concealed by smoke and supported by direct-fire weapons, an assaulting platoon attacks the first isolated building. The platoon must close on the building quickly while the enemy is still stunned by supporting fire. The company commander must closely coordinate the assault with its supporting fire so the fire is shifted at the last possible moment.

(b) The squads and platoons clear each building. After seizing the block, the company consolidates and reorganizes to repel a counterattack or to continue the attack.

(c) A mechanized infantry company would be organized on similar lines. The assault platoons should be dismounted. The Bradley fighting vehicle's (BFV's) 25-mm gun and attached tanks can provide direct-fire support.

b. <u>Attack on an Enemy Outpost</u>. Earlier, this part of the lesson discussed the

65

actions of a task force when it encountered an enemy outpost. This example discusses the actions of the company team ordered to make the hasty attack (Figure 1-56).

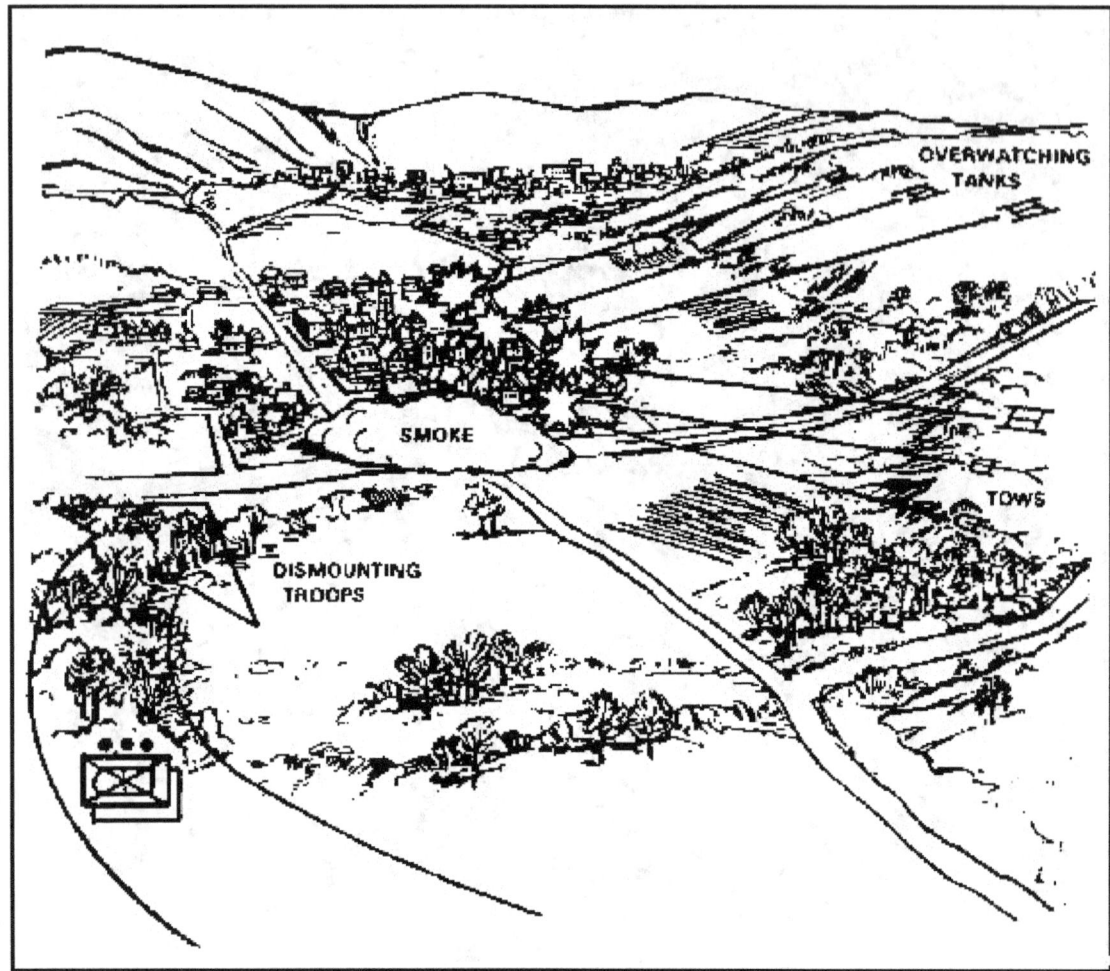

Figure 1-56. Hasty attack of an outpost

(1) The company team commander uses a form of fire and movement. His tanks and TOWs assume overwatch positions from which they can fire on the outposts, keep the enemy from escaping, and destroy any reinforcements.

(2) The rifle platoons then move into the area. They do not attack head on, but from a covered route so as to hit the outpost at a vulnerable point. As the platoons approach the outpost, smoke is employed to screen their movement and supporting fires are shifted. Once the platoons close on the outpost, they clear the buildings quickly and consolidate. The company is then ready to continue operations.

c. Seizure of a Traffic Circle. A company may have to seize a traffic circle either to secure it for friendly use or to deny it to the enemy (Figure 1-57). This operation consists of seizing and clearing the buildings that control the traffic circle and bringing direct-fire weapons into position to cover it. This is

66

accomplished by either clearing the routes of mines and obstacles so they can be used by friendly traffic, or by laying mines on the routes to prevent enemy use.

(1) After gathering all available intelligence on the terrain, enemy, and population, the commander plans for the following steps:

- Isolate the objectives.

- Seize and clear the buildings along the traffic circle under cover of tanks, ATGMs, and machine guns.

- Consolidate and prepare for counterattack.

(2) Friendly troops should not venture into the traffic circle until it is under friendly control. A traffic circle is a natural kill zone.

(3) The company should be organized as follows:

- A security element (charged with isolating the traffic circle and neutralizing enemy troops defending it) -- one rifle platoon with engineers.

- An assault element -- two rifle platoons reinforced with engineers.

- A support element (providing direct-fire support for the assault element) -- the company's TOWs and attached tanks.

- A reserve -- one rifle platoon.

(4) At various stages in this operation, those roles may change. For example, the assault element may clear buildings until the support element can no longer support it. Then the reserve can be committed to the assault. It may also happen that one of the assault platoons is in a better position to isolate the traffic circle. At that time, the isolating platoon would become an assault platoon.

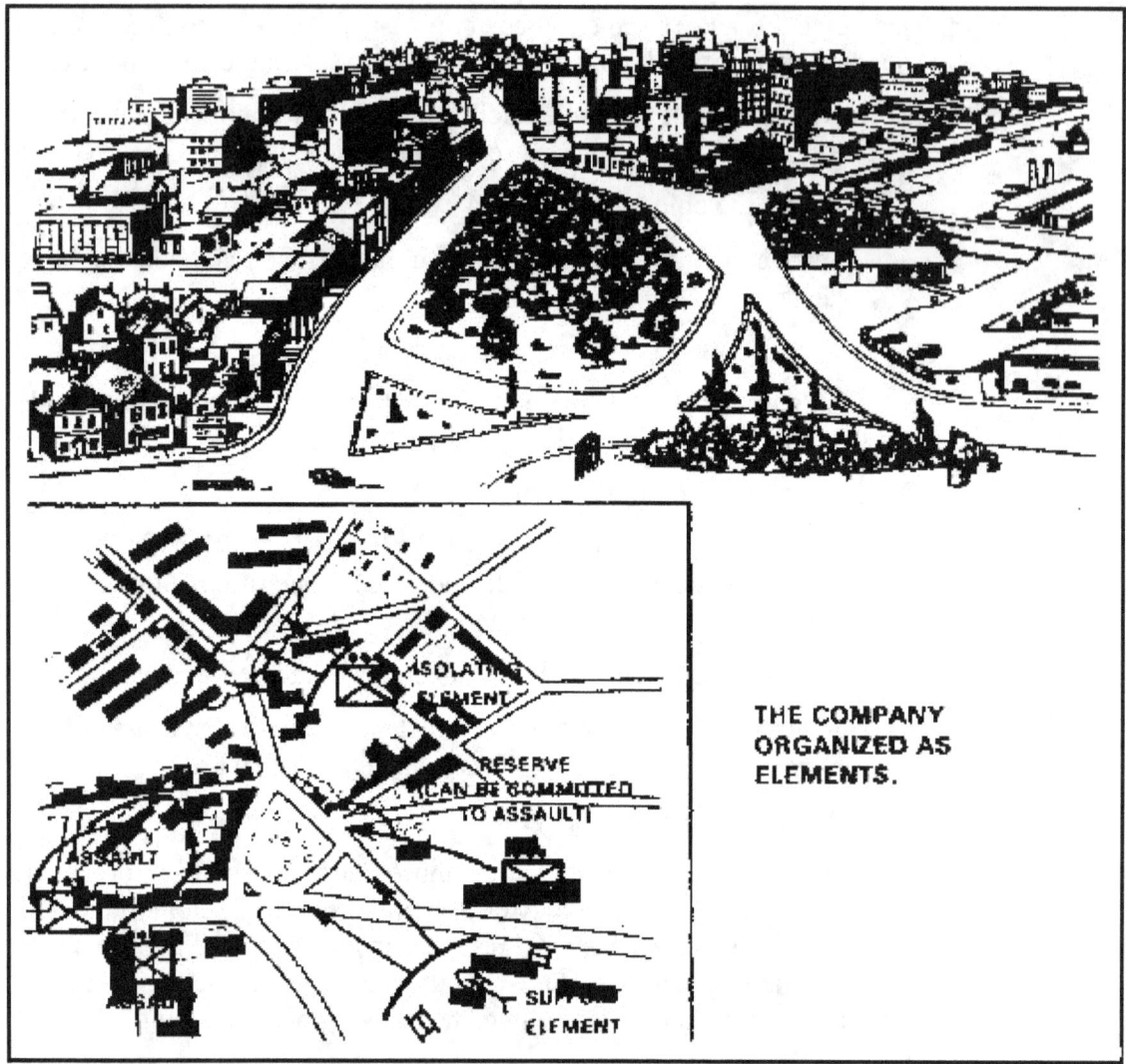

Figure 1-57. Seizure of a traffic circle

d. <u>Seizure of Key Terrain</u>. A bridge or overpass spanning a canal, highway, or railroad is an example of key terrain in a city. Therefore, seizing such a crossing point intact and securing it for friendly use is a likely mission for a rifle company.

(1) For this mission, a rifle company should take the following actions:

- Clear the buildings on the near bank that permit a clear view of the bridge and provide good fields of fire for supporting weapons.

- Quickly suppress enemy weapons on the far bank with direct fire.

- Use screening smoke to limit enemy observation and reduce interference with friendly direct fires.

- Seize a bridgehead (buildings dominating the bridge) on the far bank by an assault across the bridge.

- Secure a perimeter around the bridge so engineers can clear any obstacles and remove demolitions on the bridge.

68

(2) The first step in seizing a bridge is to clear the buildings on the near bank. Find out which buildings dominate approaches to the bridge. Buildings permitting you to employ light antitank weapons (LAWs), Dragons, machine guns, and riflemen are cleared while supporting fire prevents the enemy from reinforcing his troops on the far bank and keeps enemy demolition parties away from the bridge.

(3) In suppressing the enemy's positions on the far bank, give priority to those positions from which the enemy can fire directly down the bridge. Tanks and machine guns are effective in this role. TOWs, Dragons, and, in some cases, LAWs can be used against enemy tanks covering the bridge. The company fire support officer (FSO) should plan artillery and mortar fires to suppress infantry and antitank weapons.

The objectives of the assaulting platoons are buildings dominating approaches to the bridge. One or two platoons assault across the bridge using all available cover while concealed by smoke. They are supported by the rest of the company and attached tanks. Once on the other side, they call for the shift of supporting fire and start clearing buildings. When the first buildings are cleared, supporting fire is shifted again and the assault continues until all the buildings in the objective area are cleared.

(4) At this point, the engineers clear the bridge and its approaches of all mines, demolitions, and obstacles. The company commander may expand his perimeter to prepare for counterattack. Once the bridge is cleared, the tanks and other support vehicles are brought across to the far bank (Figure 1-58).

BUILDINGS THAT
DOMINATE APPROACHES
ARE OBJECTIVES.

Figure 1-58. Seizure of a bridge

e. Reconnaissance. In a fast-moving situation, a company may have a movement to contact through a built-up area along a highway. Similarly, a company may have to reconnoiter such a route to prepare for a battalion task force attack. This type of mission is best accomplished by a mechanized infantry company with an attached tank platoon, if available.

(1) This operation is characterized by alternating periods of rapid movement to quickly cover distances and much slower movement for security. The speed of movement selected depends on the terrain and enemy situation (Figure 1-59).

(2) In open areas where rapid movement is possible, a tank section should lead. In closer terrain, the infantry should lead while overwatched by the tanks. Another mechanized rifle platoon and the other tank section should move on a parallel street. Artillery fire should be planned along the route. Engineers accompany the lead platoon on the main route to help clear obstacles and mines.

70

**Figure 1-59. Movement to contact along a highway
through a city (commerical ribbon)**

(3) The team should seize the key points on the highway (crossroads, bridges, and overpasses) by combinations of the following actions:

- Between key points, the team moves with the infantry mounted when contact is not likely.

- At key points or when enemy contact is likely, the team moves dismounted to clear enemy positions or to secure the key point. Tanks support the dismounted troops.

(4) In peripheral or strip areas, this advance should be on one axis with the lead unit well forward and security elements checking side streets as they are reached. In the city core, this operation is conducted as a coordinated movement on two or three axes for more flank security.

(5) Enemy positions can be either destroyed by the team itself or, if the need for speed is great, bypassed and left to following units.

(6) The subunits of the team must coordinate their action. The company commander reports all information collected to the battalion task force.

5. Platoon Attack on a Built-up Area.

Platoons seldom perform independent operations in combat in built-up areas, but because of the type of combat to be expected, they can become isolated and seem to be alone. These paragraphs discuss techniques that might be employed by a platoon under such conditions. These operations are conducted as part of a company operation.

a. Attack of a Building. The most common platoon offensive mission in a built-up area is the attack of a building. The platoon must kill the defenders and secure the building.

(1) The attack involves isolating the building to prevent the escape or reinforcement of its defenders (normally coordinated at company level); suppressing the defenders with tank, machine gun, and mortar fire; entering the building at the least-defended point or, through a hole breached by tank fire; and clearing the building. To clear it, troops normally go quickly to the top floor and clear from the top down. There must be close coordination between the assault and support elements of the platoon using radios, telephones, arm-and-hand signals, or pyrotechnics.

(a) If a platoon is attacking a building independently, it should be organized with an assault element, support element, and security element to cover its flanks and rear. In addition to its own support elements, the platoon can be supported by tanks and other elements of the company.

(b) If one platoon is attacking, supported by the rest of the company, security may be provided by the other rifle platoons. The assault has three steps:

STEP 1: Isolate the building.

STEP 2: Enter the building.

STEP 3: Clear the building methodically room by room and floor by floor.

(c) The clearing is performed by the rifle squads, which pass successively through each other (leapfrogging) as rooms and floors are secured. Platoons clearing buildings should be reinforced with engineers to help with demolition (Figure 1-60).

Figure 1-60. Attack of a building

b. <u>Movement Down a Street</u>. When moving in built-up areas, a platoon follows the same principles of movement as in other areas. However, some movement techniques must be modified to adjust to a built-up area. This discussion focuses on the movement down the street of the lead platoon of a rifle company, either mechanized or nonmechanized.

(1) The platoon members must be prepared to return fire immediately. They must also be alert for any signs of the enemy and report this information promptly.

(2) The speed of movement depends on the type of operation, terrain, and degree of enemy resistance. In outlying or lightly defended areas, a mechanized infantry platoon proceeds along the street mounted, but sends dismounted men forward to reconnoiter key points (crossroads, bridges). In the center of a built-up area or in situations when there is heavy fighting, the platoon moves on foot with two squads leading -- one an each side of the road -- using all available cover. They move through the buildings, if feasible, to avoid exposure on the streets. The squads give each other mutual support.

(3) Enemy action against the platoon might consist of an ambush on the street, enfilade fire down the streets, sniper fire from rooftops, or artillery or mortar fire.

(4) For protection from those dangers, the platoon should move through buildings and along walls, use tanks for fire support, station men on the roofs or upper stairs for overwatch, and search for defenders in all three dimensions.

(5) The platoon moves in two elements: a maneuver element (one squad on narrow streets, two squads on wide streets) that moves forward, scouts danger areas, and closes with the enemy; and an overwatch element (the rest of the platoon and its supporting weapons) that moves behind the maneuver elements secures the flanks and rear and provides fire support. These two elements, or parts of them, can exchange roles (Figure 1-61).

c. Counterattacks. A platoon may be given the mission of counterattacking for one of two reasons: recapturing a defensive position or a key point, destroying or ejecting an enemy foothold; or stopping an enemy attack by striking his flank, forcing him to stop and adopt a hasty defense.

(1) Platoon counterattacks are planned at company level to meet each probable enemy penetration. They must be well coordinated and executed violently. Preferably, counterattacks should be directed at an enemy flank and supported with direct and indirect fire.

(2) In outlying areas, where the terrain is relatively open, a mechanized infantry platoon accompanied by tanks can approach the counterattack objective mounted for speed. The tanks destroy the enemy's tanks and heavy weapons while the infantry dismounts to clear the objective. In central or more congested areas, the tanks progress deliberately, from point to point, providing close support to the dismounted troops. Counterattacks require the following:

Figure 1-61. Movement down a street

- An analysis of the probable avenues of enemy approach.

- Reconnaissance and rehearsal along each counterattack route and of each proposed overwatch position.

- Construction of obstacles and fighting positions to canalize or block the enemy.

- Gaps or lanes through these obstacles if the counterattacks are to be quick enough to affect the action.

- Rapid and aggressive execution -- leaders must set the example.

- Flexibility to react to unforeseen circumstances.

PART D - DEFENSIVE OPERATIONS

In a built-up area, the defender takes advantage of the abundant cover and concealment. He also considers restrictions to the attacker's maneuverability and observation abilities. By using the terrain and fighting from well-prepared and mutually supporting positions, a

75

defending force can inflict heavy losses on, or defeat a larger attacking force.

1. Defense Considerations.

You must decide whether defending a built-up area is needed to successfully complete your mission. Consider the issues covered in the following paragraphs while making your decision.

a. Reasons for Defending Built-up Areas. The following are appropriate reasons for defending built-up areas.

(1) Certain built-up areas contain strategic, industrial, transportation, or economic complexes which must be defended for strictly psychological or national morale purposes even if they do not offer a tactical advantage to the defender. Because of the sprawl of such areas, combat power is required for their defense. Thus, the decision to defend these complexes is the responsibility of political authorities or the theater commander.

(2) Your needs to shift and concentrate combat power and to move large amounts of supplies over a wide battle area, dictate that you retain vital transportation centers. Since most transportation centers serve large areas, you must defend all of the built-up area to control such centers.

(3) The worldwide increase in sprawling built-up areas has made it impossible for forces conducting combat operations to avoid cities and towns. Most avenues of approach are straddled by small towns every few kilometers and must be controlled by defending forces. These areas can be used as battle positions or strongpoints. Blocked streets can canalize attacking armor into mined areas or zones covered by antiarmor fire. If an attacker tries to bypass a built-up area, he may encounter an array of tank-killing weapons. To clear such an area, the attacker must sacrifice speed and momentum, and expend many resources. A city or town can easily become a major obstacle.

(4) Forces can be concentrated in critical areas. Due to the tactical advantages to the defender, a well-trained force defending a built-up area can inflict major losses on a superior attacking force. Have the bulk of your combat power available for use in open terrain. However, defenders in built-up areas perform an economy-of-force role.

(5) Forces can be well concealed in built-up areas. Aerial photography, imagery, and sensory devices cannot detect forces deployed in cities. Command posts (CPs), reserves, CSS complexes, and combat forces emplaced well in built-up areas are hard to detect.

b. Reasons For Not Defending Built-up Areas. Consider the following reasons for not defending built-up areas.

(1) The location of the built-up area does not support the overall defensive plan. If the built-up area is too far forward or back in a unit's defensive sector, is isolated, or is not astride an enemy's expected avenue of approach, you may choose not to defend it.

(2) Nearby terrain allows the enemy to bypass on covered or concealed routes. Some built-up areas, mainly smaller ones, are bypassed by main roads and highway systems. An easily bypassed built-up area -- normally will be.

(3) Structures within the built-up area do not adequately protect the defenders. Extensive areas of lightly built or flammable structures offer you little protection. You may choose not to defend built-up areas near flammable or hazardous industrial areas, such as refineries or chemical plants.

(4) Dominating terrain is close to the built-up area. If the built-up area can be dominated by an enemy force occupying close terrain, you might choose to defend from there rather than the built-up area. This applies mainly to small built-up areas such as villages.

(5) Better fields of fire exist outside the built-up area. You may choose to base all or part of your defense on the long-range fields of fire existing outside a built-up area. This applies mainly to armor-heavy forces defending sectors with multiple, small, built-up areas surrounded by farm areas.

(6) The built-up area has cultural, religious, or historical significance. The area may have been declared an "open city," in which case, by international law, it is demilitarized and must be neither defended nor attacked. The presence of large numbers of noncombatants, hospitals, or wounded personnel may also affect your decision not to defend a built-up area.

2. Characteristics of Built-up Areas.

The defense of a built-up area is organized around key terrain features, buildings, and areas preserving the integrity of the defense and providing ease of movement. Organize and plan your defense by considering fire hazards, obstacles, communications restrictions, cover and concealment, avenues of approach, and fields of fire and observation.

a. Fire Hazards. A defender's detailed knowledge of the terrain permits him to avoid areas likely to be fire hazards. All cities are vulnerable to fire, especially those with many wooden buildings. You can deliberately set fires to accomplish the following:

- To disrupt and disorganize the attackers.

- To canalize the attackers into more favorable engagement areas.

- To obscure the attacker's observation.

b. Obstacles. A city itself is an obstacle since it canalizes and impedes an attack. Likely avenues of approach should be blocked by obstacles and covered by fire. Barriers and obstacles should be emplaced in three belts.

(1) The first belt the enemy will encounter is at the nearest buildings

across from and parallel to the main defensive position. This belt consists of wire and improvised barriers, both inside buildings and outside, in open areas, danger areas, and dead space. These barriers and obstacles should be heavily booby trapped. This belt impedes enemy movement, breaks up and disorganizes attack formations, and inflicts casualties.

(2) The second belt is placed between the first belt and the main defensive position buildings, but out of handgrenade range from defensive positions. It impedes movement, channels the enemy into the best fields of fire, breaks up attack formations, and inflicts casualties. This belt is not meant to stop enemy soldiers permanently. It should be constructed efficiently to give the most benefit -- not to be an impenetrable wall. It consists mainly of wire obstacles, improvised barriers, road craters, and mine fields. It should be boobytrapped heavily (including trip-wire-activated Claymores). Triple-strand concertina is placed along the M60's final protective line (FPL) (as designated earlier with engineer tape) to slow the enemy on the FPL and allow the machine gun to be used effectively.

(3) The third belt is the defensive position's denial belt. It consists of wire obstacles placed around, through, and in the defensive buildings and close-in mine fields. It impedes and complicates the enemy's ability to gain a foothold in the defensive area. It should be booby trapped and Claymores should be used extensively, both trip-wire activated and command detonated. The booby traps and Claymores should be placed where they will not cause friendly casualties.

(4) All avenues of approach (surface and subsurface) must be denied. Do not overlook the use of field-expedient obstacles such as carts, light poles, and so on (Figure 1-62), or the emplacement of antipersonnel and antitank mines.

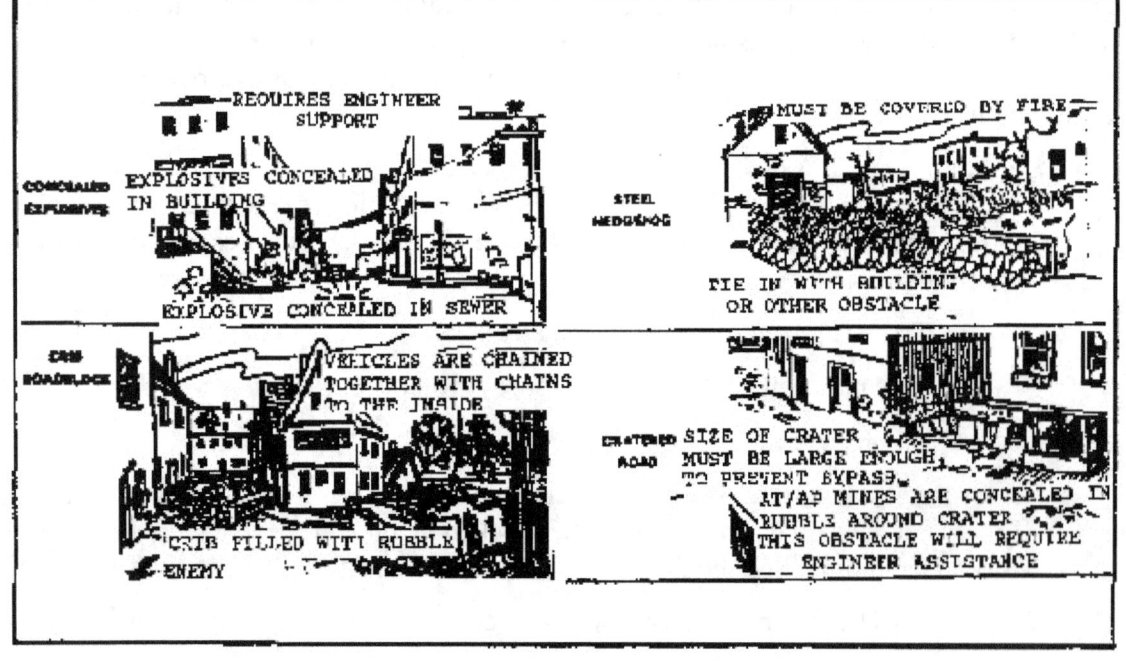

Figure 1-62. Examples of field-expedient obstacles

c. Communications Restrictions. Wire is the primary means of communication for controlling the defense of a city and for enforcing security. However, wire can be compromised if it's interdicted by the enemy. Radio communication in built-up areas is normally degraded by structures and a high concentration of electrical power lines. The new family of radios may correct this problem, but all units within the built-up area may not have these radios. Therefore, radio is an alternate means of communication. Messengers can be used well as another means of communication. Visual signals may also be used but are often not effective because of the screening effects of buildings, walls, and so forth. Signals must be planned, widely disseminated, and understood by all assigned and attached units. Increased noise (the din of battle) makes the effective use of sound signals difficult.

d. Cover and Concealment. Prepare positions using the protective cover of walls floors, and ceilings. Soldiers should always improve positions using materials at hand. When the defender must move, he can reduce his exposure by doing the following:

- Using prepared breaches through buildings.

- Moving through reconnoitered and marked underground systems.

- Using trenches and sewage systems.

- Using the concealment offered by smoke and darkness to cross open areas.

To accomplish his mission, the attacker must advance by crossing streets and open areas between buildings where he is exposed to fires from concealed weapons positions.

e. Avenues of Approach. As the defender, you must not only consider the conventional avenues of approach into and out of the city, but also the avenues within built-up areas above and below ground level. The defender normally has the advantage. He knows the city and can move rapidly from position to position through buildings and underground passages.

f. Fields of Fire and Observation. Position weapons to obtain maximum effect and mutual supporting fire. This allows for engagements out to maximum effective ranges. Artillery forward observers (FOs) should be well above street level to adjust fires on the enemy at maximum range. Fires and final protective fires (FPFs) are planned on the most likely approaches to allow for their rapid shifting to threatened areas.

3. Defensive Plan at Battalion Level.

The built-up area defensive plan at battalion level depends on the size and location of the area. Many factors must be considered before instituting such a plan.

a. Defense of a Village. A battalion task force (TF) assigned a defensive sector that includes a village could incorporate the village as a strongpoint in its defense (Figure 1-63). This use of a built-up area is most common where the village stands astride a high-speed avenue of approach or where it lies between two difficult obstacles. To incorporate such an area into its defense, the battalion TF must control the highground on either side of the village to prevent the enemy from firing from those areas into the village.

(1) The majority of the TF tanks should be employed where the maneuver room is the greatest (on the key terrain to the flanks of the village). This is also where the TF TOWs should be employed. As the security force withdraws and the company/team assumes the fight, TOWs can assume overwatching positions in depth.

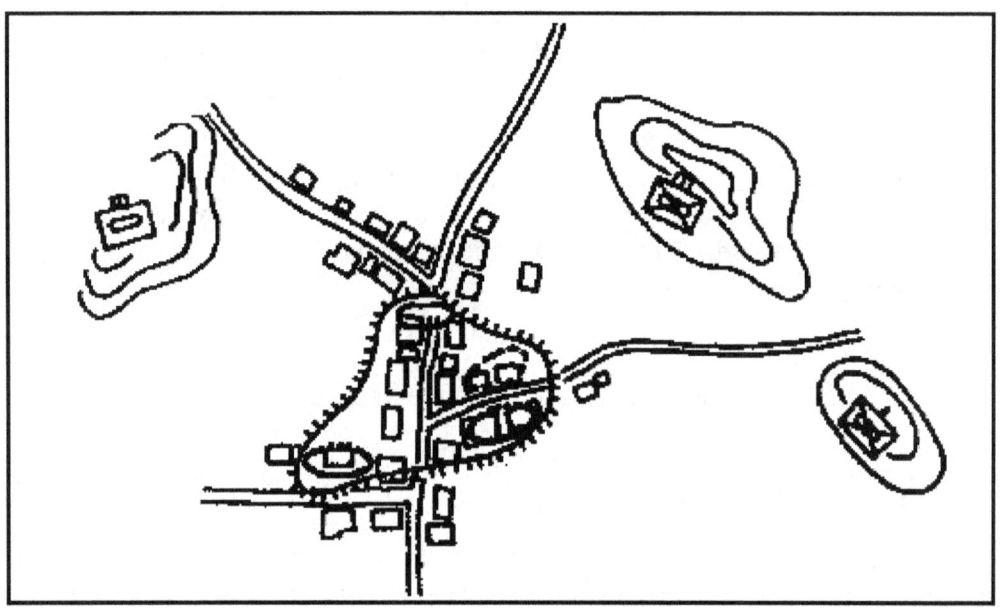

Figure 1-63. Defense of a village

(2) Although the battalion TF's disposition should prevent large enemy forces from threatening the rear and flanks of the village, the danger of small-unit enemy infiltration means the village must be prepared for all-round defense.

(3) Engineers required for team mobility operations should stay with the company/team in the town to provide continuous engineer support if that company/team becomes isolated. Engineer support for the rest of the TF should be centrally controlled by the TF commander. Engineer assets may be in direct support (DS) of the other company/teams. The priority of barrier materials, demolitions, and mines should go to the company/team in the village.

(4) The TF commander should use the key terrain on the village's flanks for maneuver to prevent the village's defense from becoming isolated. The strongpoints in the town should provide a firm location where the enemy can be stopped, around which counterattacks can be launched.

b. Defense of a Sector. Along with defending a village, a battalion TF may be given the mission of defending a sector in a city (Figure 1-64). The battalion should take advantage of the outlying structures to provide early warning and to

80

delay the enemy. Advantage is also taken of the tougher interior buildings to provide fixed defense. This defense should cover an area of about four to twelve blocks square.

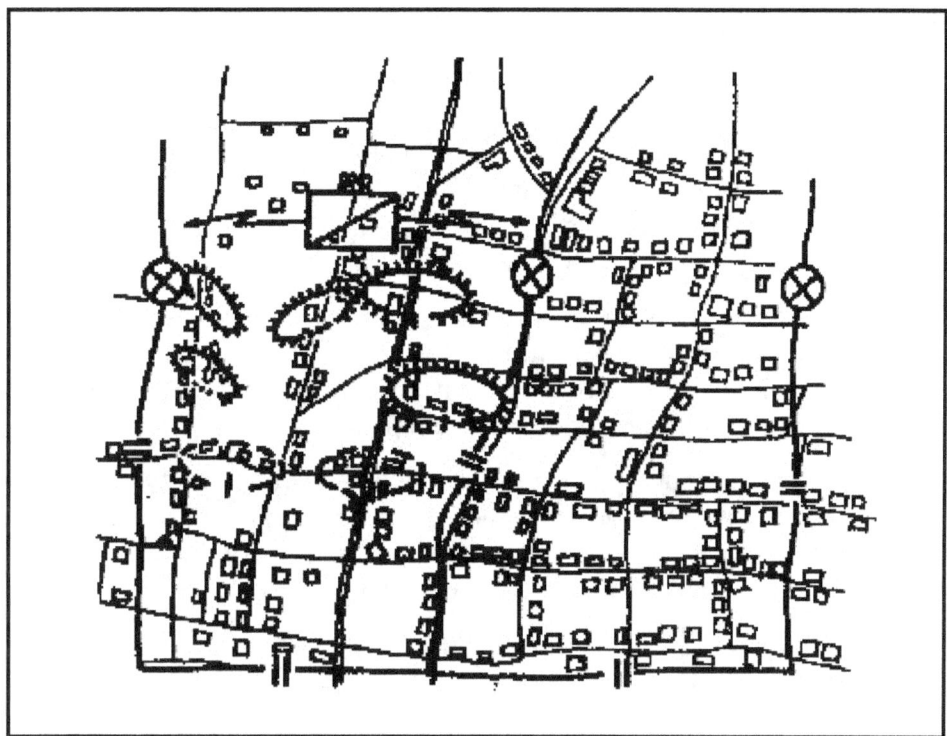

Figure 1-64. Defense of a built-up sector

(1) The battalion TF deployment begins with the reconnaissance platoon reconnoitering the built-up area to provide an area reconnaissance and location of the enemy. At the edge of the area, where fields of fire are the greatest, the battalion TF should deploy BFVs and ITVs and other antiarmor weapon systems to provide long-range antiarmor defense.

(2) The forward edge of battle area (FEBA) should include the most formidable buildings in the sector. Forward of the FEBA, the battalion TF organizes a guard force which could be a reinforced company. The guard force concentrates on causing the enemy to deploy without engaging the enemy in decisive combat. This can be done through maximum use of ambushes and obstacles, and of covered and concealed routes through buildings for disengagement. The guard force inflicts casualties and delays the enemy but avoids decisive engagement since buildings beyond the FEBA do not favor the defense. As the action nears the FEBA, the guard force detects the location of the enemy's main attack. Upon reaching the FEBA, the guard force can be used as a reserve and reinforce other elements of the battalion, or it can counterattack to destroy an enemy strongpoint.

(3) The defense along the FEBA consists of a series of strongpoints set up similar to that earlier described in the company defense of the village. Key terrain features such as strong buildings, road junctions, and good firing

81

positions should be the center of the strongpoint defense. Buildings should be prepared for defense as discussed in Lesson 2, Part C of this subcourse.

(4) The battalion's attached tanks are normally used to engage enemy tanks, cover obstacles by fire, and engage in counterattacks. Employ them in platoons where possible, but in contested areas they may be employed in sections.

(5) Use artillery fire to suppress and blind enemy overwatch elements, to engage enemy infantry and the approaches to the door, to provide counterbattery fire, and to support counterattacks using both indirect and direct fire.

(6) Attach engineers to the delaying force to help in laying mines and constructing obstacles, clearing fields of fire, and preparing routes to the rear. These routes should also have obstacles. Engineers are in support of the force in the strongpoints to help prepare fighting positions.

c. Delay Along a Commercial Ribbon. Delays weaken the enemy and gain enough time to organize a strong defense. They are often conducted by covering force units forward of a main battle area (MBA) defense. This type mission is best assigned to a mechanized infantry battalion TF.

(1) A delay along a commercial ribbon consists of a succession of ambushes and battle positions (Figure 1-65).

(a) Ambushes are planned on overwatching obstacles and are closely coordinated but decentrally executed. The deployment of the battalion TF is realigned at important cross streets. The ambushes can be combined with limited-objective attacks on the enemy's flanks. These are usually effective in the edge of open spaces, parks, wide streets, and so on. They should be executed by tanks and supported by infantry.

Figure 1-65. Delay along a commercial ribbon

(b) Place your battle positions where heavy weapons, such as tanks,

82

antitank weapons, and machine guns, will have the best fields of fire. Such locations are normally found at major street intersections, parks, and at the edges of open residential areas. Prepare your battle positions carefully and deliberately. Reinforce them by obstacles and demolished buildings and support them by artillery and mortars. They should inflict maximum losses on the enemy and cause him to deploy for a deliberate attack.

(2) Tanks and antitank weapons have prepared primary and alternate positions to reduce their vulnerability. Coordination must be continuous with withdrawing ambushes until they are safely within the battle position.

(3) The battalion TF is most effective when deployed in two delaying echelons, alternating between conducting ambushes and fighting from battle positions. As the enemy threatens to overrun a battle position, the company disengages and delays using ambush tactics back toward the next battle position. As the company passes through the company to the rear, it establishes another battle position. Use smoke and demolitions to aid in the disengagement. You can employ security elements on the flank to prevent the enemy from out-flanking the delay. A small reserve can be used to react to unexpected enemy action and to conduct continued attacks on the enemy's flank.

(4) Use engineers to support the TF. The direction of engineer effort is centralized to support the preparation of battle positions. It should be decentralized to support the force committed to ambush.

(5) The width of the TF zone depends on the nature of the buildings and obstacles along the street and the time the enemy must be delayed.

4. Defensive Plan At Company Level.

The defensive plan in built-up areas at company level depends on the size and location of the area. You have many factors to consider before instituting such a plan.

a. Defense of a Village. Once the company commander has completed his reconnaissance of the village, he scouts the surrounding terrain and, with the information assembled, develops his plan for the defense (Figure 1-66). One of his first decisions is whether to defend with his infantry on the leading edge of the village, or farther back within the village.

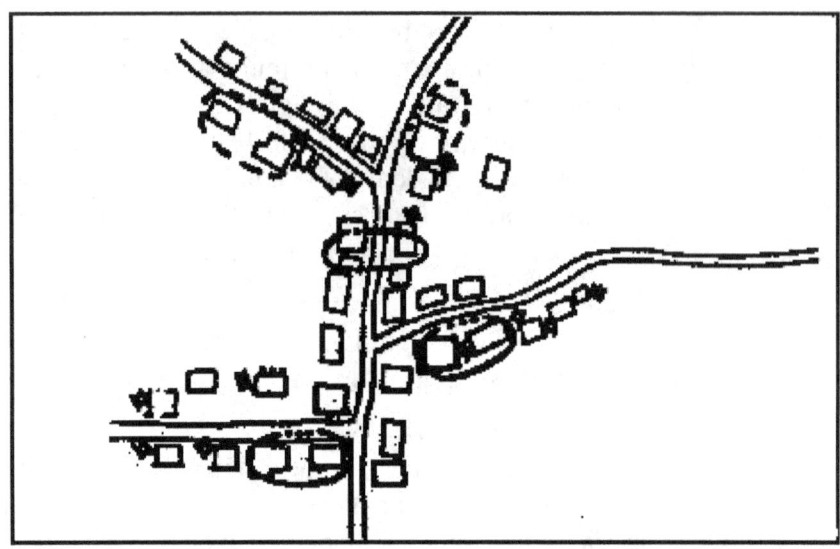

Figure 1-66. Defense of a village

(1) Several factors will influence your decision. First, you must know the type of enemy your company will defend against. If the threat is mainly dismounted infantry, the greater danger is allowing them to gain a foothold in the town. If the threat is armor or motorized infantry, the greatest danger is that massive direct fire will destroy the company's defensive positions. You must also consider the terrain forward and to the flanks of the village from which the enemy can direct fires against your positions.

(2) Platoons are given a small group of buildings in which to prepare their defense, permitting the platoon leader to establish mutually supporting squad-sized positions. This increases the area the platoon can control and hampers the enemy's ability to isolate or bypass a platoon. A platoon is responsible for the road through the village. The rest of the company is positioned to provide all-round security and defense in depth.

(3) A position for the company mortars must be chosen that protects mortars from direct fire and allows for overhead clearance. The company's BFVs/APCs are placed in positions to the rear of the buildings and interior courtyards where their weapon systems can provide added rear and flank security. Combat vehicles are assigned primary, alternate, and supplementary positions as well as primary and secondary sectors of fire. They should be positioned in defilade behind rubble and walls or inside buildings for movement into and out of the area. Control of the platoon's BFVs/APCs by the platoon leader is required for resupply, MEDEVAC, and rapid repositioning during the battle.

(4) Locate a forward CP where you can position your company trains. Choose a location near the highway to ease recovery and maintenance operations. Establish a company OP where the fields of observation are best.

(5) You must also decide which buildings must be rubbled. To defeat the enemy you need good fields of fire, but rubbling the buildings too soon or

rubbling too many, may disclose your exact locations and destroy cover from direct fire. Position the company's TOWs on high ground in and around the town to attain good fields of fire to the front and flanks.

(6) If a tank platoon is available from the TF, place the tanks along the leading edge where rapid fire will complement the TOWs and Dragons. The tank platoon leader selects the exact firing positions and assigns sectors of fire. If faced by enemy infantry, the tanks move to alternate positions with the protection of the infantry. These alternate positions allow the tanks to engage to the front, as well as the flanks, with as little movement as possible. After they are withdrawn from the leading edge of the town, the tanks can provide a mobile reserve for the team.

(7) Plan the FPFs to address the biggest threat to the platoon -- enemy infantry. When firing an FPF inside a built-up area, mortars are more effective than artillery. This is true because their higher angle of fall gives them a greater chance of impacting on the street.

(8) Obstacles, mainly antivehicle obstacles, are easily constructed in a built-up area. You need to stop enemy vehicles without interfering with your own movement in the village. Therefore, execute the emplacement of cratering charges at key street locations on order. Emplace mines on the outskirts of the town and along routes the company will not use.

(9) Supporting engineers use C4 and other explosives to make firing ports, mouseholes, and demolition obstacles. Based upon your priority of work, tell the engineer squad leader to assist each of the infantry platoons preparing the village for defense, and to execute the team's obstacle plan. The squad leader's mission is to tell the infantrymen exactly where to place the demolitions and how much is needed for the desired effect. He also assists in the emplacement and recording of the minefields as well as the preparation of fighting positions.

(10) Ammunition expenditure is usually high when fighting in a built-up area. To avoid moving around the village with ammunition resupply during the battle, direct more ammunition be stockpiled in each occupied platoon and squad position. Also order the platoons to stockpile firefighting equipment, drinking water, food, and first-aid supplies at each squad position. Other factors you should consider are the following:

- Resupply.
- MEDEVAC.
- Communications.
- Firefighting.
- Sleep and alert periods.
- Security.
- Limited visibility.

- Civilian control.

(11) To ensure adequate communications, the company installs a wire net and develops a plan for pyrotechnic signals. Backup wire should be laid in case primary lines are cut by vehicles or enemy fires. Also plan for the use of messengers throughout the village.

b. Defense of a Block. A company in a built-up area may have to defend a block in a core periphery or residential area. It conducts this operation according to the defensive scheme of the battalion. The operation is coordinated with the action of security forces charged with delaying to the front of the company's position. The defense takes advantage of the protection of buildings dominating the roads.

(1) A well-organized company defense does the following:

- Stops the enemy's attack on the roads by using obstacles and enfilade fire.

- Destroys the enemy by ambush and direct fire from prepared positions.

- Ejects the enemy from footholds or remains in place for a counterattack conducted by battalion.

(2) The operation of the company is more effective if it has time to reconnoiter the terrain and to prepare obstacles and fire lanes. Vehicles not needed for the defense should be grouped in the combat trains at battalion. The OPs should be supplemented by patrols, mainly at night, and communications should be wire. Organize the company to provide a series of OPs, a defense, and a reserve tasked with counterattacks.

(3) The defensive forces ambush on the avenues of approach, cover the obstacles by fire, and prepare a strong defense inside the buildings. The reserve can be tasked with the following:

- Reinforce the fires of the defense.

- React to a danger on the flank.

- Counterattack to throw the enemy from a foothold.

(4) Engineers are centrally controlled at company level. They construct obstacles, prepare access routes, and assist in preparing defensive positions. A company or section of tanks attached to the company provides heavy direct-fire support, engages enemy tanks, and supports counterattacks.

c. Company Delay. A company delay can be part of a battalion's defense (Figure 1-67). Its operations destroy enemy reconnaissance elements forward of the outskirts of the town, prevent their penetration of the built-up areas, and gain and maintain contact with the enemy to determine the strength and location of the main attack.

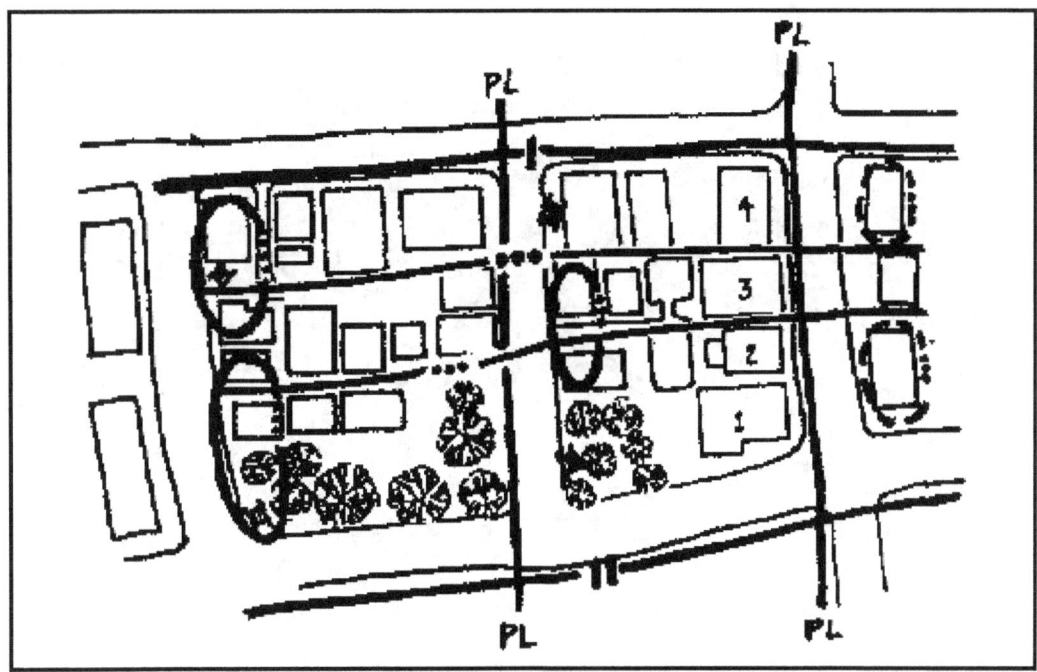

Figure 1-67. Delay in a built-up area

(1) Prepare the company's sector with obstacles to increase the effect of the delay. Engineers prepare obstacles on main routes, but avoid some covered and concealed routes known by the friendly troops for reinforcement, displacement, and resupply. These routes are destroyed when no longer needed.

(2) Antitank guided missiles are positioned on the outskirts of the town to destroy the enemy at maximum range. They should be located in defilade positions or in prepared shelters. They fire at visible targets and then fall back or proceed to alternate positions. Platoons are assigned sectors from 500 to 700 meters wide. They are reinforced with sensors or ground surveillance radars (GSRs) placed on the outskirts or on higher ground. Platoons delay by using patrols, OPs, and ambushes and by taking advantage of all obstacles. Each action is followed by a disengagement and withdrawal. By day the defense is dispersed; at night it is more concentrated. Close coordination is vital.

(3) Tanks support the platoon by engaging enemy tanks, providing reinforcing fires, aiding the disengagement of the platoons, and covering obstacles by fire.

d. <u>Defense of a Traffic Circle</u>. A rifle company or team may be assigned the mission of defending a key traffic circle in a built-up area to prevent the enemy from seizing it (Figure 1-68).

(1) If you are tasked with this mission, analyze enemy avenues of approach and the buildings dominating those avenues. Plan all possible fire power on the traffic circle itself and on the approaches to it. You should also plan for all-round defense of the buildings dominating the

87

traffic circle to prevent encirclement. Prepare as many covered and concealed routes between these buildings as possible. This makes it easier to mass or shift fires, and to execute counterattacks.

Figure 1-68. Defense of traffic circle

(2) Obstacles can also deny the enemy the use of the traffic circle. Obstacle planning in this case must consider if friendly forces are supposed to use the traffic circle. TOWs and Dragons can fire across the traffic circle if fields of fire are long enough. Tanks engage enemy tanks and provide heavy direct-fire support for counterattacks.

5. Defensive Plan at Platoon Level.

The defensive plan in built-up areas at platoon level depends on the size and location of the area. Again, many factors must be considered before you institute such a plan.

a. Defense of a Stronqpoint. One of the most common defensive tasks a platoon will be given is the strongpoint defense of a building, part of a building, or a group of small buildings (Figure 1-69). The platoon's defense is normally integrated into the company's mission (defense of a traffic circle, and so forth). The platoon must keep the enemy from gaining a foothold in the buildings. It makes the best use of its weapons and supporting fires, organizes all-round defense, and counterattacks or calls for a company counterattack to eject an enemy who has gained a foothold. The platoon leader analyzes his defensive sector to recommend to the company commander the best use of obstacles and supporting fires.

(1) The platoon is organized into a series of firing positions located to cover avenues of approach, to cover obstacles, and to provide mutual support. Snipers may be located on the upper floors of the buildings. Unengaged elements should be ready to counterattack, fight fires, or reinforce other elements of the platoon.

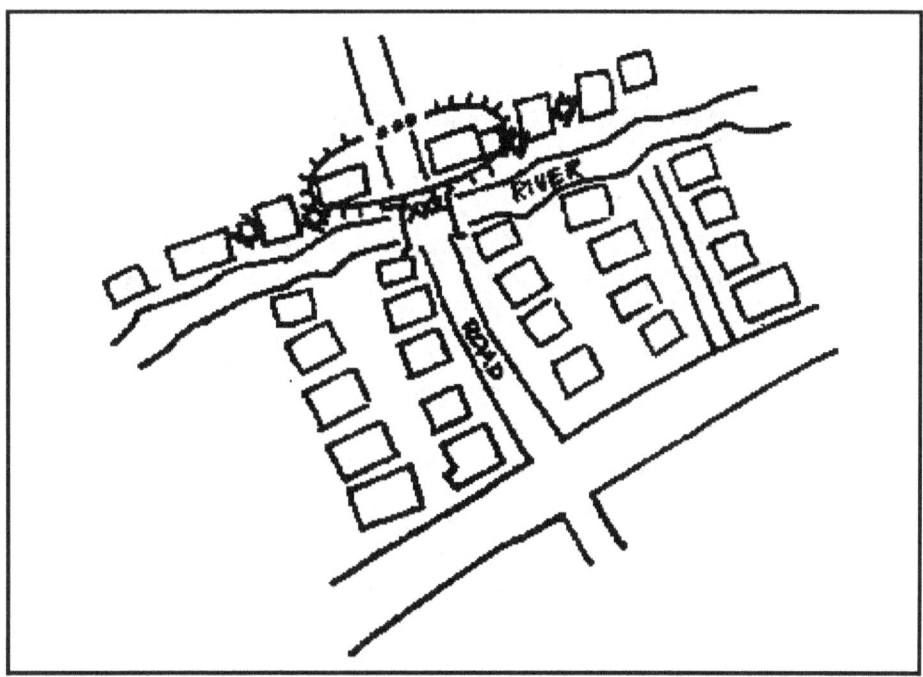

Figure 1-69. Defense of a strongpoint

(2) Depending on the length of the mission, the platoon should stockpile the following:

- Pioneer equipment, (axes, shovels, hammers, picket pounders).

- Barrier material (barbed wire, sandbags).

- Munitions (especially grenades).

- Food and water.

- Medical supplies.

- Firefighting equipment.

b. <u>Defense Against Armor and Antiarmor Ambushes</u>. The terrain common to built-up areas is well-suited for an infantry's defense against armored forces. Armored forces try to avoid built-up areas but may be forced to pass through them. A well-trained infantry can inflict heavy casualties on such armored forces.

(1) Built-up areas have certain traits which favor infantry antitank operations.

(a) Rubble in the streets can be used to block enemy vehicles, conceal mines, and cover and conceal defending infantry.

(b) The streets restrict armor maneuver, fields of fire, and communications, thereby reducing the enemy's ability to reinforce.

(c) Buildings provide cover and concealment for defending infantry.

(d) Rooftops, alleys, and upper floors provide good firing positions.

89

(e) Sewers, storm drains, and subways provide underground routes for infantry forces.

(2) Antiarmor operations in built-up areas involve the following planning steps:

(a) STEP 1: Choose a good engagement area. Enemy tanks should be engaged where most restricted in their ability to support each other. The best way for infantrymen to engage tanks is one at a time, so they can destroy one tank without being open to the fires of another. Typical locations include narrow streets, turns in the road, "T" intersections, bridges, tunnels, split-level roads, and rubbled areas. Less obvious locations can also be used by using demolitions or mines to create obstacles.

(b) STEP 2: Select good weapons positions. The best weapons positions are places where the tank is weakest and the infantry is most protected. A tank's ability to see and fire are limited, mainly to the rear and flanks if the tanks are buttoned up. Figure 1-70 shows the weapons and visual dead space of a buttoned-up tank against targets located at ground level. Similar dead space exists against targets located overhead.

- To the infantry force, the best places to fire on tanks are at the flanks and rear at ground level, or at the top of tanks if the force is in an elevated position in a building. A suitable antitank defense might be set up as shown in Figure 1-71.

- The best place to engage a tank from the flank is over the second road wheel at close range. This is best done at a corner so the tank cannot traverse the turret to counterattack.

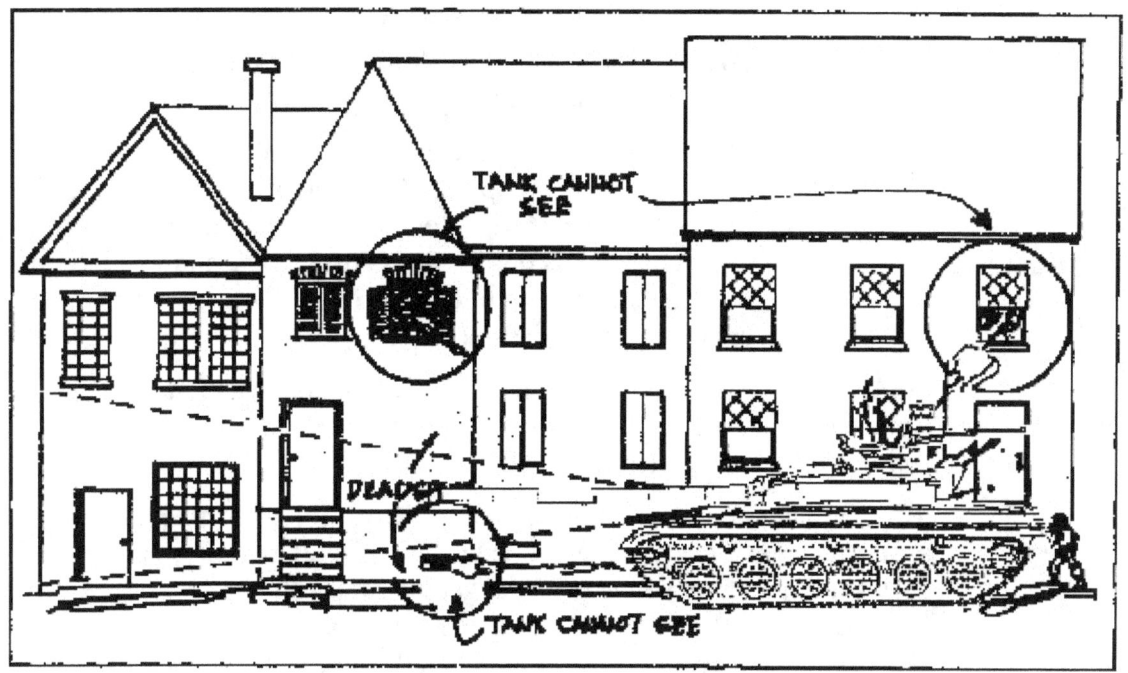

Figure 1-70. Tanks cannot fire at close-range, street-level, and overhead targets

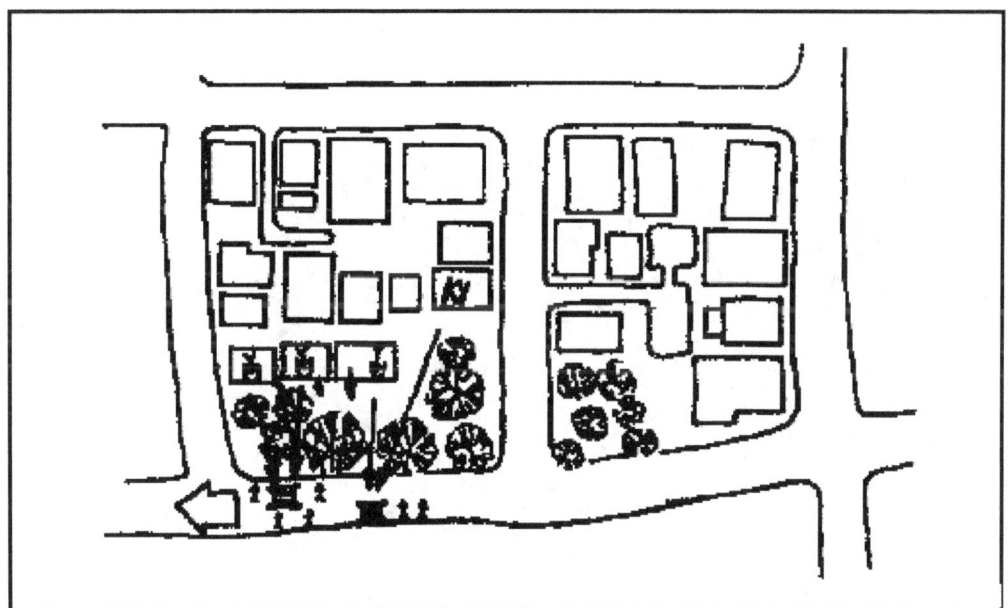

Figure 1-71. A platoon's antiarmor defense

- For safe engagement from an elevated position, infantrymen should allow the tank to approach to a range three times the elevation of the weapons (Figure 1-70).

- To engage at a greater range is to risk counterfire since the weapon's position will not be in the tank's overhead dead space. However, overhead fire at the rear or flank of the

91

tank is even more effective. Alternate and supplementary positions should be selected to enforce all-round security and to increase flexibility.

(c) STEP 3: Coordinate target engagement. Tanks are most vulnerable when buttoned up. The first task of the tank-killing force is to force the tanks to button up using mortar fire and sniper fire. The next task is to coordinate the fires of the antitank weapons so that if there is more than one target in the engagement area, all targets are engaged at the same time.

(3) Armored vehicles are often accompanied by infantry in built-up areas. Antiarmor weapons must be supported by an effective all-round antipersonnel defense (Figure 1-72).

(4) At a planned signal, (for example the detonation of a mine) all targets are engaged. If all targets cannot be engaged simultaneously, they are engaged in the order of the most dangerous first. Although tanks present the greatest threat, infantry fighting vehicles such as the Soviet BMPs are also dangerous because their infantry can dismount and destroy friendly antiarmor positions. If the friendly force is not secured by several infantrymen, priority of engagement might be given to enemy APCs. Rubble and mines should be used to reduce target mobility and acquire more targets.

Figure 1-72. Coordinated antitank ambush

d. Conduct of an Armored Ambush. A rifle company can use its attached tank platoon to conduct an armored ambush in a built-up area (Figure 1-73). To do so,

92

the armored platoon should be reinforced with an M2 BFV or an M113A2 armored personnel carrier (APC) and one or two squads from the rifle company. The ambush can be effective against enemy armor if it is conducted in an area cleared and reconnoitered by friendly forces.

(1) The operation involves maneuver on an obstacle-free road network. Obstacles outside the ambush area can be used to channelize and delay the enemy. The ambushing tank platoon must know the area.

(2) The ambushing armor should be located in a dispersed, camouflaged position situated about 1,000 meters from the expected enemy avenue of approach. A security post located at a choke point observes and reports the approach, speed, security posture, and activity of the enemy. This role is assigned to a scout who uses the BFV/APC to move from OP to OP. When the enemy is reported at a center point, the tank platoon leader knows how much he must move his tanks into ambush position.

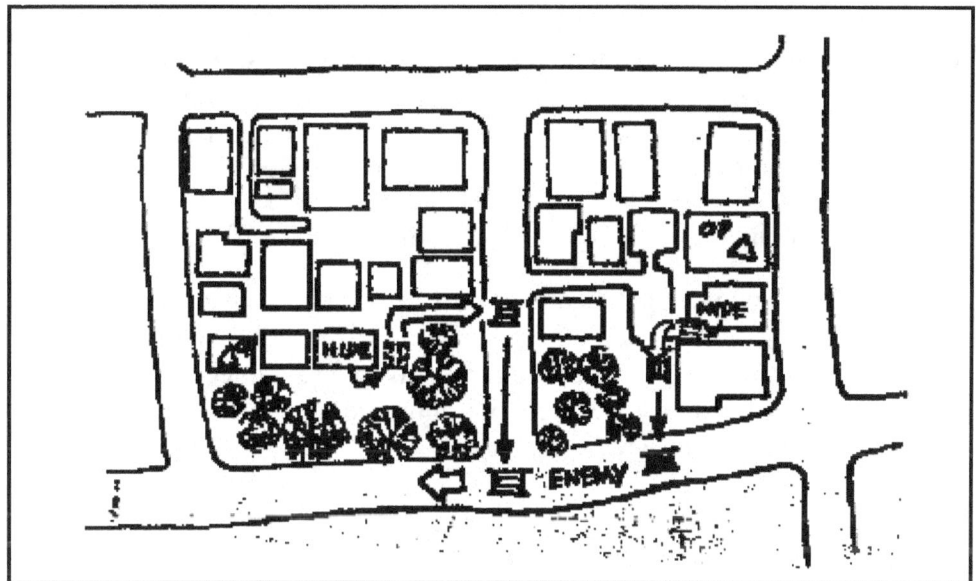

Figure 1-73. Armored ambush

(3) The tanks move quickly from their hide positions to firing positions, taking advantage of all available concealment. They try for flank shots on the approaching enemy -- the average range is 300 to 400 meters. Such long ranges do not expose tanks to the enemy infantry. Once the enemy is engaged, tanks break contact and move to a rally point with close security provided by an infantry squad. They then move to a new ambush site.

LESSON 2

COMBAT TECHNIQUES IN BUILT-UP AREAS

OVERVIEW

In this lesson you will learn the fundamental urban combat skills of movement, entry, firing, navigation, and camouflage. The lesson also covers the employment and effects of weapons in built-up areas, subterranean operations, and other military operations on urban terrain (MOUT).

TERMINAL LEARNING OBJECTIVE:

ACTION: Identify the fundamental urban combat skills, the principles of weapon employment and effects in built-up areas, subterranean operations, urban fighting positions, and techniques used to attack and clear buildings.

CONDITION: You will be given information from FM 90-10-1.

STANDARD: The fundamental combat skills, principles of weapon employment and effects in built-up areas, subterranean operations, and urban fighting positions, and techniques used to attack and clear buildings will be identified in accordance with FM 9-10-1.

REFERENCES: The material contained in this lesson was derived from the following publication:

FM 90-10-1

INTRODUCTION

Successful combat operations in built-up areas depend on the proper employment of the rifle squad. Each member must be skilled in the techniques of combat in built-up areas: moving, entering buildings, clearing buildings, employing hand grenades, selecting and using firing positions, navigating in built-up areas, and camouflaging.

PART A - FUNDAMENTAL COMBAT SKILLS IN A BUILT-UP AREA.

1. <u>Movement</u>.

Movement in built-up areas is the first fundamental skill the soldier must master. Movement techniques must be practiced until they become habitual. To reduce exposure to enemy fire, the soldier avoids silhouetting himself, avoids open areas, and selects his next covered position before movement.

   a. <u>Crossing a Wall</u>. You must learn the correct method of crossing a wall (Figure 2-1). After you have reconnoitered the other side, quickly roll over the wall, keeping a low silhouette. The speed of your move and a low silhouette deny the enemy a good target.

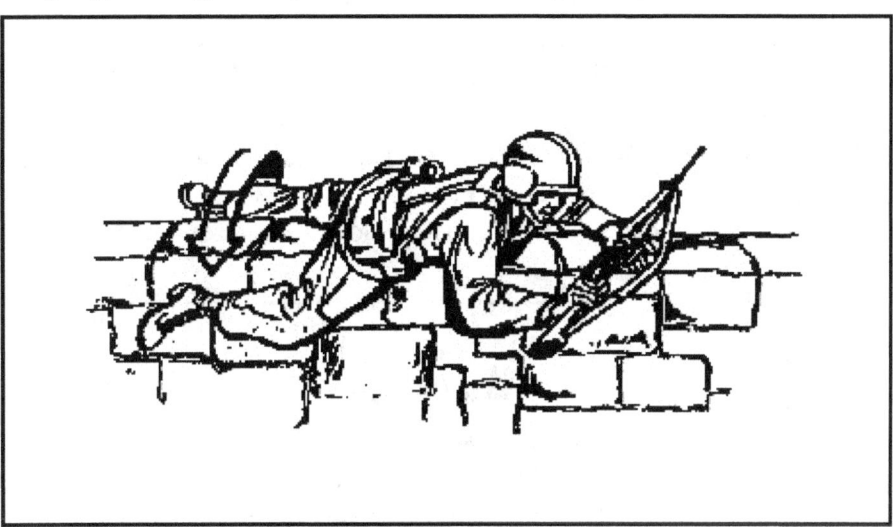

Figure 2-1. Soldier crossing a wall

   b. <u>Movement Around Corners</u>. The area around a corner must be observed before you move beyond it. The most common mistake a soldier makes at a corner is allowing his weapon to extend beyond the corner, thus, exposing his position. You should show your head below the height an enemy soldier would expect to see it. The correct technique for looking around a corner (Figure 2-2), is to lay flat on the ground and do not extend your weapon beyond the corner of the building. Wear your kevlar helmet and expose your head (at ground level) only enough to permit observation.

Figure 2-2. Correct technique for looking around a corner

c. <u>Movement Past Windows</u>. Windows present another hazard to the soldier and small-unit leader. The most common mistake in passing a window is exposing your head. If you show your head (Figure 2-3), an enemy gunner inside the building could engage you through the window without exposing himself to friendly covering fires.

Figure 2-3. Soldier moving past a window

(1) When using the correct technique for passing a window, the soldier stays below the window level. He makes sure he does not silhouette himself in the window; he "hugs" the side of the building. An enemy gunner inside the building would have to expose himself to covering fires if he tried to engage the soldier.

(2) The same techniques used in passing first-floor windows are used when passing basement windows (Figure 2-4); however, the most common

mistake in passing a basement window is not being aware of it. Do not walk or run past a basement window, since you present a good target to an enemy gunner inside the building. The correct procedure for negotiating a basement window is to stay close to the wall of the building and step or jump past the window without exposing your legs.

Figure 2-4. Soldier passing basement windows

d. <u>Use of Doorways</u>. Doorways should not be used as entrances or exits since they are normally covered by enemy fire. If you must use a doorway as an exit, move quickly through it to your next positions staying as low as possible to avoid silhouetting yourself (Figure 2-5). Preselection of positions, speed, a low silhouette, and the use of covering fires must be emphasized in exiting doorways.

Figure 2-5. Soldier exiting a doorway

e. <u>Movement Parallel to Buildings</u>. Soldiers and small units may not always be able to use the inside of buildings as a route of advance. Therefore, they must move on the outside of the buildings (Figure 2-6). Smoke and covering fires, and cover and concealment should be used to hide movement. Correctly moving on the outside of a building, the soldier "hugs" the side of the building, stays in the shadow, presents a low silhouette, and moves rapidly to his next position (Figure 2-7). If an enemy gunner inside the building fires on a soldier, he exposes himself to fire from other squad members. Furthermore, an enemy gunner farther down the street would have difficulty detecting and engaging the soldier.

Figure 2-6. Soldier moving outside a building

Figure 2-7. Selection of the next position

f. Crossing Open Areas. Open areas such as streets, alleys, and parks should be avoided when possible. They are natural kill zones for enemy crew-served weapons. They can be crossed safely only if certain fundamentals are applied by the individual or small-unit leader.

(1) When crossing an open area, the soldier develops a plan for his own movement. (Whenever possible, use smoke to conceal the movement of all soldiers.) He runs the shortest distance between the buildings and moves along the far building to the next position (Figure 2-7, A and B). By doing so, he reduces the time he is exposed to enemy fire.

(2) Before moving to another position, the soldier should make a visual reconnaissance and select the position for the best cover and concealment. At the same time, he should select the route he will take to get to that position.

g. Fire Team Employment. Moving as a fire team, from building to building or between buildings, presents a problem because a fire team presents a large target to enemy fire (Figure 2-8). When moving from the corner of one building to another, the fire team should move across the open area in a group. Moving from the side of one building to the side of another presents a similar problem, and the technique of movement employed is the same. The fire team uses the building as cover. In moving to the adjacent building, team members should keep a distance of 3 to 5 meters between themselves and, using a planned signal, make an abrupt flanking movement (on line) across the open area to the next building.

Figure 2-8. Fire team movement

h. Movement Between Positions. When moving from position to position, each soldier must be careful not to mask his supporting fires. When he reaches his next position he must be prepared to cover the movement of other members of his fire team or squad. He uses his new position effectively, and fires his weapon from either shoulder.

99

(1) The most common error a soldier can make when firing from a fighting position is firing over the top of his cover and thus silhouetting himself against the building to his rear, providing the enemy with an easy target. The correct technique for firing from a covered position is to fire around the side of the cover, reducing your exposure to the enemy (Figure 2-9).

Figure 2-9. Soldier firing from a covered position

(2) Another common error is for a right-handed firer to try to fire from the right shoulder around the left corner of a building. Firing left-handed around the left corner of a building takes advantage of the cover afforded by the building (Figure 2-10). Right-handed and left-handed soldiers should be trained to adapt cover and concealment to fit their manual orientation. Also, soldiers should be able to fire from their opposite shoulders if needed.

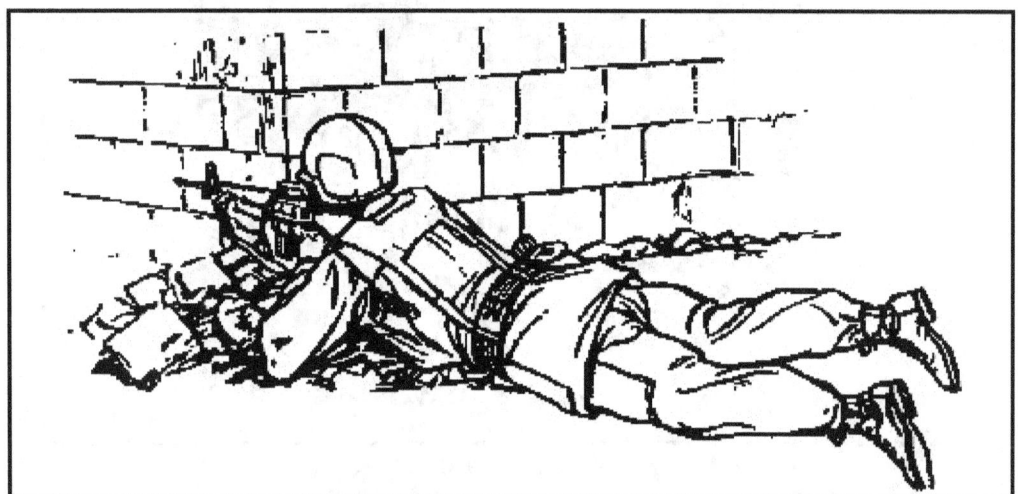

Figure 2-10. Firing lefthanded around the corner of a building

i. <u>Movement Inside a Building</u>. When moving within a building under attack (Figure 2-11), avoid silhouetting yourself in doors and windows. If forced to use a hallway (Figure 2-12), stay against the wall to avoid presenting a target to the enemy.

100

Figure 2-11. Movement within a building under attack

Figure 2-12. Hallway procedures

(1) The enemy often boobytraps windows and doors. When entering a room, avoid using the door handle. Instead, fire a short burst of automatic fire through the door around the latch and then kick it open. If boobytraps are detected, they should be marked, reported, and bypassed.

(2) Before entering each room, "cook off" a hand grenade by removing the grenade's safety pin, releasing the safety lever, counting by thousands (one thousand and one, one thousand and two), and then throwing the grenade into the room. Be careful of thin walls and floors. Voice alerts should be given while throwing grenades. The MK3 A2 concussion (offensive) hand grenade is the preferred hand grenade during offensive operations, since it will not produce fragments which can go through the wall and injure the soldiers outside and will reduce civilian casualties during precision and surgical MOUT operations. When friendly forces throw grenades, the command is "Frag Out!" When an enemy grenade has been identified,

101

friendly forces shout "Grenade!"

WARNING.

Fragments from hand grenades may injure
soldiers outside the room. Also, cooking
off hand grenades can be dangerous unless
properly performed.

(3) Get in fast and spray the room with automatic fire. As soon as the hand grenade goes off, rush into the room (Figure 2-13), spray the room with fire, and quickly back against a near wall to observe the entire area. The second man enters immediately behind you, engages any targets with a short burst of automatic fire, and then systemically searches the room. Meanwhile, the support party, in position outside the room being cleared, provides outside security.

Figure 2-13. Procedures for the first soldier entering a room

(4) Always use voice alerts. Voice alerts and signals within the assault team are extremely important. You must always let others in the assault team know where you are and what you are doing. Once a room has been cleared, the assault team yells, "Clear!" to inform the support party. Before leaving the room and rejoining the support party, the assault team yells "Coming out!" When moving up or down a staircases the assault team yells "Coming up" or "Coming down."

(5) Mouseholes measure about 2 feet wide and are blown or cut through a wall so soldiers can enter a building or a room (Figure 2-14). They are safer entrances than doors because doors can be easily booby trapped and

should be avoided. As with any entry, a hand grenade is thrown in first.

Figure 2-14. Soldiers entering through a mousehole

2. <u>Entry Techniques</u>.

When entering a building, enter with minimum exposure. Select the entry point before moving toward the building. Avoid windows and doors. Use smoke to conceal your advance to the building. Use demolitions, tank rounds, combat engineer vehicles (CEVs), and so on, to make new entrances. Precede your entry with a grenade. Enter immediately after the grenade explodes, and be covered by one of your buddies.

a. <u>Upper Building Levels</u>. Clearing a building from the top down is the preferred method. Clearing or defending a building is easier from an upper story. Gravity and the building's floor plan become assets when throwing hand grenades and moving from floor to floor.

(1) An enemy who is forced to the top of a building may be cornered and fight desperately or escape over the roof. But an enemy who is forced down to the ground level will likely withdraw from the building, thus exposing himself to friendly fires from the outside.

(2) Various means, such as ladders, drain pipes, vines, helicopters, or the roofs and windows of adjoining buildings may be used to reach the top floor or roof of a building. In some cases, one soldier can climb onto the shoulders of another and reach high enough to pull himself up. Another method is to attach a grappling hook to the end of a scaling rope so a rifleman can scale a wall, spring from one building to another, or gain entrance through an upstairs window.

b. <u>Use of Ladders</u>. Ladders offer the quickest method to gain access to the upper levels of a building (Figure 2-15). Units can get ladders from local civilians or stores, or material to build ladders can be obtained through supply channels. If required, ladders can be built with resources available throughout the urban area. For example, lumber can be taken from inside the walls of buildings (Figure 2-16). Although ladders will not permit access to the top of some buildings, they will offer security and safety through speed.

Figure 2-15. Using ladders to get to upper levels

Figure 2-16. Getting lumber from inside the walls

c. <u>Use of the Grappling Hook</u>. Select a suitable grappling hook and rope. The grappling hook should be sturdy, portable, easily thrown, and equipped with hooks that can hold inside a window. The scaling rope should be 5/8 to 1 inch in diameter and long enough to reach the objective window. Tie knots in the rope at l-foot intervals to make climbing easier. Follow the procedures outlined below.

(1) When throwing the grappling hook, stand as close to the building as possible (Figure 2-17). The closer you stand, the less exposure to enemy fires. The closer the range, the less horizontal distance you must throw the hook.

(2) Make sure there is enough rope to reach the target. Hold the hook and a few coils of rope in the throwing hand. The remainder of the rope, in loose coils, should be in the other hand. Allow the rope to play out freely. The throw should be a gentle, even, upward lob of the hook with the other hand releasing the rope as it plays out.

(3) Once the grappling hook is inside the window (or on the roof), pull on the rope to obtain a good hold before beginning to climb. When using a window, pull the hook to one corner to ensure chances of a good "bite" and to reduce exposure to lower windows during the climb.

Figure 2-17. Grappling hook thrown at close range

(4) The use of grappling hooks is the least preferred method for gaining entry to upper levels of buildings. They should be used only as a last resort and away from potential enemy positions. This method may potentially be used on adjacent buildings offering concealed locations and a connecting roof to enemy positions.

d. <u>Scaling Walls</u>. When forced to scale a wall during exposure to enemy fire, use all available concealment. Smoke and diversionary measures improve the chances of a successful exposed movement. When using smoke for concealment, plan for

105

wind direction and effects of the smoke. Use fire, shouting, and fake movement to distract the enemy.

(1) A soldier scaling an outside wall is vulnerable to enemy sniper fire. Soldiers who are moving from building to building and climbing buildings should be covered by friendly fire. Areas between buildings offer good fields of fire to the enemy. Properly positioned friendly weapons can suppress and eliminate enemy fire. The M203 grenade launcher is effective in clearing the enemy from rooms inside buildings (Figure 2-18).

Figure 2-18. Using the M203 grenade launcher to clear enemy gunfire

(2) The soldier scaling a wall with a rope should avoid silhouetting himself in windows of uncleared rooms and avoid exposing himself to enemy fires from lower windows. He should climb with his weapon slung over the firing shoulder to quickly bring it to a firing position. He should clear the lower room with a hand grenade before ascending outside the windows. The soldier does this by first loosening the safety pin so he only needs one hand to throw the grenade. The objective upper-story window should not be entered before a hand grenade has been thrown in.

(3) The soldier enters the objective window with a low silhouette (Figure 2-19). Entry can be head first; however, a preferred method is to hook a leg over the window sill and enter sideways, straddling the ledge as shown in the figure.

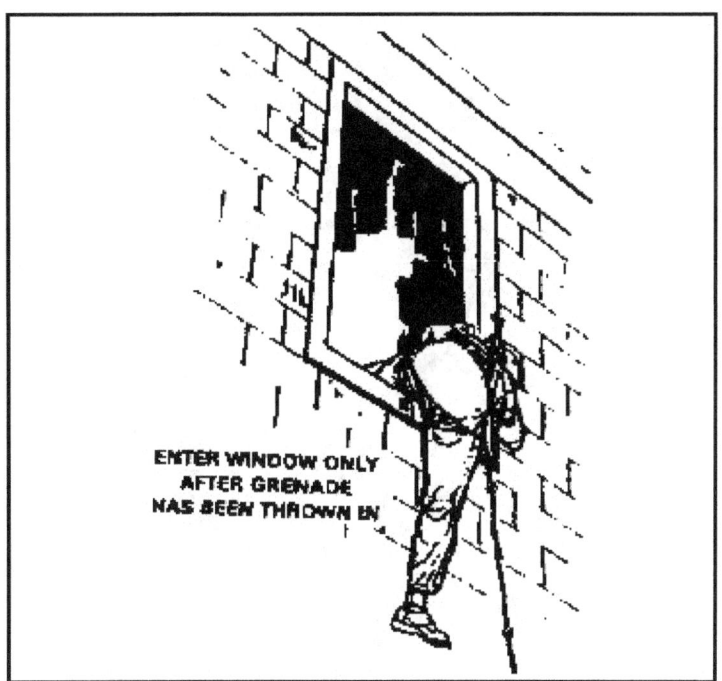

Figure 2-19. Soldier entering the objective window

e. Rappelling. Rappelling (Figure 2-20) is a combat technique soldiers can use to descend from the rooftop of a tall building into a window. Urban fighters should learn the basic seat-hip rappel.

> (1) To set up the rappel site, be sure the rope reaches the bottom. Carefully test the anchor point and inspect to see that the rope will run around it when pulled from below. Pad friction points along the edge of the wall to prevent the rope from being cut.

> (2) In the seat-hip rappel, the main friction is taken up by a snaplink inserted in a rope seat fastened to the body. This is a fast method of getting down a wall; it is also used in rappelling from helicopters.

> (3) Before attaching the Swiss seat (Figure 2-21) and hook snaplink, tuck your battle dress uniform (BDU) jacket into your trousers -- loose clothing or equipment around the waist may be pulled into the snaplink, locking the rappel.

Figure 2-20. Rappelling

(4) To rappel, put on leather work gloves and stand to one side of the ropes (when braking with the right hand, stand on the left side; when braking with the left hand, stand on the right). Snap the ropes into the snaplink.

(5) Take up some slack in the ropes between the snaplink and anchor point; bring the ropes underneath, around, and over the snaplink, snapping into the ropes again. (This results in a turn of the ropes around the solid shaft of the snaplink that does not cross itself when under tension. When using a single rope, make two turns.)

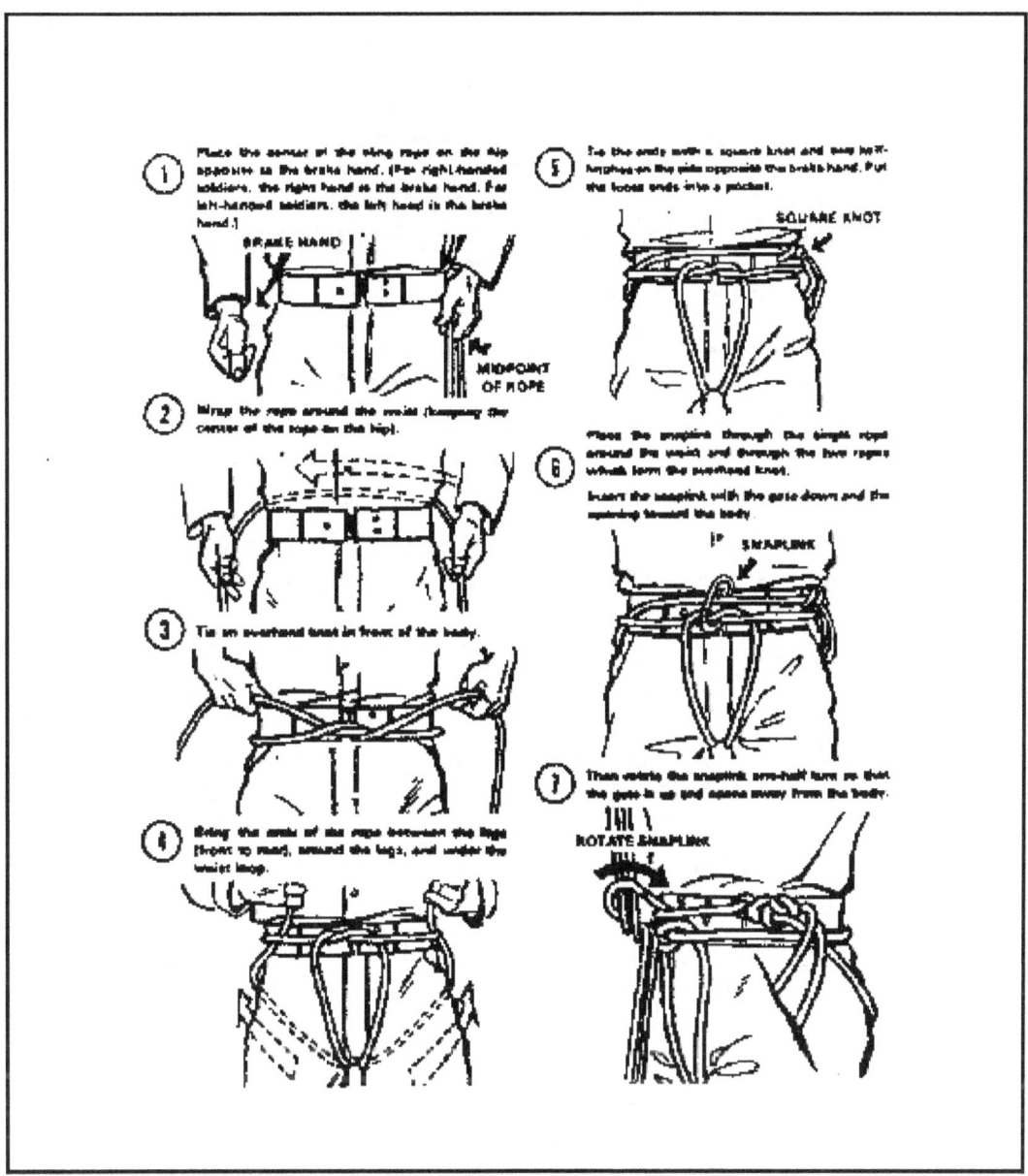

Figure 2-21. Tying of the Swiss seat

(6) Facing the anchor point, carefully back over the edge of the obstacle and lean well out, almost at a right angle to the surface; this is the "L" position (Figure 2-22). Give the signal "On rappel." If the tactical situation requires silence, use planned visual signals.

Figure 2-22. The "L" position

(7) Descend using the upper hand as a guide and the lower hand to brake. Hold the braking hand behind and slightly above the hip. Brake by closing the hand and pressing the rope against the body.

(8) Continue to "walk" down, looking at the ground over the braking hand. To go faster, push off the wall with a slight hop and descend in bounds with the brake hand extended toward the ground.

(9) Give the signal "Off rappel" upon reaching the bottom, and straighten the ropes. (When silence is required, use a planned signal for pulling on the ropes.)

(10) When the last man is down, recover the rope by pulling on one side of the double rope. Pulling it smoothly prevents the rising end from whipping around and binding the rope. Stand clear of the falling rope.

f. <u>Entry at Lower Levels</u>. Buildings should be cleared from the top down. However, it may be impossible to enter a building at the top; therefore, entry at the bottom or a lower level may be the only course of action. When entering a building at the lower level, soldiers avoid entry through windows and doors since both can be easily boobytrapped and are usually covered by enemy fire.

(1) Ideally, when entering at lower levels, demolitions, artillery, tank fire, antitank weapons fire, or similar means are used to create a new entrance to avoid booby traps. Quick entry is required to follow up the effects of the blast and concussion.

(2) When the only entry to a building is through a window or door, supporting fire should be directed at that location. If no supporting fire is available, LAWs can be employed instead.

(3) Before entering, soldiers throw a cooked-off hand grenade into the new entrance to reinforce the effects of the original blast. When making a new entrance in a building, they consider the effects of the blast on the building and adjacent buildings. If there is the possibility of a fire in an adjacent building, soldiers coordinate with adjacent units and obtain permission before starting the operation. In wooden frame buildings, the blast may cause the building to collapse. In stone, brick, or cement buildings, supporting fires are aimed at the corner of the building or at weak points in

110

the building construction. (Specific lower-level entry techniques are shown in Figures 2-23 through 2-25.)

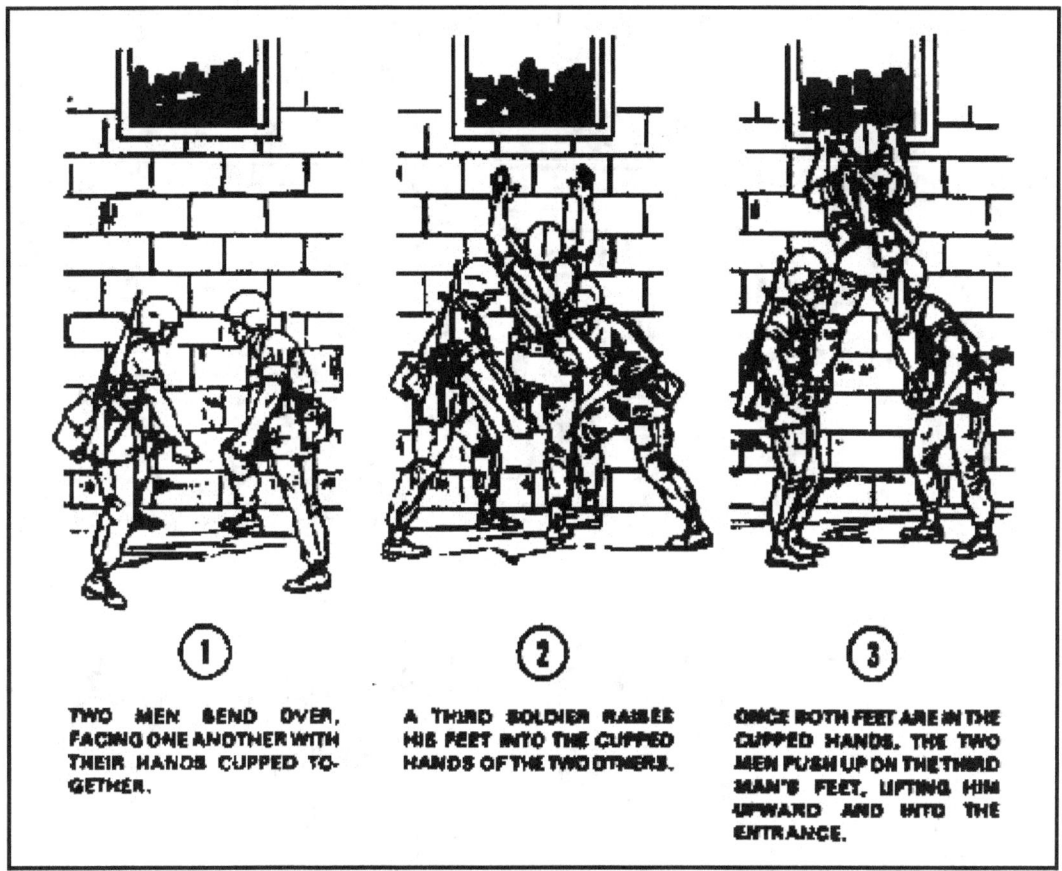

Figure 2-23. Lower-level entry techniques

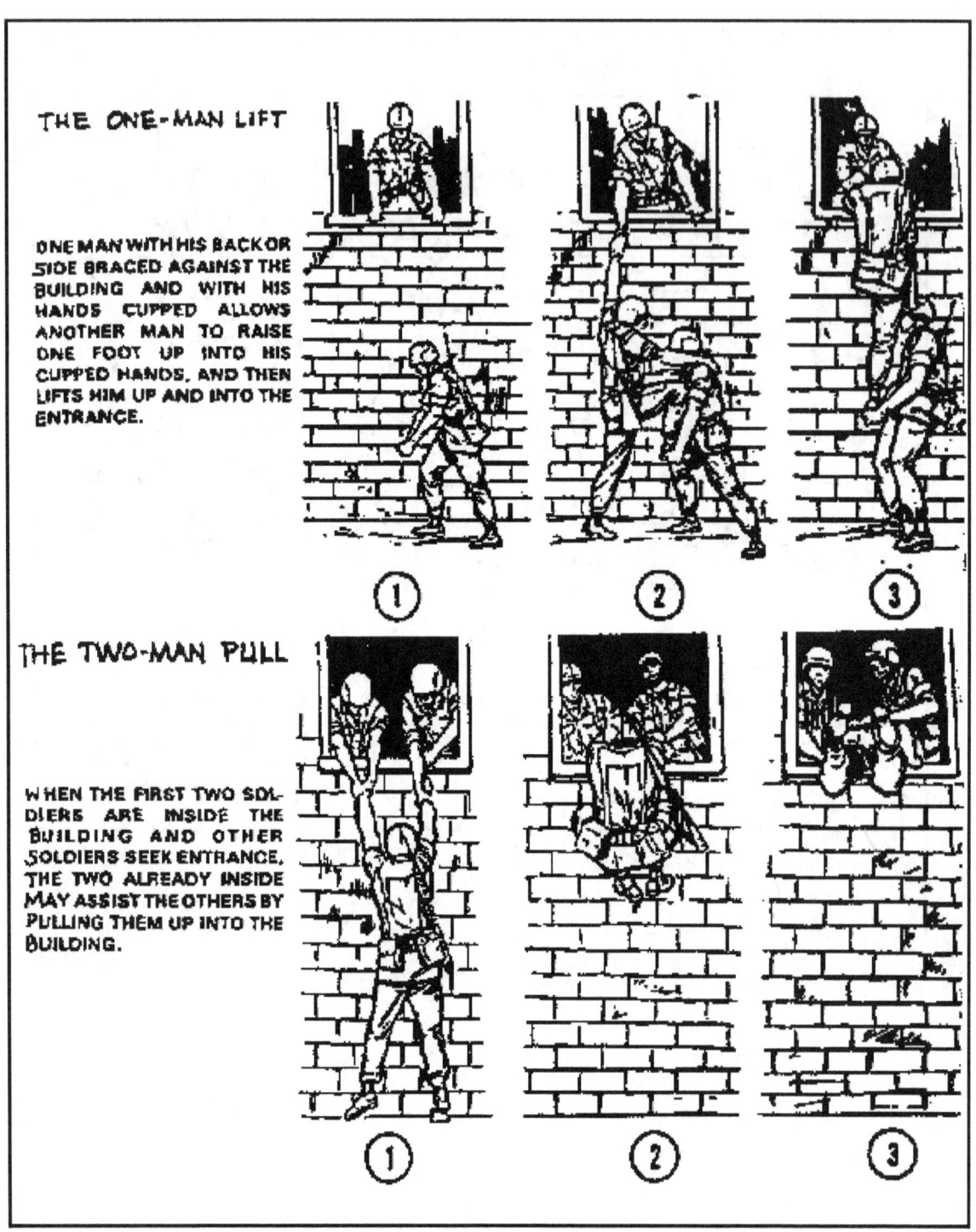

THE ONE-MAN LIFT

ONE MAN WITH HIS BACK OR SIDE BRACED AGAINST THE BUILDING AND WITH HIS HANDS CUPPED ALLOWS ANOTHER MAN TO RAISE ONE FOOT UP INTO HIS CUPPED HANDS, AND THEN LIFTS HIM UP AND INTO THE ENTRANCE.

THE TWO-MAN PULL

WHEN THE FIRST TWO SOLDIERS ARE INSIDE THE BUILDING AND OTHER SOLDIERS SEEK ENTRANCE, THE TWO ALREADY INSIDE MAY ASSIST THE OTHERS BY PULLING THEM UP INTO THE BUILDING.

Figure 2-24. Lower-level entry techniques (continued)

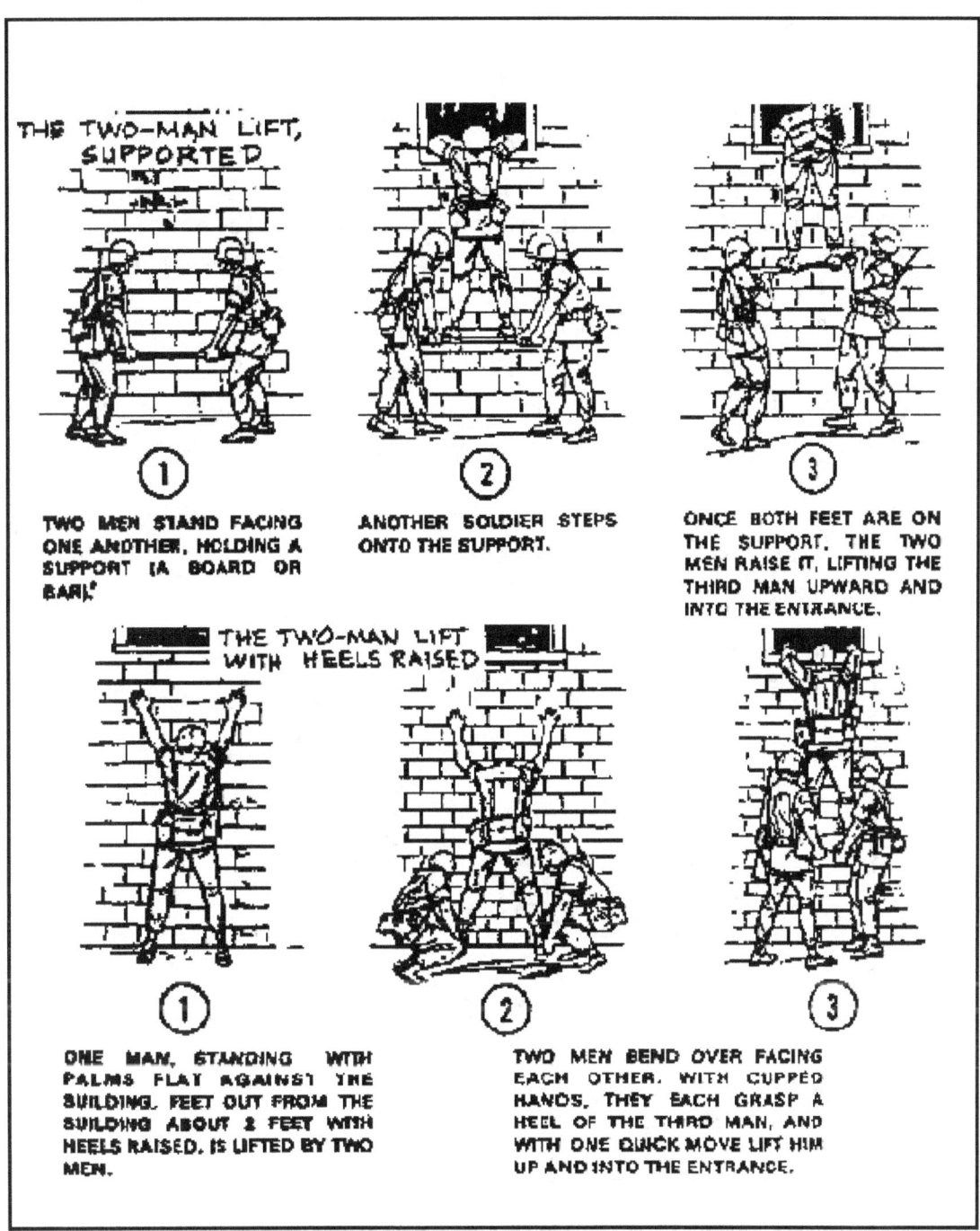

Figure 2-25. Lower-level entry techniques (continued)

g. <u>Hand Grenades</u>. Combat in built-up areas (mainly during the attack) requires extensive use of hand grenades since one must be used to clear each room of a building. Throw a grenade before negotiating staircases, mouseholes, and so on. This usually requires the use of both hands and the overhand and underhand methods of throwing. The grenade should be allowed to "cook off" for two seconds to prevent the enemy from grabbing the grenade and tossing it back.

Note: "Cooking off" a hand grenade involves pulling the

113

safety pin, releasing the safety lever or "spoon," counting two seconds (one thousand and one, one thousand and two), throwing the hand grenade, and immediately taking cover.

(1) The construction material used in the building being cleared influences the use of grenades. If the walls of a building are made of thin material, such as sheetrock or thin plyboard, the soldier must either lie flat on the floor with his helmet pointing towards the area of detonation, or move away from any wall that might be penetrated by grenade fragments.

(2) Soldiers should throw grenades in an opening before entering a building to eliminate enemy who might be near the entrance (Figure 2-26). The M203 grenade launcher is the best method for putting a grenade in an upper story window.

(3) When a hand grenade must be used, the soldier throwing the grenade should stand close to the building, using it for cover. At the same times the individual and the rest of the element should have a planned area to move to for safety if the grenade does not go through the window but falls back to the ground.

Figure 2-26. Throwing a grenade in an upper-level opening

(4) The soldier throwing the grenade should allow the grenade to cook off for at least two seconds, and then step out far enough to lob the grenade in the upper-story opening. Your weapon should be kept in the nonthrowing

114

hand so it can be used if needed. Your weapon should never be laid outside or inside the building. Once the grenade has been thrown into the opening (Figure 2-27), assaulting troops move swiftly to enter the building.

Note: The correct method for throwing a grenade through a window requires the soldier to stand close to the building, using it for cover. The soldier indicates a grenade has been thrown by yelling "Frag out."

Figure 2-27. Hand grenade thrown through a window

WARNING.

After throwing the grenade, the soldier must immediately announce loudly that a grenade has been thrown and then take cover since the grenade may bounce back or be thrown back, or the enemy may fire at him.

(5) If soldiers must enter the building by the stairs, they first look for booby traps. Then they throw a grenade through the stairwell door, let it detonate, and quickly move inside. They can use the staircase for cover.

(6) The best way to enter a building is to breach the exterior wall. Again, a grenade must be thrown through the hole using all available cover, such as the lower corner of the building (Figure 2-28).

115

(7) When a door is the only means of entering a room, soldiers must beware of fire from enemy soldiers within the room and beware of booby traps. Doors can be opened by using the hand, by kicking, by firing, or by using pioneer tools such as an axe. When opening a door, soldiers must not expose themselves to firers through the door. A two-man team should be used when doors are opened by hand. Each soldier should stay close to one side of the doorway so as not to expose himself in the open doorframe. However, it is better to open the door by kicking or firing. When kicking, one man stands to the side while the other kicks (Figure 2-29).

Figure 2-28. Lower corner of a building used for cover

(8) Once the door is open, a hand grenade is tossed in. After the grenade explodes, soldiers move in while firing short bursts of automatic fire. If the doorframe is sturdy and cannot be kicked open, soldiers must shoot the door open or break it down with an axe. The procedure for entering the room is the same as for kicking the door open.

(9) Another way to enter a room is to blast mouseholes with demolitions. In moving from room to room through mouseholes, soldiers must use grenades as in moving through doorways. As they enter the mousehole, they should use the floor or adjacent wall for cover.

116

Figure 2-29. Soldier kicking a door open.

(10) While clearing the bottom floor of a building, soldiers may encounter stairs which must also be cleared. Once again, grenades play an important role. To climb the stairs, soldiers should first inspect for booby traps, then toss a grenade to the head of the stairs or the next landing (Figure 2-30). Remember to use voice commands when throwing grenades. Once the grenade has detonated, throw another grenade over and behind the staircase banister and into the hallway, destroying any enemy hiding to the rear. Using the staircase for cover, throw the grenade underhand to reduce the risk of it bouncing back and rolling back down the stairs.

(11) After the stairs have been cleared, assaulting forces move to the top floor and clear it, using the methods already described. Upon securing the top floor, forces move downstairs to clear the center and bottom floors, and to continue with the mission.

Note: Since large quantities of hand grenades are used when clearing buildings, a continuous supply must be available to forces having this mission within a built-up area.

Figure 2-30. Soldier tossing a grenade up a stairway

3. <u>Firing Positions</u>.

Whether a unit is attacking, defending, or conducting retrograde operations, its success or failure depends on the ability of the individual soldier to place accurate fire on the enemy with the least exposure to return fire. Consequently, the soldier must immediately seek and properly use firing positions.

a. <u>Hasty Firing Position</u>. You normally occupy a hasty firing position in the attack or the early stages of the defense. It is a position from which you can place fire upon the enemy while using available cover for protection from return fire. You may occupy it voluntarily, or be forced to occupy it due to enemy fire. In either case, the position lacks preparation before occupation. Some of the more common hasty firing positions in a built-up area and techniques for occupying them are: corners of buildings, firing from behind walls, firing from windows, firing from unprepared loopholes, and firing from the peak of a roof.

(1) <u>Corners of Buildings</u>. The corner of a building provides cover for a hasty firing position if used properly.

(a) You must be capable of firing your weapon both right- and left-handed to be effective around corners. A common error made in firing around corners is firing from the wrong shoulder. This exposes more of your body to return fire than necessary. By firing from the proper shoulder, you can reduce the target exposed to

118

enemy fire.

(b) Another common mistake when firing around corners is firing from the standing position. You expose yourself at the height the enemy would expect a target to appear, and risk exposing the entire length of your body as a target for the enemy.

(2) <u>Walls</u>. When firing behind walls, you fire around cover -- not over it (Figure 2-31).

Figure 2-31. Firing around cover

(3) <u>Windows</u>. In a built-up area, windows provide convenient firing ports. Normally you would want to avoid firing from the standing position since it exposes most of your body to return fire from the enemy and could silhouette you against a light-colored interior beyond the window. This is an obvious sign of the firer's position, especially at night when the muzzle flash can easily be observed. When properly firing from a window (Figure 2-32), the soldier is well back into the room to prevent the muzzle flash from being seen, and he is kneeling to limit exposure and avoid silhouetting himself.

Figure 2-32. Soldier firing from a window

(4) <u>Loopholes</u>. You can fire through a hole torn in the wall and avoid windows (Figure 2-33). Stay well back from the loophole so the muzzle of the weapon does not protrude beyond the walls and the muzzle flash is concealed.

Figure 2-33. Soldier firing from a loophole

(5) <u>Roof</u>. The peak of a roof provides a vantage point for snipers increasing their field of vision and the ranges at which they can engage targets (Figure 2-34). A chimney, a smokestack, or any other object protruding from the roof of a building can reduce the size of the target exposed and should be used as shown in the figure.

Figure 2-34. Soldier firing from the peak of a roof

(6) When the soldier is subjected to enemy fire and none of the positions mentioned above are available, he must try to expose as little of himself as possible. When a soldier in an open area between buildings (a street or alley) is fired upon by an enemy in one of the buildings to his front and no cover is available, he should lie prone as close as possible to a building on the same side of the open area as the enemy. To engage the soldier, the enemy must then lean out the window and expose himself to return fire.

(7) When no cover is available, target exposure can be reduced by firing from the prone position, by firing from shadows, and by presenting no silhouette against buildings.

b. Prepared Firing Position. A prepared firing position is one built or improved to allow the firer to engage a particular area, avenue of approach, or enemy positions reducing his exposure to return fire. Examples of prepared positions include the following:

Barricaded windows.

Fortified loopholes.

Sniper positions.

Antitank positions.

Machine gun positions.

(1) The natural firing port provided by windows can be improved by barricading the window, leaving a small hole for the firer's use (Figure 2-35). The barricading may be accomplished with materials torn from the interior walls of the building or any other available material. When

121

barricading windows, avoid the following:

Figure 2-35. Window firing position

- Barricading only the windows to be used as firing ports. The enemy will soon determine the barricaded windows are firing positions.

- Neat, square, or rectangular holes easily identified by the enemy. A barricaded window should not have a neat, regular firing port. The window should keep its original shape so the position of the firer is hard to detect. Firing from the bottom of the window gives the firer the advantage of the wall because the firing port is less obvious to the enemy. Sandbags are used to reinforce the wall below the window and to increase protection for the firer. All glass must be removed from the window to prevent injury to the firer. Lace curtains permit the firer to see out and prevent the enemy from seeing in. Wet blankets should be placed under weapons to reduce dust. Wire mesh over the window keeps the enemy from throwing in hand grenades.

(2) Although windows usually are good firing positions, they do not always allow the firer to engage targets in his sector.

(a) To avoid establishing a pattern of always firing from windows, an alternate position is required such as the prepared loophole (Figure 2-36). This involves cutting or blowing a small hole into the wall to allow the firer to observe and engage targets in his sector.

Figure 2-36. Prepared loopholes

(b) Sandbags are used to reinforce the walls below, around, and above the loophole. Two layers of sandbags are placed on the floor under the firer to protect him from an explosion on a lower floor (if the position is on the second floor or higher). A wall of sandbags, rubble, furniture, and so on, should be constructed to the rear of the position to protect the firer from explosions in the room.

(c) A table, bedstead, or other available material provides overhead cover for the position. This prevents injury to the firer from falling debris or explosions above his position.

(d) The position should be camouflaged by knocking other holes in the wall, making it difficult for the enemy to determine which hole the fire is coming from. Siding material should be removed from the building in several places to make loopholes less noticeable.

(3) A chimney or other protruding structure provides a base from which a sniper position can be prepared. Part of the roofing material is removed to allow the sniper to fire around the chimney. He should stand inside the building on the beams or on a platform with only his head and shoulders above the roof (behind the chimney). Sandbags placed on the sides of the position protect the sniper's flanks.

(4) When the roof has no protruding structure to provide protection, the

123

sniper position should be prepared from underneath on the enemy side of the roof. The position is reinforced with sandbags, and a small piece of roofing material should be removed to allow the sniper to engage targets in his sector (Figure 2-37). The missing piece of roofing material should be the only sign a position exists there. However, other pieces of roofing should be removed to deceive the enemy as to the true sniper position. The sniper should be invisible from outside the building, and the muzzle flash must be hidden from view.

(5) Some rules and considerations for selecting and occupying individual firing positions are as follow:

Make maximum use of available cover and concealment.

Avoid firing over cover; when possible fire around it.

Avoid silhouetting against light-colored buildings, the skyline, and so on.

Carefully select a new firing position before leaving an old one.

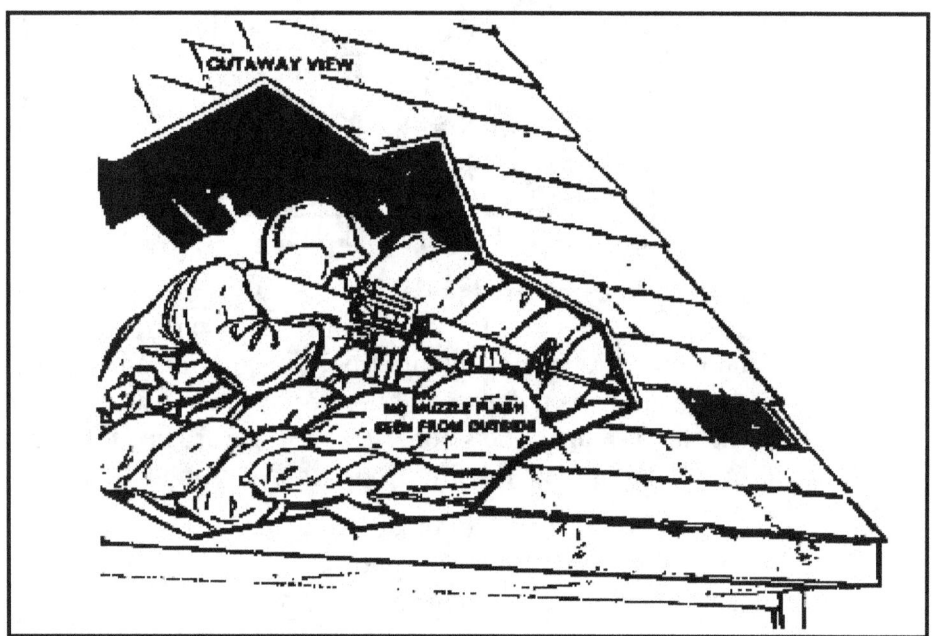

Figure 2-37. Sniper position

- Avoid setting a pattern; fire from both barricaded and unbarricaded windows.

- Keep exposure time to a minimum.

- Begin improving a hasty position immediately after occupation.

- Use construction material for prepared positions that is readily available in a built-up area.

- Remember, positions providing cover at ground level may not provide cover on higher floors.

(6) The rifle squad, during an attack on and in defense of a built-up area, is often reinforced with attached antitank weapons. Therefore, the rifle squad leader must be able to choose good firing positions for the antitank weapons under his control.

(7) Various principles of employing antitank weapons have universal applications such as: making maximum use of available cover; trying to achieve mutual support; and allowing for the backblast when positioning recoilless weapons, TOWs, Dragons, and LAWs.

(8) Operating in a built-up area presents new considerations. Soldiers must select numerous alternate positions, particularly when the structure does not provide cover from small-arms fire. They must position their weapons in the shadows and within the building.

(9) In attacking a built-up area, the recoilless weapon and ATGM crews are severely hampered in choosing firing positions due to the backblast of their weapons. They may not have enough time to knock out walls in buildings and clear backblast areas. They should select positions which allow the backblast to escape such as corner windows (Figure 2-38) where the round fired goes out one window and the backblast escapes from another. The corner of a building can be improved with sandbags to create a firing position.

Figure 2-38. Corner firing position

(10) A 90-mm recoilless rifle (RCLR) crew firing from the top of a building can use the chimney for cover (Figure 2-39). The rear of this position should be reinforced with sandbags and could also be used by a Dragon team.

Figure 2-39. 90-mm recoilless rifle team firing from rooftop

(11) Employ recoilless weapons and ATGMs in streets and other open areas to make use of rubble, corners of buildings, destroyed vehicles, and anything affording cover (Figure 2-40).

Figure 2-40. Prepared positions using building for overhead cover

They can move along rooftops to obtain a better angle in which to engage enemy armor. When buildings are elevated, positions can be prepared using a building for overhead cover. Care must be taken in placement of the weapons so the backblast under the building does not damage or collapse the building or injure the crew.

(12) The machine gun has no backblast, so it can be positioned almost anywhere. In the attacks, windows and doors offer ready-made firing ports (Figure 2-41). However, the enemy normally has windows and doors under observation and fire during combat, so avoid obvious emplacements. Any opening in walls created during the fighting may be used. When other holes are not present, small explosive charges can create loopholes (Figure 2-42). Regardless of what openings are used, machine guns should be well within the building and in the shadows.

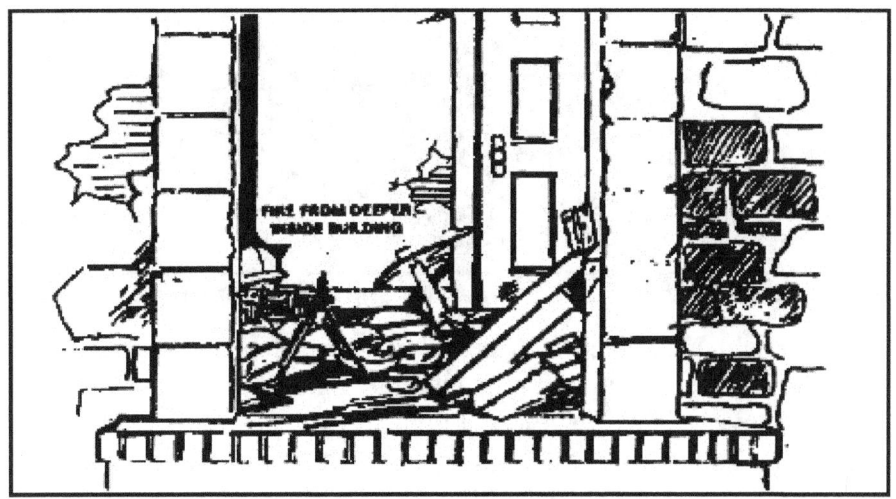

Figure 2-41. Emplacement of a machine gun in a doorway

Figure 2-42. Use of a loophole with a machine gun

(13) Upon occupying a building, soldiers often board up all windows and doors. By leaving small gaps between the slots, soldiers can use windows and doors as good alternative firing positions.

(14) Loopholes should be used extensively in the defense. They should not be constructed in any logical pattern, nor should they all be at floor or table-top level. Varying their height and location makes them hard to pinpoint and identify. Dummy loopholes, shingles knocked off, or holes cut that are not intended to be used as fighting positions, aid in the deception. Loopholes located behind shrubbery, under doorjambs, and under the eaves of a building are hard to detect. In the defense, as in the offense, a firing position can be constructed using the building for overhead cover.

(15) Increased fields of fire can be obtained by locating the machine gun in the corner of the building or sandbagged under a building (Figure 2-43).

127

Figure 2-43. Sandbagged machine gun emplacement under a building

Available materials, such as desks, overstuffed chairs, couches, and other items of furniture, should be integrated into the construction of bunkers to add cover and concealment (Figure 2-44).

Figure 2-44. Corner machine gun bunker

(16) Although grazing fire is desirable when employing the machine gun, it may not always be practical or possible. Where destroyed vehicles, rubble, and other obstructions restrict the fields of grazing fire, the gun can be elevated to where it can fire over obstacles. Therefore, firing from loopholes on the second or third story may be necessary. A firing platform can be built under the roof (Figure 2-45) and a loophole constructed. Again, the exact location of the position must be concealed by knocking off shingles in isolated patches over the entire roof.

Figure 2-45. Firing platform built under a roof

c. <u>Target Acquisition</u>. Built-up areas provide unique challenges to units. Buildings mask movement and the effects of direct and indirect fires. The rubble from destroyed buildings, along with the buildings themselves, provide concealment and protection for attackers and defenders, making target acquisition difficult. A city offers definite avenues of approach which can easily be divided into sectors.

 (1) The techniques of patrolling and using observation posts apply in the city as well as in wooded terrain. These techniques enable units to locate the enemy, to develop targets for direct and indirect fires in the defense, and to find uncovered avenues of approach in the offense.

 (2) Most weapons and vehicles have distinguishing signatures. These come from design features or from the environment in which the equipment is used. Some examples follow:

  ● Firing a tank main gun in dry, dusty, and debris-covered streets raises a dust cloud.

  ● A tank being driven in built-up areas produces more noise than one moving through an open field.

  ● Soldiers moving through rubble on a street or in the halls of a damaged building create more noise than in a wooded area.

Soldiers must recognize signatures so they can locate and identify targets. Seeing, hearing, and smelling assist in detecting and identifying signatures leading to target location, identification, and rapid engagement. Soldiers must look for targets in areas where they are most likely to be employed.

 (3) Target acquisition is continuous, whether halted or moving. Built-up areas provide both the attacker and defender with good cover and

129

concealment, but it usually favors the defender because of the advantages achieved. This makes target acquisition extremely important since the side firing first may win the engagement.

(4) When a unit is moving and enemy contact is likely, the unit must have an overwatching element. This principle applies in built-up areas just as it does in other kinds of terrain. However, in built-up areas the overwatching element must observe both the upper floors of buildings and street level.

(5) Stealth should be used when moving in built-up areas since little distance separates attackers and defenders. Use only arm- and-hand signals until contact is made. The unit should stop periodically to listen and watch, ensuring it is not being followed or the enemy is not moving parallel to the unit's flank for an ambush. Routes should be carefully chosen so buildings and piles of rubble can be used to mask the unit's movement.

(6) Observation duties must be clearly given to squad members to ensure all-round security as they move. This security continues at the halt. All the senses must be used to acquire targets, especially hearing and smelling. Soldiers soon recognize the sounds of vehicles and people moving through rubble-littered streets. The smell of fuel, cologne, and cooking food can disclose enemy positions.

(7) Observation posts are positions from which soldiers can watch and listen to enemy activity in a specific sector. They warn the unit of an enemy approach and are ideally suited for built-up areas. OPs can be positioned in the upper floors of buildings, giving soldiers a better vantage point than at street level.

(8) In the defense, a platoon leader positions OPs for local security as ordered by the company commander. The platoon leader selects the general location but the squad leader sets up the OP (Figure 2-46). Normally, there is at least one OP for each platoon. An OP consists of two to four men and is within small-arms supporting range of the platoon. Look for positions with good observation of the target sector. Ideally, an OP has a field of observation overlaying those of adjacent OPs. The position selected for the OP should have cover and concealment for units moving to and from the OP. Use the upper floors of houses or other buildings. Ensure the squad leader does not select obvious positions, such as water towers or church steeples, which attract the enemy's attention.

A squad leader is given the general location of the OP by the platoon leader. The squad leader selects the exact position.

Leaders look for positions that—

● have good observation of the desired area or sector (ideally, an OP has a field of observation which overlaps those adjacent OPs).

● have cover and concealment (good observation of the sector may require the OP to accept less cover and concealment and require troops to selectively clear fields of observation).

Figure 2-46. Selection of OP location

(9) Teach your soldiers how to scan a target area from OPs or from their fighting positions. Use of proper scanning techniques enable squad members to quickly locate and identify targets. Without optics, a soldier searches quickly for obvious targets, using all his senses to detect target signatures. If no targets are found and time permits, he makes a more detailed search (using binoculars, if available) of the terrain in the assigned sector using the 50-meter method. First, he searches a strip 50 meters deep from right to left; then he searches a strip from left to right that is farther out, overlapping the first strip. This process is continued until the entire sector is searched. In the city core or core periphery where the observer is faced with multi-story buildings, the overlapping sectors may be going up rather than out.

(10) Soldiers who man OPs and other positions should employ target acquisition devices. These devices include binoculars, image-intensification devices, thermal sights, ground surveillance radar (GSR), remotely employed sensors (REMS) and platoon early warning systems (PEWS). All of these devices enhance the unit's ability to detect and engage targets. Several types of devices should be used since no single device can meet every need of a unit. A mix might include PEWS sensors to cover out-of-sight areas and dead space, image-intensification devices for close range, thermal sights for camouflage, and smoke penetration for low-light conditions. A mix of devices is best because several devices permit overlapping sectors and more coverage, and the capabilities of one device can compensate for limitations of another.

(11) Target acquisition techniques used at night are similar to those used during the day. At night, whether using daylight optics or the unaided eye, a soldier does not look directly at an object but a few degrees off to the side. The side of the eye is more sensitive to dim light. When scanning with off-center vision, he moves his eyes in short abrupt, irregular moves.

131

At each likely target area, he pauses a few seconds to detect any motion.

(12) Sounds and smells can aid in acquiring targets at night since they transmit better in the cooler, damper, night air. Running engines, vehicles, and soldiers moving through rubble-covered streets can be heard for great distances. Odors from diesel fuel, gasoline, cooking food, burning tobacco, after-shave lotion, and so on, reveal enemy and friendly locations.

d. Flame Operations. Incendiary ammunition, special weapons, and the ease with which incendiary devices can be constructed from gasoline and other flammables make fire a true threat in built-up area operations. During defensive operations, firefighting should be a primary concern. The proper steps must be taken to reduce the risk of a fire that could make a chosen position indefensible.

(1) Soldiers choose or create positions without large openings. These positions provide as much built-in cover as possible to prevent penetration by incendiary ammunition. All unnecessary flammable materials are removed, including ammunition boxes, furniture, rugs, newspapers, curtains, and so on. Any electricity and gas coming into the building must be shut off.

(2) A building of concrete-block construction, with concrete floors and a tin roof, is an ideal place for a position. However, most buildings have wooden floors or subfloors, wooden rafters, and wooden inner walls, which require improvement. Inner walls are removed and replaced with blankets to resemble walls from the outside. Spread sand two inches deep on floors and in attics to retard fire.

(3) All available firefighting gear is prepositioned so it can be used during actual combat. For the individual soldier such gear includes entrenching tools, helmets, sand, and blankets. These items are supplemented with fire extinguishers not in use.

(4) Fire is so destructive it can easily overwhelm personnel regardless of extraordinary precautions. Soldiers plan routes of withdrawal so a priority of evacuation can be sent from fighting positions. This allows soldiers to exit through areas which are free from combustible material and provide cover from enemy direct fire.

(5) The confined space and large amounts of combustible material in built-up areas influence the enemy to use incendiary devices. Two major first-aid problems that are more urgent than in the open battlefield are: burns, and smoke and flame inhalation which creates a lack of oxygen. These can easily occur in buildings and render the victim combat ineffective. Although there is little defense against flame inhalation and lack of oxygen, smoke inhalation can be greatly reduced by wearing the individual protective mask. Regardless of the fire hazard, defensive planning for combat in built-up areas must include aidmen. Aidmen must reach victims and must have extra supplies for the treatment of burns and inhalation injuries.

(6) Offensive operations also require plans for firefighting. The success of the mission can easily be threatened by fire. Poorly planned use of incendiary munitions can make fires so extensive they become obstacles to offensive operations. The enemy may use fire to cover his withdrawal and to create obstacles and barriers to the attacker.

(7) When planning offensive operations, the attacker must consider all available weapons. The best two weapons for creating fires are the M202 FLASH and the flamethrower, which is currently out of Army inventory but can be obtained by special request through logistics channels. The flamethrower is the better training weapon since water can be substituted for the flame and the effect of the weapon can be measured by the penetration of the water. There is currently no training round for the M202. When using fire in an operation, firefighting support must be available to avoid using combat soldiers to fight fires. Choose your targets during your initial planning to avoid accidentally destroying critical facilities within the built-up area. When using flame operations in a built-up area, set priorities to determine which critical installations (hospitals, power stations, radio stations, and historical landmarks) should have primary firefighting support.

(8) Every soldier participating in the attack must be ready to deal with fire. The normal firefighting equipment available includes the entrenching tool, helmet (for carrying sand or water), and blankets (for snuffing out small fires). Fire extinguishers are available on each of the vehicles supporting the attack.

4. Navigation in Built-up Areas.

Built-up areas present a different set of challenges involving navigation. Deep in the city core, the normal terrain features depicted on maps may not apply -- buildings become the major terrain features and units become tied to streets. Fighting in the city destroys buildings whose rubble blocks streets. Street and road signs are destroyed during the fighting if they are not removed by the defenders. Operations in subways and sewers present other unique challenges. However, maps and photographs are available to help the unit overcome these problems. The global positioning system can provide navigation abilities in built-up areas.

a. Military Maps. The military city map is a topographical map of a city, usually a 1:12,500 scale, delineating streets and showing street names, important buildings, and other urban elements. The scale of a city map can vary from 1:25,000 to 1:5,000, depending on the importance and size of the city, density of detail, and intelligence information.

(1) Special maps, prepared by supporting topographic engineers, can assist units in navigating in built-up areas. These maps have been designed or modified to give information not covered in a standard map, which includes maps of road and bridge networks, railroads, built-up areas, and electric power fields. They can be used to supplement military city maps and topographical maps.

(2) Once in the built-up area, soldiers use street intersections as reference points much as they would use hills and streams in rural terrain. City maps supplement or replace topographic maps as the basis of navigation. These maps enable units moving in the built-up area to know where they are and to move to new locations even though streets have been blocked or a key building destroyed.

(3) The old techniques of compass reading and pace counting can still be used, especially in a blacked-out city where street signs and buildings are not visible. Compass azimuth readings can be thrown off from the high metal content and presence of electrical fields in the city. Carefully observe your compass so you will be aware of this condition. Sewers must be navigated in much the same way. Maps providing the basic layout of the sewer system are maintained by city sewer departments. This information includes directions the sewer lines run and distances between manhole covers. Along with basic compass and pace count techniques, such information enables a unit to move through the city sewers.

(4) City utility workers are assets to units fighting in built-up areas. They can provide maps of sewers and electrical fields and information about the city. This is important especially with regard to the use of the sewers. Sewers can contain pockets of methane gas which is highly toxic to humans, City sewer workers know the locations of these danger areas and can advise a unit how to avoid them.

b. Aerial Photographs. Current aerial photographs are also excellent supplements to military city maps and can be substituted for a map. A topographic map or military city map could be obsolete if it was compiled many years ago. A recent aerial photograph shows changes which have taken place since the map was made. This could include destroyed buildings and streets blocked by rubble as well as enemy defensive preparations. More information can be gained by using aerial photographs and maps together than using either one alone.

5. Camouflage.

To survive and win in combat in built-up areas, you must supplement cover and concealment with camouflage. To properly camouflage men, carriers, and equipment, soldiers must study the surrounding area and make positions look like the local terrain.

a. Application. Only the material needed for camouflaging a position should be used since excess material could reveal the position. Gather the camouflage material from a wide area. For example, if defending the city park, all of the park is used for resources -- do not denude a small area near a fighting position for camouflage material. This will make it stick out like a "sore thumb."

(1) Buildings provide numerous concealed positions. Armored vehicles can often find isolated positions under archways or inside small industrial or commercial structures. Thick masonry, stone, or brick walls offer excellent protection from direct fire and provide concealed routes.

(2) After camouflage is completed, the soldier inspects positions from the

134

enemy's viewpoint. He makes routine checks to see if the camouflage remains natural looking and actually conceals his position. If it does not look natural, the soldier must rearrange or replace it.

(3) Positions must be progressively camouflaged as they are prepared. Work should continue until all camouflage is complete. When the enemy has air superiority, work may be possible only at night. Shiny or light-colored objects which could attract attention from the air must be hidden. Fires can only be lit in enclosed or hidden areas to avoid being seen by the enemy.

(4) Shirts should be worn since exposed skin reflects light and attracts the enemy. Even dark skin reflects light because of its natural oils.

(5) Camouflage face paint is issued in three standard, two-tone sticks. When issue-type face-paint sticks are not available, burnt cork, charcoal, or lampblack can be used to tone down exposed skin. Use mud as a last resort since it dries and peels off, leaving the skin exposed. It may also contain harmful bacteria.

b. Use of Shadows. Buildings in built-up areas throw sharp shadows which can be used to conceal vehicles and equipment (Figure 2-47). Soldiers should avoid areas not in shadows. Vehicles may have to be moved periodically as shadows shift during the day. Emplacements inside buildings provide better concealment.

(1) Soldiers should avoid the lighted areas around windows and loopholes. They will be better concealed if they fire from the shadowed interior of a room (Figure 2-48).

(2) A lace curtain or piece of cheesecloth provides additional concealment to soldiers in the interior of rooms if curtains are common to the area. Interior lights are prohibited.

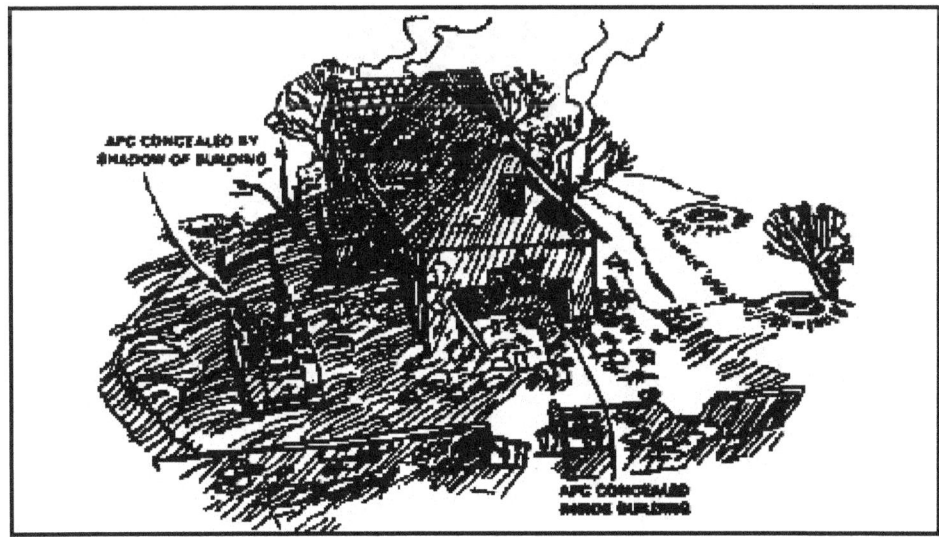

Figure 2-47. Use of shadows for concealment

Figure 2-48. Concealment inside a building

c. <u>Color and Texture</u>. Standard camouflage pattern painting of equipment is not as effective in built-up areas as a solid, dull, dark color hidden in shadows. Since repainting vehicles before entering a built-up area is not always practical, the lighter sand-colored patterns should be subdued with mud or dirt.

(1) The need to break up the silhouette of helmets and individual equipment exists in built-up areas the same as it does elsewhere. However, burlap or canvas strips are a more effective camouflage than foliage (Figure 2-49). Predominant colors are normally browns, tans, and sometimes grays rather than greens, but each camouflage location should be evaluated.

Figure 2-49. Helmet camouflaged with burlap strips

(2) Weapons emplacements should use a wet blanket (Figure 2-50), canvas, or cloth to keep dust from rising when the weapon is fired.

Figure 2-50. Wet blanket used to keep dust down

(3) Command posts and logistical emplacements are easier to camouflage and better protected if located underground. Antennas can be remoted to upper stories or to higher buildings based on remote capabilities. Field telephone wire should be laid in conduits, in sewers, or through buildings.

(4) Soldiers should consider the background to ensure they are not silhouetted or skylined, but rather blend into their surrounding. To defeat enemy urban camouflage, soldiers should be alert for the following common camouflage errors:

- Tracks or other evidence of activity.

- Shine or shadows.

- An unnatural color or texture.

- Muzzle flash, smoke, or dust.

- Unnatural sounds and smells.

- Movement.

(5) Dummy positions can be used effectively to distract the enemy and make him reveal his position by firing.

(6) Built-up areas afford cover, resources for camouflage, and locations for concealment. The following basic rules of cover, camouflage, and concealment should be adhered to:

(a) Use the terrain and other camouflage habits to suit your

137

surroundings.

(b) Employ deceptive camouflage of buildings.

(c) Continue to improve positions. Reinforce fighting positions with sandbags or other shrapnel and blast-absorbent material.

(d) Maintain the natural look of the area.

(e) Keep positions hidden by clearing away minimal debris for fields of fire.

(f) Choose firing ports in inconspicuous spots when available.

Note: Remember, a force that covers and conceals itself has a significant advantage over a force that does not.

PART B - EMPLOYMENT AND EFFECTS OF WEAPONS IN BUILT-UP AREAS

This part of the lesson describes weapons' capabilities and effects against generic targets. It focuses on specific employment considerations pertaining to combat in built-up areas, and it addresses both organic infantry weapons and combat support weapons.

1. Effectiveness of Weapons and Demolitions.

The characteristics and nature of combat in built-up areas affect the results and employment of weapons. Leaders at all levels must consider the following factors in various combinations when choosing their weapons.

a. Hard, smooth, flat surfaces are characteristic of urban targets. Rarely do rounds impact perpendicular to these flat surfaces, but at some angle of obliquity. This reduces the effect of most rounds and increases the threat of ricochets. The tendency of rounds to strike glancing blows against hard surfaces means that up to 25 percent of impact-fuzed explosive rounds may not detonate when fired onto rubbled areas.

b. Engagement ranges are close. Studies and historical analyses have shown that only five percent of all targets are more than 100 meters away. About 90 percent of all targets are located 50 meters or less from the identifying soldier. Few personnel targets will be visible beyond 50 meters and usually occur at 35 meters or less. Minimum arming ranges and troop safety from backblast or fragmentation effects must be considered.

c. Engagement times are short. Enemy personnel present only fleeting targets. Enemy-held buildings or structures are normally covered by fire and often cannot be engaged with deliberate, well-aimed shots.

d. Depression and elevation limits for some weapons create dead space. Tall buildings form deep canyons that are often safe from indirect fires. Some weapons can fire rounds to ricochet behind cover and inflict casualties. Target engagement

138

from oblique angles, both horizontal and vertical, demands superior marksmanship skills.

e. Smoke from burning buildings, dust from explosions, shadows from tall buildings, and the lack of light penetrating inner rooms all combine to reduce visibility and to increase a sense of isolation. Added to this is the masking of fires caused by rubble and man-made structures. Targets, even those at close range tend to be indistinct.

f. Urban fighting often becomes a confused melee with several small units attacking on converging axes. The risks from friendly fires, ricochets, and fratricide, must be considered during the planning phase of operations and control measures continually adjusted to lower these risks.

g. Both the firer and target may be inside or outside buildings, or they may both be inside the same, or separate buildings. The enclosed nature of combat in built-up areas means you must consider the weapon's effect, such as muzzle blast and backblast, as well as the round's impact on the target.

h. Usually the man-made structure must be attacked before enemy personnel inside are attacked. Therefore, you choose weapons and demolitions based on their effects against masonry and concrete rather than against enemy personnel.

i. Modern engineering and design improvements mean most large buildings constructed since World War II are resilient to the blast effects of bomb and artillery attack. Even though modern buildings may burn easily, they often retain their structural integrity and remain standing. Once high-rise buildings burn out, they are still useful to the military and are almost impossible to damage further. A large structure can take 24 to 48 hours to burn out and get cool enough for soldiers to enter.

j. The most common worldwide building type is the 12- to 24-inch brick-wall building. The table in Figure 2-51 lists the frequency of occurrence of building types worldwide.

TYPE OF BUILDING	FREQUENCY OF OCCURRENCE (PERCENTAGE)
30-inch Stone	1
8- to 10-inch Reinforced Concrete	6.9
12- to 24-inch Brick	63
6-inch Wood	16
14-inch Steel and Concrete (Heavy Clad)	2
7-inch Steel and Concrete (Light Clad)	12

Figure 2-51. Types of buildings and frequency of occurrence

2. <u>M16 Rifle and Squad Automatic Weapon</u>.

The M16A1/M16A2 rifle is the most common weapon fired in built-up areas. The

M16A1/M16A2 rifle is used to kill enemy personnel, to suppress enemy fire and observation, and to penetrate light cover. You can use 5.56-mm tracer fire to designate targets for other weapons.

a. Employment. Close combat is the predominant characteristic of urban engagements. Riflemen must be able to hit small fleeting targets, bunker apertures, windows, and loopholes. This requires pinpoint accuracy with weapons fired in the semiautomatic mode. Killing an enemy through an 8-inch loophole at a range of 50 meters may be a challenge, but one that will be common in combat in built-up areas.

(1) When fighting inside buildings, three-round bursts or rapid semiautomatic fire should be used. To suppress defenders while entering a room, a series of rapid three-round bursts should be fired at all identified targets and likely enemy positions. This is more effective than long bursts or spraying the room with automatic fire. Fire from an underarm or shoulder position; not from the hip.

(2) When targets reveal themselves in buildings, the most effective engagement is the quick-fire technique with the weapon up and both eyes open. Accurate, quick fire not only kills enemy soldiers, but also gives the attacker fire superiority.

(3) Within built-up areas, burning debris, reduced ambient light, strong shadow patterns of varying density, and smoke, all limit the effect of night vision and sighting devices. The use of aiming stakes in the defense and of the pointing technique in the offense, both using three-round bursts, are night-firing skills required of all infantrymen. The individual laser aiming light can sometimes be used effectively with night vision goggles (NVGs). Ensure any soldier using NVGs is teamed with at least one soldier not wearing them.

b. Weapon Penetration. The penetration achieved with a 5.56-mm round depends on the range to the target and the type of material being fired against. The M16A2 and SAW achieve greater penetration than the older M16A1, but only at longer ranges. At close range, both weapons perform the same. Single 5.56-mm rounds are not effective against structural materials (as opposed to partitions) when fired at close range -- the closer the range, the less the penetration.

(1) For the 5.56-mm round, maximum penetration occurs at 200 meters. At ranges less than 25 meters penetration is greatly reduced. At 10 meters penetration by the M16 round is poor due to the tremendous stress placed on this high-speed round which causes it to yaw upon striking a target. Stress causes the projectile to break up and the resulting fragments are often too small to penetrate.

(2) Even with reduced penetration at short ranges, interior walls made of thin wood paneling, sheetrock, or plaster are no protection against 5.56-mm rounds. Common office furniture such as desks and chairs cannot stop these rounds, but a layer of books 18 to 24 inches thick can.

(3) Wooden frame buildings and single cinder block walls offer little protection from 5.56-mm rounds. When clearing such structures soldiers must ensure friendly casualties do not result from rounds passing through walls, floors, or ceilings.

(4) Armor-piercing rounds are slightly more effective than ball ammunition in penetrating urban targets at all ranges. They are more likely to ricochet than ball ammunition, especially when the target presents a high degree of obliquity.

c. Protection. The following common barriers in built-up areas stop a 5.56-mm round fired at less than 50 meters:

One thickness of sandbags.

A 2-inch thick concrete wall (unreinforced).

A 55-gallon drum filled with water or sand.

A small ammunition can filled with sand.

A cinder block filled with sand (the block will probably shatter).

A plate glass windowpane at a 45-degree angle (glass fragments will be thrown behind the glass).

A brick veneer.

A car body (an M16A1/M16A2 rifle penetrates but normally will not exit).

d. Wall Penetration. Although most structural materials repel single 5.56-mm rounds, continued and concentrated firing can breach some typical urban structures (see Figure 2-52).

TYPE	PENETRATION	ROUNDS REQUIRED
8-inch reinforced concrete	Initial / Loophole	35 / 250
14-inch triple brick	Initial / Loophole	90 / 160
12-inch cinder block with single-brick veneer	Loophole / Breach hole	60 / 250
9-inch double brick	Initial / Loophole	70 / 120
16-inch tree trunk or log wall	Initial*	1 to 3
12-inch cinder block (filled with sand)	Loophole	35
24-inch double sandbag wall	Initial*	220
3/8-inch mild steel door	Initial*	1

*Penetration only; no loophole.

Figure 2-52. Structural penetration capabilities of the 5.56 round
against typical urban targets (range 25 to 100 meteres)

(1) The best method for breaching a masonry wall is by firing short bursts (three to five rounds) in a unshaped pattern. The distance from the gunner to the wall should be minimized for best results -- ranges as close as 25 meters are relatively safe from ricochet. Ballistic eye protection, protective vest, and helmet should be worn.

(2) Ball ammunition and armor-piercing rounds produce almost the same results but armor-piercing rounds are more likely to fly back at the firer. The 5.56-mm round can be used to create either a loophole (about 7 inches in diameter) or a breach hole (large enough for a man to enter). When used against reinforced concrete, the M16 rifle and SAW cannot cut the reinforcing bars.

3. Machine Guns (7.62 mm and .50 caliber).

In the urban environment, the Browning .50-caliber machine gun and the 7.62-mm M60 machine gun provide high-volume, long-range automatic fires for the suppression or destruction of targets. They provide final protective fire along fixed lines and can be used to penetrate light structures -- the .50-caliber machine gun is most effective in this role. Tracers from both machine guns are likely to start fires but the .50-caliber tracer is more apt to do so.

a. Employment. The primary consideration impacting on the employment of machine guns within built-up areas is the limited availability of long-range fields

142

of fire. Although machine guns should be emplaced at the lowest level possible, grazing fire at ground level is often obstructed by rubble.

(1) The .50-caliber machine gun is often employed on its vehicular mount during both offensive and defensive operations. If necessary it can be mounted on the M3 tripod mount for use in the ground role or in the upper levels of buildings. When mounted on a tripod, the 50-caliber machine gun can be used as an accurate long-range weapon and can supplement sniper fires.

(2) The M60 machine gun is cumbersome, making it difficult to use inside while clearing a building. However it is useful outside to suppress and isolate enemy defenders. The M60 can be fired from either the shoulder or the hip to provide a high volume of assault and suppressive fires. The use of the long sling to support the weapon and ammunition is preferred.

(3) Because of their reduced penetration power, M60 machine guns are less effective against masonry targets than .50-caliber machine guns. However their availability and light weight make them well suited to augment heavy machine gun fire or to be used in areas where .50-caliber machine guns cannot be positioned, or as a substitute when heavy machine guns are not available. The M60 machine gun can be employed on its tripod to deliver accurate fire along fixed lines and then can quickly be converted to bipod fire to cover alternate fields of fire.

b. Penetration. The ability of the 7.62-mm and .50-caliber rounds to penetrate are also affected by the range to the target and type of material fired against. The 7.62-mm round is affected less by close ranges than the 5.56-mm; the .50-caliber's penetration is reduced least of all.

(1) At 50 meters the 7.62-mm ball round cannot penetrate a single layer of sandbags. It can penetrate a single layer at 200 meters, but not a double layer. The armor-piercing round does only slightly better against sandbags. It cannot penetrate a double layer but can penetrate up to 10 inches at 600 meters.

(2) The penetration of the 7.62-mm round is best at 600 meters, but most urban targets are closer. The longest effective range is usually 200 meters or less. The table in Figure 2-53 explains the penetration capabilities of a single 7.62-mm (ball) round at closer ranges.

RANGE (meters)	PINE BOARD (inches)	DRY LOOSE SAND (inches)	CINDER BLOCK (inches)	CONCRETE (inches)
25	13	5	8	2
100	18	4.5	10	2
200	41	7	8	2

Figure 2-53. Penetration capabilities of a single 7.62-mm round

(3) The .50-caliber round is also optimized for penetration at long ranges (about 800 meters). For hard targets, .50-caliber penetration is affected by obliquity and range. Both armor-piercing and ball ammunition penetrate 14 inches of sand or 28 inches of packed earth at 200 meters, if the rounds impact perpendicular to the flat face of the target. The table in Figure 2-54 explains the effect of a 45-degree obliquity on a .50-caliber machine gun's penetration.

THICKNESS (feet)	100 METER (rounds)	200 METERS (rounds)
2	300	1,200
3	450	1,800
4	600	2,400

Figure 2-54. Number of rounds needed to penetrate a reinforced concrete at a 25-degree obliquity

c. Protection. Barriers offering protection against 5.56-mm rounds are also effective against 7.62-mm rounds with some exceptions. The 7.62-mm round can penetrate a windowpane at a 45-degree obliquity, a hollow cinder block, or both sides of a car body. It can also easily penetrate wooden frame buildings. The .50-caliber round can penetrate all of the commonly found urban barriers except a sand-filled 55-gallon drum.

d. Wall Penetration. Continued and concentrated machine gun fire can breach most typical urban walls. Such fire cannot breach thick reinforced concrete structures or dense natural stone walls. Internal walls, partitions, plaster, floors, ceilings, common office furniture, home appliances, and bedding can be easily penetrated by both 7.62-mm and .50-caliber rounds (Figures 2-55 and 2-56).

TYPE	THICKNESS (inches)	HOLE DIAMETER (inches)	ROUNDS REQUIRED
Reinforced concrete	8	7	100
Triple brick wall	14	7	170
Concrete block with single brick veneer	12	6	30
		24	200
Cinder block (filled)	12	*	18
Double brick wall	9	*	45
Double sandbag wall	24	*	110
Log wall	16	*	1
Mild steel door	3/8	*	1
* Penetration only, no loophole.			

Figure 2-55. Structure penetrating capabilities of 7.62-mm round (NATO ball) against typical urban targets (range 25 meters)

TYPE	THICKNESS (inches)	HOLE DIAMETER (inches)	ROUNDS REQUIRED
Reinforced concrete	10	12	50
		24	100
	18	7	140
Triple brick wall	12	8	15
		26	50
Concrete block with single brick veneer	12	10	25
		33	45
Armor plate	1	*	1
Double sandbag wall	24	*	5
Log wall	16	*	1
* Penetration only, no loophole			

Figure 2-56. Structure penetrating capabilities of .50-caliber ball against typical urban targets (range 25 meters)

(1) The M60 machine gun can be hard to hold steady to repeatedly hit the same point on a wall. The dust created by the bullet strikes also makes precise aiming difficult. Firing from a tripod is usually more effective-than without, especially if sandbags are used to steady the weapon. Short bursts of three to five rounds fired in a U-type pattern are best.

(2) Breaching a brick veneer presents a special problem for the M60 machine gun. Rounds penetrate the cinder block, but leave a net-like

145

structure of unbroken block. Excessive ammunition is required to destroy a net since most rounds only pass through a previously eroded hole. One or two minutes work with an E-tool, crowbar, or axe can remove this web and allow entry through the breach hole.

(3) The .50-caliber machine gun can be fired accurately from the tripod using the single-shot mode. This is the most efficient method for producing a loophole. Automatic fire in three- to five-round bursts in a U-type pattern, is more effective in producing a breach.

4. Grenade Launchers (40-mm M203 and MK 19).

Both the M203 dual-purpose weapon and the MK 19 grenade machine gun fire 40-mm high-explosive (HE) and high-explosive, dual-purpose (HEDP) ammunition. Ammunition for these weapons is not interchangeable, but the grenade and fuze assembly that actually hits the target are identical. Both weapons provide point and area destructive fires as well as suppression. The MK 19 has a much higher rate of fire and a longer range. The M203 is much lighter and more maneuverable.

a. Employment. The main consideration affecting the employment of 40-mm grenades within built-up areas is the typically short engagement range. The 40-mm grenade has a minimum arming range of 14 to 28 meters. If the round strikes an object before it is armed, it will not detonate. Both the HE and HEDP rounds have 5-meter casualty radii against exposed troops, which means the absolute minimum safe-firing range for combat is 31 meters. The 40-mm grenades can be used to suppress the enemy in a building, or inflict casualties by firing through apertures or windows. The MK 19 can use its high rate of fire to concentrate rounds against light structures. This concentrated fire can create extensive damage. The 40-mm HEDP round can penetrate the armor on the flank, rear, and top of Soviet BMPs and BTRs. Troops can use the M203 from upper stories to deliver accurate fire against the top decks of armored vehicles. Multiple hits are normally required to achieve a kill.

b. Weapon Penetration. The 40-mm HEDP grenade has a small shaped charge that penetrates better than the HE round. It also has a thin wire wrapping that bursts into a dense fragmentation pattern, creating casualties out to five meters. Because they explode on contact, 40-mm rounds achieve the same penetration regardless of range. The table in Figure 2-57 explains the penetration capabilities of the HEDP round.

TARGET	PENETRATION (inches)
Sandbags	20 (double layer)
Sand-filled cinder block	16
Pine logs	12
Armor plate	2

Figure 2-57. Penetration capabilities of the HEDP round

(1) If projected into an interior room, the 40-mm HEDP can penetrate all interior partition-type walls. It splinters plywood and plaster walls making a hole large enough to fire a rifle through. It is better to have HEDP rounds pass into a room and explode on a far wall even though much of the round's energy is wasted penetrating the back wall (see Figure 2-58). The fragmentation produced in the room causes more casualties than the high-explosive jet formed by the shaped charge.

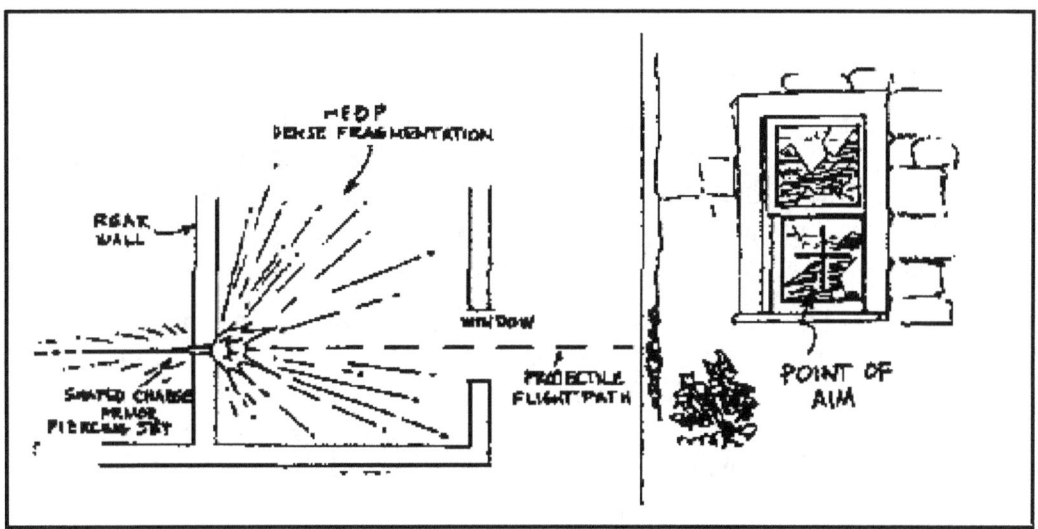

Figure 2-58. Aim point for 40-mm HEDP

(2) Fragments from the HEDP round do not reliably penetrate interior walls. They are also stopped by office furniture, sandbags, helmets, and protective vests (flak jackets). The M203 dual-purpose weapon has the inherent accuracy to place grenades into windows at 125 meters and bunker apertures at 50 meters. These ranges are significantly reduced as the angle of obliquity increases. Combat experience shows that M203 gunners cannot consistently hit windows at 50 meters when forced to aim and fire quickly.

c. Wall Penetration. The M203 cannot reasonably deliver the rounds needed to breach a typical exterior wall. The MK 19 can concentrate its fire and achieve wall penetration. Firing from a tripod, using a locked-down traversing and elevating mechanism is best for this role. Brick, cinder block, and concrete can be breached using the MK 19. Individual HEDP rounds can penetrate six to eight inches of brick. The only material proven to be resistant to concentrated 40-mm fire is dense stone, such as that used in some European building construction. No precise data exist as to the number of rounds required to produce loopholes or breach holes with the MK 19. However, the rounds' explosive effects are dramatic and should exceed the performance of the .50-caliber machine gun.

5. Light and Medium Recoilless Weapons.

Light recoilless weapons are used to attack enemy personnel, field fortifications, and light armored vehicles. They have limited capability against main battle tanks, especially those

147

equipped with reactive armor, except when attacking from the top, flanks, or rear. This category of weapons includes the following:

- M72 light antitank weapon (LAW).
- AT4/8.
- M47 Dragon.
- 90-mm recoilless rifle (RCLR).
- Shoulder-launched, multipurpose assault weapon (SMAW).
- Available foreign weapons such as the RPG-7.

a. Employment. Other than defeating light armored vehicles, the most common task for which light recoilless weapons are used is to neutralize fortified firing positions. Due to their small warhead, they are not as effective in this role as heavier weapons such as a tank main-gun round. Their light weight does allow soldiers to carry several and they can be used from inside or on top of buildings.

(1) Light and medium recoilless weapons, with the exception of the SMAW and AT8, employ shaped-charge warheads. As a result, the hole they punch in wall is too small to use as a loophole. The fragmentation and spall these weapons produce are limited. Shaped-charge warheads do not neutralize enemy soldiers behind walls unless they are located directly in line with the point of impact.

(2) Against structures, shaped-charge weapons should be aimed about six inches below, or to the side of a firing aperture (see Figure 2-59). This enhances the probability of killing the enemy behind the wall. A round that passes through a window wastes much of its energy on the back wall. Since these shaped-charge rounds lack the wire wrapping of the 40-mm HEDP, they burst into few fragments and are often ineffective casualty producers.

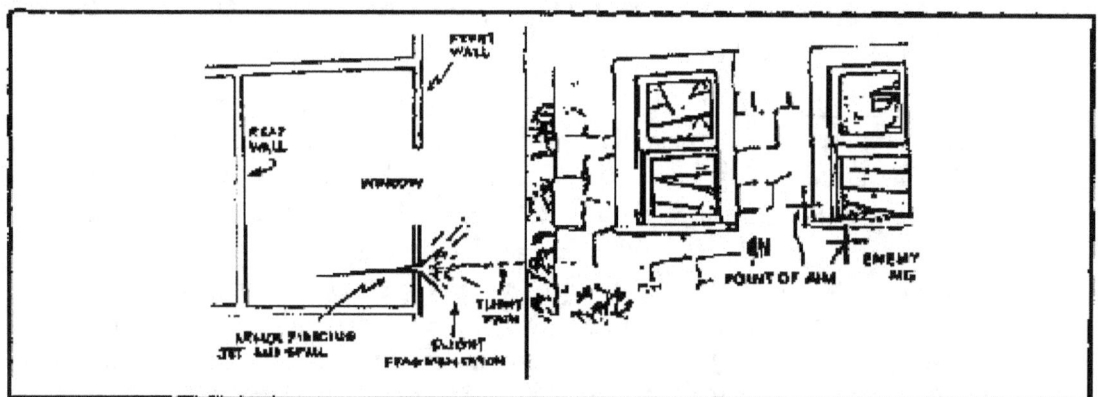

**Figure 2-59. Point of aim for a shaped-charge weapon
against a masonry structure**

(3) Sandbagged emplacements present a different problem (see Figure 2-60). Because sandbags absorb much of the energy from a shaped-charge,

the rounds should be aimed at the center of the firing aperture. Even if the round misses the aperture, the bunker wall area near it is usually easiest to penetrate.

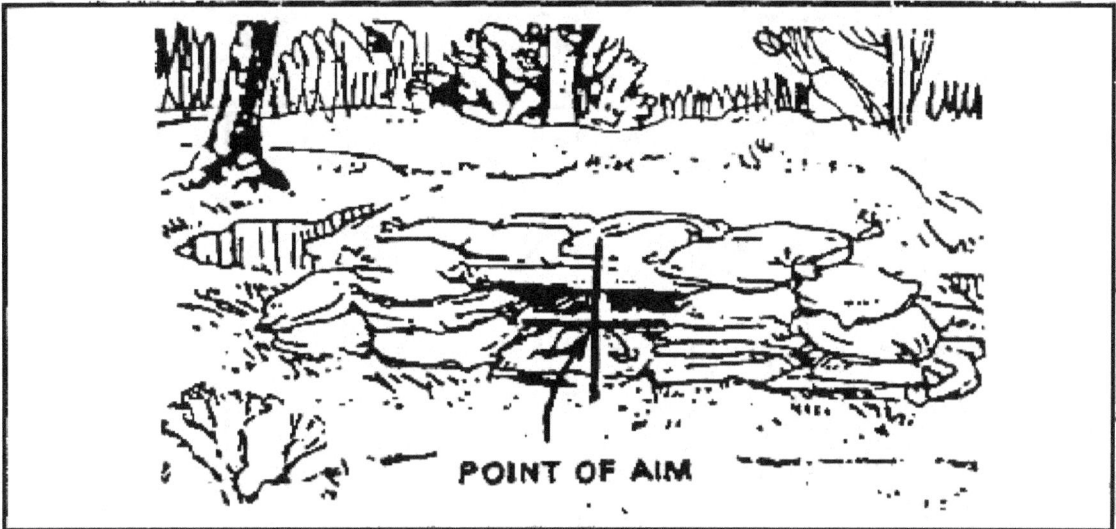

Figure 2-60. Point of aim for a sandbagged emplacement

(4) Light and medium recoilless weapons obtain their most effective short-range antiarmor shots by firing from upper stories, or from the flanks and rear. When firing at main battle tanks, these weapons should always be employed against these weaker areas in volley, series, or paired firings. They normally require multiple hits to achieve a kill on a tank. Flanks, top, and rear shots hit the most vulnerable parts of armored vehicles. Firing from upper stories protects the firer from tank main gun and coaxial machine gun fire since tanks cannot sharply elevate their cannons. The BMP-2 can elevate its 30-mm cannon to engage targets in upper stories. The BTR-series armored vehicles can also fire into upper stories with their heavy machine gun.

(5) Modern infantry fighting vehicles such as the BMP-2 and the BTR-80, have significantly improved frontal protection against shaped-charge weapons. Many main battle tanks have some form of reactive armor in addition to their thick armor plate. Head-on, ground-level shots against these vehicles have little probability of obtaining a kill. Even without reactive armor, modern main battle tanks are hard to destroy with a light antiarmor weapon.

(6) The easiest technique to use to improve the probability of hitting and killing an armored vehicle, is to increase the firing depression angle. A 45-degree downward firing angle doubles the probability of a first-round hit as compared to a ground-level shot (see Figure 2-61).

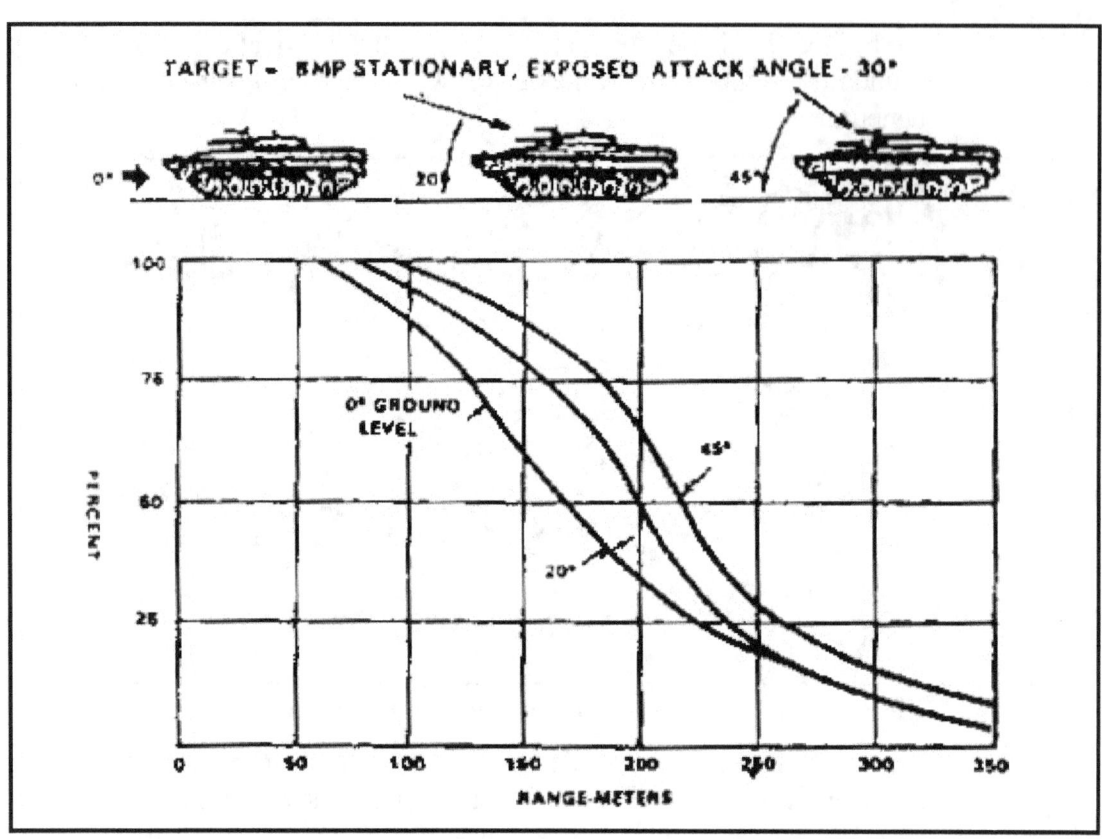

Figure 2-61. Probability of achieving at hit at different angles using an M72A2 LAW

b. <u>Backblast</u>. Backblast characteristics must be considered when employing all recoilless weapons. During combat in built-up areas, the backblast area in the open is more hazardous due to all the loose rubble and the channeling effect of the narrow streets and alleys. Figure 2-62 shows the backblast areas of United States light and medium recoilless weapons in the open.

(1) When firing recoilless weapons in the open, soldiers should protect themselves from blast and burn injuries caused by the backblast. All personnel should be out of the danger zone. Anyone not able to vacate the caution zone should be behind cover. Soldiers in the caution zone should wear helmets, protective vests, and eye protection. The firer and all soldiers in the area should wear earplugs.

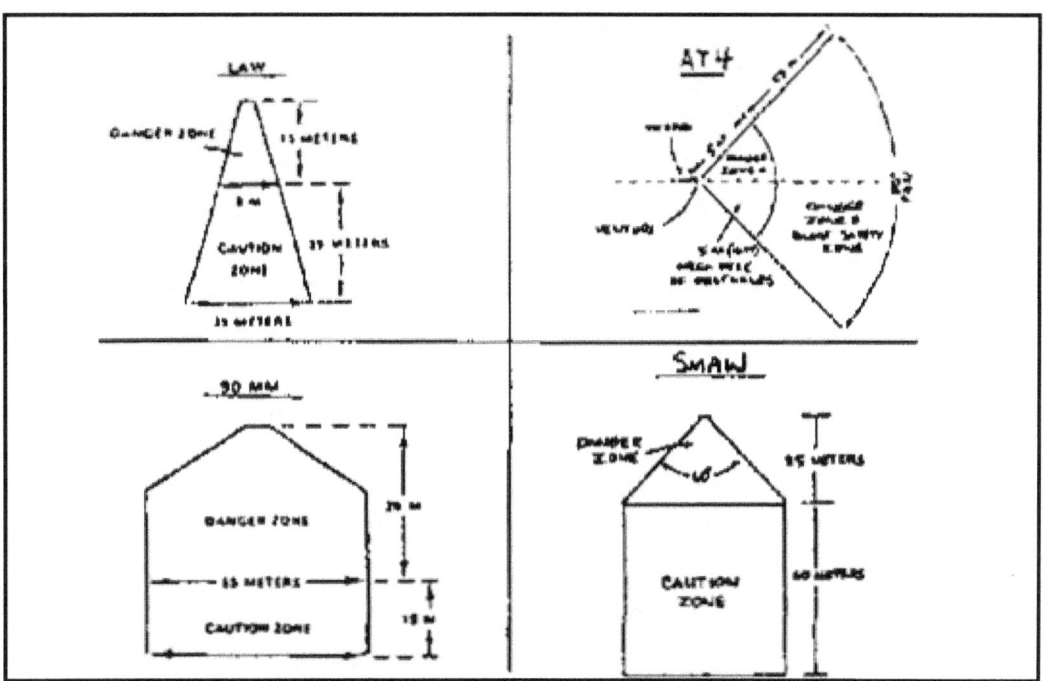

Figure 2-62. Backblast areas of light recoilless weapons in the open

(2) Since the end of World War II, the U.S. Army has conducted extensive testing on the effects of firing recoilless weapons from within enclosures. Beginning as early as 1948, tests have been conducted on every type of recoilless weapon available. In 1975 the U.S. Army Human Engineering Laboratory at Aberdeen Proving Grounds in Maryland conducted extensive firing of LAWs, Dragons, 90-mm RCLRs, and TOW from masonry and frame buildings and from sandbag bunkers. These tests showed firing these weapons from enclosures presented no serious hazards, even when the overpressure was enough to produce structural damage to the building. The following are other findings of this test.

(a) Little hazard exits to the gunnery or crew from any type of flying debris. Loose items were not hurled around the room.

(b) No substantial degradation occurred to the operator's tracking performance as a result of obscuration or blast overpressure.

(c) The most serious hazard that can be expected is hearing loss. This must be evaluated against the advantage gained in combat from firing from cover. To place this hazard in perspective, a gunner wearing earplugs and firing the loudest combination (the Dragon from within a masonry building) is exposed to less noise hazard than if he fired a LAW in the open without earplugs.

(d) The safest place for other soldiers in the room with the firer is against the wall from which the weapon is fired. Plastic ignition plugs are a hazard to anyone standing directly behind a LAW or TOW when it is fired.

(e) Firers should take advantage of all available sources of

151

ventilation by opening doors and windows. Ventilation does not reduce the noise hazard, but it helps clear the room of smoke and dust, and reduces the effective duration of the overpressure.

(f) The only difference between firing these weapons from enclosures and firing them in the open, is the duration of the pressure fluctuation.

(g) Frame buildings, especially small ones can suffer structural damage to the rear walls, windows, and doors. Large rooms suffer slight damage if any.

(3) Recoilless weapons fired from within enclosures create some obscuration (smoke) inside the room, but almost none from the gunner's position looking out. Inside the room, obscuration can be intense, but the room remains inhabitable. The table in Figure 2-63 shows the effects of smoke and obscuration.

(4) The Dragon causes the most structural damage, but only in frame buildings. There does not seem to be any threat of injury to the gunner, since the damage is usually to the walls away from the gunner. The most damage and debris is from flying plaster chips and pieces of wood trim. Large chunks of plasterboard can be dislodged from ceilings. The backblast from LAW, Dragon, or TOW rarely displaces furniture. Figure 2-64 shows the test results of structural damage and debris.

BUILDING	WEAPON	FROM GUNNERS POSITION LOOKING OUT	INSIDE THE ROOM	FROM OUTSIDE AT A DISTANCE
Masonry	LAW	None	Moderate	Slight smoke
	Dragon	Slight	Moderate	Small flash
Bunker	Dragon	None	Slight	Moderate flash
	TOW	None	Slight	Moderate smoke
Small Frame	LAW	None	Moderate	Moderate
	Dragon	None	Severe	Moderate
Medium Frame	LAW	None	Slight	Moderate
	Dragon	None	Severe	Slight flash
Large Frame	LAW	None	Slight	None
	Dragon	Slight	Severe	Slight flash
	TOW	None	Severe	Slight smoke

Figure 2-63. Smoke and obscuration

152

| | | DAMAGE | | |
BUILDING	WEAPON	STRUCTURE	WALL COVERING	DEBRIS MOVEMENT
Masonry	LAW	None	Slight	Slight
	Dragon	None	Slight	Slight
Bunker	Dragon	None	None	None
	TOW	None	None	Leaves and dust disturbed
Small Frame	LAW	None	Slight	None
	Dragon	Severe	Severe	None
Medium Frame	LAW	None	None	Slight
	Dragon	Slight	Slight	Lamp and chair overturned
Large Frame	LAW	None	Slight	Slight
	Dragon	Slight	Moderate	None
	TOW	Slight	Severe	None

Figure 2-64. Structural damage and debris movement

(5) To fire a LAW from inside a room the following safety precautions must be taken (see Figure 2-65).

Figure 2-65. Firing a LAW inside a room

(a) At least 4 feet of clearance should exist between the rear of the LAW and the nearest wall.

(b) At least 20 square feet of ventilation (an open 7- by 3-foot door is sufficient) should exist to reduce or prevent structural damage to the building -- the more ventilation the better.

153

(c) All glass should be removed from windows.

(d) All personnel in the room should be forward of the rear of the weapon and should wear helmets, protective vests, ballistic eye protection, and earplugs.

(e) All combustible material should be removed from the rear of the weapon.

(f) Ceiling height should be at least 7 feet.

(6) To fire a 90-mm RCLR, AT4/8, or SMAW from inside a room, the following safety precautions must be taken (see Figure 2-66.)

(a) The building must be of sturdy construction.

(b) The ceiling should be at least 7 feet high with any loose plaster or ceiling boards removed.

Figure 2-66. Firing a 90-mm RCLR, AT4/8, or SMAW from inside a building

(c) The floor size should be at least 15 feet by 12 feet. (The larger the room, the better.).

(d) At least 20 square feet of ventilation (room openings) should exist to the rear or side of the weapon. An open 7- by 3-foot door would provide minimum ventilation.

(e) All glass should be removed from windows and small loose objects removed from the room.

(f) Floors should be wet to prevent dust and dirt from blowing around and obscuring the gunner's vision.

(g) All personnel in the room should be forward of the rear of the weapon.

(h) All personnel in the room should wear helmets, protective vests, ballistic eye protection, and earplugs.

154

(i) If the gunner is firing from the prone position, his lower body must be perpendicular to the bore of the weapon or the blast could cause injury to his legs.

c. Weapon Penetration. The most important tasks to be performed against structures are the neutralization of fortified firing positions, personnel, and weapons behind barriers. Recoilless weapons can be used in this role; none however, is as effective as heavy direct-fire weapons or standard demolitions. Each recoilless weapon has different penetrating ability against various targets. Penetration does not always mean the destruction of the integrity of a position. Usually, only those enemy soldiers directly in the path of the spall from a high-explosive antitank (HEAT) round become casualties. Other soldiers inside a fortification could be deafened, dazed, or shocked but could eventually return to action.

(1) M72 LAW. The LAW, although light and easy to use, has a small explosive charge and limited penetration. It can be defeated by a double-layer brick wall, backed by four feet of sandbags, since it cannot produce a loophole in this type construction. The LAW requires about 15 meters to arm. If it hits a target before it arms, it usually does not detonate. (The LAW is being replaced by the AT4 in the U.S. Army inventory of munitions.) The LAW can penetrate the following:

Two feet of reinforced concrete, leaving a dime-sized hole and creating little spall.

Six feet of earth, leaving a quarter-sized hole with no spall.

Eight inches of steel (flanks, rear, and top armor of most armored vehicles), leaving a dime-sized hole.

(2) M136 84-mm Launcher (AT4). The AT4 is heavier than the LAW with a diameter of 84 millimeters, which gives the warhead much greater penetration. The AT4 can penetrate more than 17.5 inches (450 mm) of armor plate. Its warhead produces highly destructive results behind the armor. Tests against typical urban targets are still ongoing, but the AT4 should penetrate at least as well as the 90-mm recoilless rifle if not better. The AT4 has a minimum arming distance of 10 meters, which allows it to be fired successfully against close targets. Gunners should be well covered by protective equipment when firing at close targets.

(3) 90-mm Recoilless rifle. The 90-mm recoilless rifle is being phased out of the U.S. Army inventory of weapons but it is still used in some units. Its light weight and maneuverability combined with great penetrating power make the 90-mm RCLR a useful weapon during combat in built-up areas. The 90-mm RCLR has an antipersonnel round effective against exposed enemy. The flechette projectiles fired by this antipersonnel round cannot penetrate structural walls, but can pierce partitions and wooden-framed buildings. The antipersonnel round has no minimum range, but the HEAT round is not armed until it has traveled 35 to 50 feet. The 90-mm HEAT

round can penetrate the following:

> Three and one half feet of packed earth, leaving a 2-inch hole with no spall.

> Two and one half feet of reinforced concrete, creating a small loophole (less than 3 inches wide) with little spall.

> Ten inches of armor plate, leaving a quarter-sized hole.

(4) <u>Shoulder-launched, Multipurpose Assault Weapon (SMAW)</u>. The SMAW is being issued to U.S. Marine Corps units. It has been type-classified and in time of war, Army units could find it available. The SMAW is a lightweight man-portable assault weapon easily carried and placed into action by one man. It is used against fortified positions, but it is also effective against light-armored vehicles. The SMAW has a 9-mm spotting rifle and a 3.8-power telescope which ensure accuracy over ranges common to combat in built-up areas. The SMAW has excellent incapacitating effects behind walls and inside bunkers, and can arm within 10 meters. It fires the same dual-mode fuzed round as the AT8 and it has another round designed for even greater effect against armored vehicles. The SMAW has the same penetration ability as the AT8 -- it can destroy most bunkers with a single hit. Multiple shots can create breach holes even in reinforced concrete.

(5) <u>RPG-7</u>. The RPG-7 is a common threat weapon worldwide. It is lightweight and maneuverable and is accurate over ranges common to combat in built-up areas. In a conflict almost anywhere in the world, U.S. forces must protect themselves against RPGs. The RPG warhead is moderately effective against armored vehicles, particularly M113 armored personnel carriers. It is less effective against common urban hard targets. It has a limited effect against reinforced concrete or stone. Typically, the round produces a small hole with little spall. The RPG produces a small hole in earth berms, with little blast effect and no spall. A triple layer of sandbags is usually protection against RPG rounds. Because of its fuze design, the RPG can often be defeated by a chain-link fence erected about 4 meters in front of a position. Even without such a barrier, a high percentage of RPG rounds fired against urban targets are duds due to glancing blows.

d. <u>Wall Breaching</u>. Wall breaching is a common combat task in built-up areas for which light recoilless weapons can be used. Breaching operations improve mobility by providing access to building interiors without using existing doors or windows. Breaching techniques can also be used to create loopholes for weapons positions or to allow hand grenades to be thrown into defended structures. Breach holes for troop mobility should be about 24 inches (60 centimeters) in diameter. Loopholes should be about 8 inches (20 centimeters) in diameter (see Figure 2-67). None of the light recoilless weapons organic to maneuver battalions (with the possible exception of the AT8 and SMAW) provide a one-shot wall-breaching ability. To breach walls a number of shots should be planned.

(1) Of all the common building materials, heavy stone is the most difficult to penetrate. The LAW, AT4, 90-mm RCLR, and RPG-7 usually will not penetrate a heavy European-style stone wall. Surface cratering is usually the only effect.

(2) Layered brick walls are also difficult to breach with light recoilless weapons. Some brick walls can be penetrated by multiple firings, especially if they are less than three bricks thick. Five LAW rounds fired at the same spot on an eight-inch (double-brick) wall normally produces a loophole. Heavier weapons, such as the AT4 and 90-mm RCLR, may require fewer rounds. The AT8 and SMAW produce a hole in brick walls that is often large enough to be a breach hole.

Figure 2-67. Tactical uses of holes in masonry walls

(3) Wooden structural walls offer little resistance to light recoilless weapons. Even heavy timbered walls are penetrated and splintered. Three LAW rounds fired at the same area of a wood-frame wall usually produce a man-sized hole. The AT8 and SMAW have a devastating effect against a wood-frame wall. A single round produces a breach hole as well as significant spall.

(4) Because of its high velocity, the AT4 may penetrate a soft target, such as a car body or frame building before exploding.

(5) None of the light recoilless weapons are as effective against structural walls as demolitions or heavier weapons such as tank main guns, field artillery, or combat engineer vehicle demolition guns. Of all the light recoilless weapons, the SMAW and AT8 are the most effective.

157

6. Antitank Guided Missiles.

Antitank guided missiles (ATGMs) are used mainly to defeat main battle tanks and other armored combat vehicles. They have a moderate capability against bunkers, buildings, and other fortified targets commonly found during combat in built-up areas. This category of weapons includes the already mentioned tube-launched, optically-sighted, wire-command-link-guided (TOW) and Dragon missiles.

a. Employment. TOWs and Dragons provide overwatch antitank fires during the attack of a built-up area and an extended range capability for the engagement of armor during the defense. Within built-up areas, they are best employed along major thoroughfares and from the upper stories of buildings to attain long-range fields of fire. Their minimum firing range of 65 meters could limit firing opportunities in the confines of densely built-up areas.

(1) Obstacles. When fired from street level, rubble or other obstacles could interfere with missile flight. At least 3.5 feet (1 meter) of vertical clearance over such obstacles must be maintained. Figure 2-68 shows the most common obstacles to ATGM flights found in built-up areas. Power lines are a special obstacle presenting a unique threat to ATGM gunners. If the power in the lines has not been interrupted, the ATGM guidance wires could create a short circuit. This would allow extremely high voltage to pass to the gunner in the brief period before the guidance wires melted. This voltage could either damage the sight and guidance system, or injure the gunner. Before any ATGM is fired over a power line, an attempt must be made to determine whether or not the power has been interrupted.

Figure 2-68. Common obstacles to ATGM flights

(2) Dead Space. Three aspects of dead space affecting ATGM fires are arming distance, maximum depression, and maximum elevation.

(a) Both the Dragon and TOW missiles have a minimum arming distance of 65 meters which severely limits their use in built-up areas. Few areas in the inner city permit fires much beyond the minimum arming distance -- ground-level, long-range fires down streets or rail lines, and across parks or plazas are possible. ATGMs may be used effectively from upper stories or roofs of buildings to fire into other buildings.

(b) The TOW is limited much more than the Dragon by its maximum depression and elevation. The maximum depression and elevation limits of the TOW mount could result in dead space and preclude the engagements of close targets (see Figure 2-69). A target located at the minimum arming range (65 meters) cannot be engaged by a TOW crew located any higher then the sixth floor of a building due to maximum depression limits. At 100 meters the TOW crew can be located as high as the ninth floor and still engage the target.

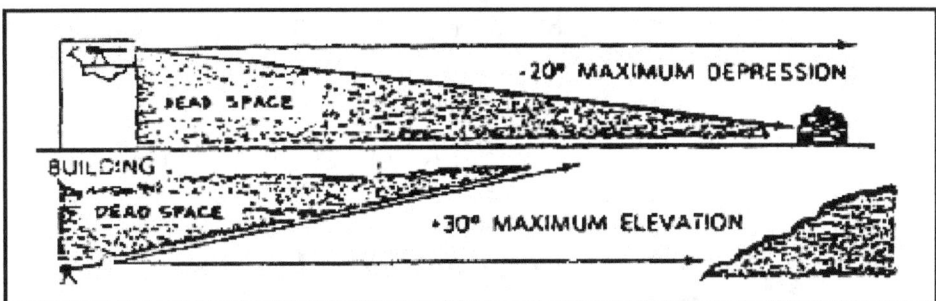

Figure 2-69. TOW maximum elevation and depression limitations

(3) Backblast. As for the light recoilless weapons, backblast for ATGMs is more of a concern during combat in built-up areas than in open country. Any loose rubble in the caution zone could be picked up and thrown by the backblast. The channelling effect of walls and narrow streets is even more pronounced and results in a greater backblast effect. If the ATGM backblast strikes a wall at an angle it can pick up debris or be deflected and cause injury to unprotected personnel (Figure 2-70). Both ATGMs (TOW and Dragon) can be fired from inside some buildings. In addition to the helmet and protective vest, eye protection and earplugs should be worn by all personnel in the room.

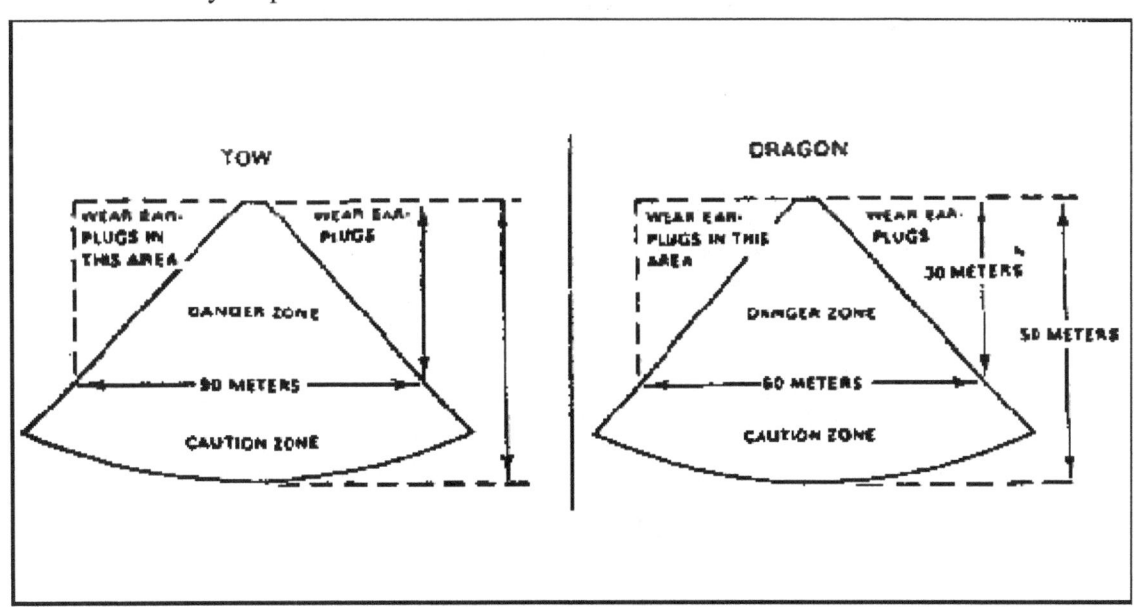

Figure 2-70. ATGM backblast in an open street

(a) To fire a TOW from inside a room, the following safety precautions must be taken (Figure 2-71):

159

- The building must be of sturdy construction.

- The ceiling should be at least 7 feet high.

- The floor size of the room should be at least 15 by 15 feet; larger if possible.

- At least 20 square feet of room ventilation should exist to the rear of the weapon. An open 7- by 3-foot door is sufficient. Additional ventilation can be created by removing sections of interior partitions.

- All glass must be removed from the windows and all small loose objects removed from the room.

Figure 2-71. TOW fired inside a room

- All personnel in the room should be forward of the rear of the TOW.

- All personnel in the room should wear ballistic eye protection and earplugs.

- Nine inches (23 centimeters) of clearance must be between the launch tube and the aperture through which it is fired.

(b) To fire a Dragon inside a room, the following safety precautions must be taken:

- The building must be of sturdy construction.

- The ceiling should be at least seven feet high.

- The floor size should be at last 15 by 15 feet; larger if possible.

- At least 20 square feet of ventilation should exist (room openings) to the rear of the weapon. An open seven- by three-foot door would provide minimum ventilation.

160

- All glass should be removed from windows, and small loose objects removed from the room.

- The room should be clean or the floors must be wet to prevent dust and dirt (kicked up by the backblast) from obscuring the vision of other soldiers in the room.

- All personnel in the room must be forward of the rear of the weapon.

- All personnel in the room must wear ballistic eye protection and earplugs.

- At least a 6-inch clearance must exist between the launch tube and aperture through which it is fired.

b. Weapon Penetration. ATGMs can penetrate and destroy heavily armored tanks. They have large warheads employing the shape-charge principle. Because of their size, these warheads can achieve significant penetration against typical urban targets. Penetration however does not mean a concurrent destruction of the structural integrity of a position. The shaped-charge warhead produces relatively little spall. Enemy personnel not standing directly behind or near the point of impact of an ATGM may escape injury.

(1) Standard TOW Missiles. The basic TOW missile can penetrate 8 feet of packed earth, 4 feet of reinforced concrete or 16 inches of steel plate. The improved TOW (ITOW), the TOW 2, and the TOW 2A all have been modified to improve their penetration. They all penetrate better than the basic TOW. All TOW missiles can defeat triple sandbag walls, double layers of earth-filled 55-gallon drums, and 18-inch log walls.

(2) TOW 2B. The TOW 2B uses a different method of defeating enemy armor. It flies over the target and fires an explosively formed penetrator down onto the top armor which is thinner. Because of this design feature, the TOW 2B missile cannot be used to attack nonmetallic structural targets. When using the TOW 2B missile against enemy armor, gunners must avoid firing directly over other friendly vehicles, disabled vehicles, or large metal objects such as water or oil tanks.

(3) Dragon Missile. The Dragon missile can penetrate 8 feet of packed earth, 4 feet of concrete, or 13 inches of steel plate. It can attain effective short-range fire from upper stories, or from the rear, or flanks of a vehicle. These engagements are targeted against the most vulnerable parts of tanks and can entrap tanks in situations where they are unable to counterfire. Elevated firing positions increase the first-round hit probability. Firing down at an angle of 20 degrees increases the chance of a hit by 67 percent at 200 meters. A 45-degree down angle doubles the first-round-hit probability compared to a ground-level shot.

c. Breaching Structural Walls. Firing ATGMs is the least efficient means to defeat structures. Because of their small basic load and high cost, ATGMs are better used against tanks or enemy-fortified firing positions. They can be effective against bunkers or other identified enemy firing positions.

7. Flame Weapons.

Flame weapons are characterized by both physical and psychological casualty-producing abilities. Flame does not need to be applied with pinpoint accuracy, but care must be taken to ensure the flames do not spread to structures needed by friendly forces. Large fires in built-up areas are catastrophic. If they burn out of control, fires can create an impenetrable barrier for hours. The most common United States flame weapons are the M202 FLASH and the M34 white phosphorus (WP) grenade. The M2A1-7 and the M9-7 portable flamethrowers are stored in war reserve status as standard "C" items. Their availability is limited.

a. Employment. Flame weapons used against fortified positions should be aimed directly at the aperture. Even if the round or burst misses, enough flaming material enters the position to cause casualties and to disrupt the enemy occupants. The M34 WP grenade is difficult to throw far, or into a small opening such as a bunker aperture. However its effects are dramatic when thrown into a room or building.

b. Effects. The three standard flame weapons have different effects against typical urban targets.

(1) M202 FLASH. The M202 FLASH can deliver area fire out to 500 meters. In combat in built-up areas, the range to targets is normally much less. Point targets, such as an alleyway or bunker, can usually be hit from 200 meters. Precision fire against a bunker aperture is possible at 50 meters.

(a) The FLASH warhead contains a thickened flame agent which ignites when exposed to air. The minimum safe combat range is 20 meters, which is the bursting radius of the rocket warhead due to splashback. If the projectile strikes a hard object along its flight path and breaks open, it will burst into flames even if the fuze has not armed. M202 rocket packs must be protected from small-arms fire and shell fragments that could ignite them. The M202 has a backblast that must be considered before firing (see Figure 2-72). Urban conditions affect this backblast exactly the same as the LAW (see paragraph B5). The same considerations for firing a LAW from an enclosed area apply to the M202.

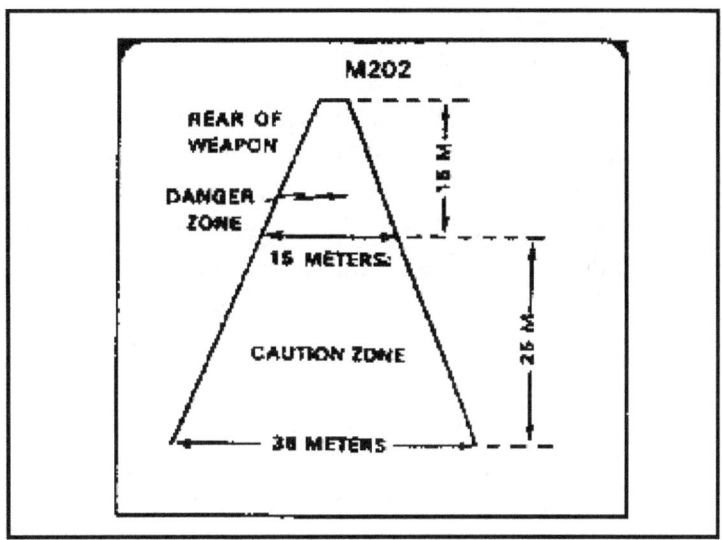

Figure 2-72. Backblast area of the M202 FLASH

(b) The M202 FLASH is not effective in penetrating typical urban targets. It can penetrate up to 1 inch of plywood at 200 meters and at close range it can penetrate some wooden doors. The rocket reliably penetrates window glass. The M202 does not damage brick or cinder block construction. The flame agent splattered against the top flanks and rear of light armored vehicles can be effective. The psychological effect of hits by flame rockets on closed-in crewmen is significant.

(c) A round detonating near or on a vehicle's rear deck or engine compartment could set the vehicle on fire. A wheeled vehicle such as the BTR could have its tires severely damaged by the M202. Modern Russian tanks and BMPs have an NBC protective overpressure system that could prevent flame from reaching the vehicle's interior.

(2) <u>M34 WP Hand Grenade</u>. The M34 is used to ignite and destroy flammable objects especially wooden structures. It is also used to create an immediate smoke cloud to conceal movement across a narrow open space such as a street. Its smoke is not toxic but can cause choking in heavy concentrations.

(a) The grenade's explosion, bright flash, smoke, and burning WP particles, all combine to make the M34 one of the most effective psychological weapons available. The M34 hand grenade throws WP fragments up to 35 meters from the point of detonation. These fragments can attach to clothing or skin and continue burning. Because of its weight, most infantrymen can throw this grenade only 30 to 40 meters.

(b) The soldier must avoid injury from friendly use of the M34. As with the M202, the M34 can ignite if the WP inside is exposed to the air. Bullets and shell fragments have been known to strike and rupture M34 grenades, therefore, grenades must be protected from enemy fire.

(c) The M34 WP grenade is an effective weapon against enemy armored vehicles when used in the close confines of combat in built-up areas. It can be thrown or dropped from upper stories onto enemy vehicles. The M34 can be combined with flammable liquids, detonating cords, blasting caps, and fuze igniters to create the "eagle fireball," a field-expedient antiarmor device.

(d) The M34 is also excellent as a screening device. A grenade can be thrown from behind cover into an open street or plaza. When it explodes, the enemy's observation is temporarily obscured. Thus friendly forces can quickly cross the open area. If the enemy fires, it is unaimed and presents less of a danger. If screening smoke is used to cover a squad's movement across short open areas, it will reduce expected casualties from small-arms fire by about 90 percent.

(3) <u>M2AI-7 and M9-7 Portable Flamethrowers</u>. Portable flamethrowers have a much shorter effective range than the M202 (20 to 50 meters) but require no special backblast consideration. The psychological and physical effects of the portable flamethrower are impressive. When used against troops behind a street barricades, the flamethrower can be fired in a traversing burst to cover a wide frontage. A blind-angle burst can be fired to exploit the splattering effect of the thickened fuel without exposing the gunner (see Figure 2-73).

(a) A burst of unlit fuel (wet shot) can be fired with the flamethrower and ignited with a subsequent shot, creating an intense fireball. This technique is effective in destroying captured equipment or for killing enemy soldiers in sewers. If the enemy has established a position in a wooden building, you can burn the building down with flame. Flame is also effective when fired onto the back deck of tanks or at vision blocks.

(b) Thickened fuel is difficult to extinguish and therefore, you must decide what can and will burn before you employ flame. Limits imposed on collateral damage, either political or tactical, are the most serious constraints to the use of flames. If the portable flamethrower is issued in combat in built-up areas, it will probably be used by specially trained personnel. Ensure the flame operator is provided adequate security as he approaches the target. The enemy will concentrate his fire on any flamethrowers he detects.

Figure 2-73. Blind-angle burst

(c) Although pinpointing targets at night is difficult, consider using flamethrowers at night for the psychological as well as destructive effect on the enemy.

8. Hand Grenades.

Hand grenades are used extensively during combat in built-up areas. Smoke grenades are used for screening and signalling. You can use riot control grenades to drive the enemy out of deep fortifications. Concussion (offensive) grenades are used to clear the enemy out of rooms and basements, and they are the most used explosive munition during intense combat in built-up areas. In World War II, it was common for a battalion fighting in a city to use over 500 fragmentation grenades each day.

a. Employment. Smoke and riot control grenades have similar employment techniques. Fragmentation grenades are used to produce enemy casualties.

(1) The AN-M8 hydrogen chloride (HC) grenade produces a dense white or grey smoke. It burns intensely and cannot be easily extinguished once it ignites. The smoke can be dangerous in heavy concentrations because it makes breathing difficult and causes choking. The M8 grenade is normally used for screening. It produces a slowly building screen of longer duration, than that of the M34 WP grenade, without the problem of collateral damage caused by scattered burning particles.

(2) The M18-series smoke grenades produce several different colors of smoke which are used for signalling. Yellow smoke is sometimes difficult to see in built-up areas. Newer versions of yellow smoke grenades are more visible than before.

165

(3) The M7A3 chemical smoke (CS) riot control grenade can be used to drive enemy troops out of fortifications when civilian casualties or collateral damage constraints are considerations. Built-up areas often create variable and shifting wind patterns. When using CS grenades, soldiers must prevent the irritating smoke from affecting friendly troops. The CS grenade burns intensely and can ignite flammable structures. Enemy troops wearing even rudimentary chemical protective masks can withstand intense concentrations of CS gas.

(4) The M67 fragmentation grenades are commonly used during combat in built-up areas. They provide suppression during room-to-room or house-to-house fighting and can be used while clearing rooms of enemy personnel. When used at close ranges the grenade can be "cooked off" for two seconds to deny the enemy time to throw it back. The fragmentation grenade can be rolled, bounced, or ricocheted into areas unreachable by 40-mm grenade launchers. Soldiers should be extra cautious when throwing grenades up stairs. This is not the most desired method of employment.

(5) The MK3A2 offensive hand grenade, commonly referred to as the concussion grenade, produces casualties during close combat while minimizing the danger to friendly personnel. The grenade produces severe concussion effects in enclosed areas. It can be used for light blasting and demolitions and for creating breach holes in interior walls. The concussion produced by the MK3A2 is much greater than that of the M67. It is very effective against enemy soldiers within bunkers, buildings, and underground passages.

b. Effects. Each type of hand grenade has its own specific effect during combat in built-up areas.

(1) The urban area effects of smoke grenades are nominal. Smoke grenades produce dense clouds of colored or white smoke which remain stationary in the surrounding area. They can cause fires if used indiscriminately. If trapped and concentrated within a small spaces, their smoke can suffocate soldiers.

(2) The M26 fragmentation grenade has more varied effects in combat in built-up areas. It produces a large amount of small high-velocity fragments which can penetrate sheetrock partitions and are lethal at short ranges (15 to 20 meters). Fragments lose their velocity quickly and are less effective beyond 25 meters. The fragments from an M26 grenade cannot penetrate a single layer of sandbags, a cinder-block or brick building, but they can perforate wood frame and tin buildings if exploded close to their walls.

(3) Fragmentation barriers inside rooms consisting of common office furniture, mattresses, doors, or books, can be effective against the M26 fragmentation grenade. For this reason a room should never be considered safe because one or two M26 grenades have been detonated inside it. Fragmentation grenades detonated on the floor not only throw fragments

166

laterally, but also send fragments and spall downward to lower floors. Predicting how much spall will occur is difficult since flooring material varies, but wooden floors are usually affected the most.

(4) Some Russian grenades throw fragments much larger than those of the M26. Light barriers and interior walls would probably would be defeated by those grenades, but not the M26. A major problem with the M26 grenade is its tendency to bounce back off hard targets. Fragmentation grenades are often directed at window openings on the ground floor or second floor. At ranges as close as 20 meters a thrower's chances of missing a standard one-meter by one-meter window are high. The M26 fragmentation grenade normally breaks through standard window glass and enters a room. If the grenade strikes at a sharp angle or the glass is thick plate, the grenade could be deflected without penetrating.

(5) Hand grenades are difficult weapons to use. They involve a high risk of fratricide. Conduct precombat training with hand grenades as part of normal preparations. Soldiers must be especially careful when throwing hand grenades up stairs.

(6) The pins of both fragmentation and concussion grenades can be replaced if the thrower decides not use the weapon. This pin replacement must be done carefully.

(7) Mission, enemy, terrain, troops, and time available (METT-T) and the rules of engagement (ROE) will dictate what type of grenade is used to clear each room. Because of the high expenditure of grenades, units should use butt packs or assault packs to carry additional grenades of all types. Additional grenades can also be carried in empty ammunition or canteen pouches.

9. Mortars.

The urban environment greatly restricts low-angle indirect fires because of overhead masking. While all indirect-fire weapons are subject to overhead masking, mortars are less affected than field artillery weapons, due to the mortar's higher trajectory. For low-angle artillery fires, dead space is about five times the height of the building behind which the target sits. For mortar fire, dead space is only about one-half the height of the building. Because of these advantages, mortars are even more important to the infantry during combat in built-up areas.

a. Employment. Not only can mortars fire into the deep defilade created by tall buildings, but they can also fire out of it. Mortars emplaced behind buildings are difficult for the enemy to accurately locate, and even harder for him to hit with counterfire. Because of their light weight, even heavy mortars can be hand carried to firing positions inaccessible to vehicles.

(1) Mortars can be fired through the roof of a ruined building if the ground-level flooring is solid enough to withstand the recoil. If there is only concrete flooring in the mortar platoon's area, mortars can be fired using sandbags as a buffer under the baseplates and curbs as anchors and

braces. Aiming posts can be placed in dirt-filled cans.

(2) The 60-mm, 81-mm, and 107-mm mortars of the U.S. Army have limited affect on structural targets. Even with delay fuzes, they seldom penetrate more than the upper stories of light buildings. However their wide area coverage and multi-option fuzes make them useful against an enemy force advancing through streets, through other open areas, or over rubble. The 120-mm mortar is moderately effective against structural targets. With a delay fuze setting, it can penetrate deep into a building and create great destruction.

(3) Mortar platoons often operate as separate firing sections during combat in built-up areas. The lack of large open areas can preclude establishing a platoon firing position. Figure 2-74 shows how two mortar sections, separated by only one street, can be effective in massing fires and be protected from counter-mortar fire by employing defilade and dispersion.

(4) All three of the standard mortar projectiles are useful during combat in built-up areas. High-explosive fragmentation is the most commonly used round. WP is effective in starting fires in buildings and forcing the enemy out of cellars and light-frame buildings. It is also the most effective mortar round against dug-in enemy tanks. Even near-misses blind and suppress the tank crew, forcing them to button up. Hits are difficult to achieve but are effective.

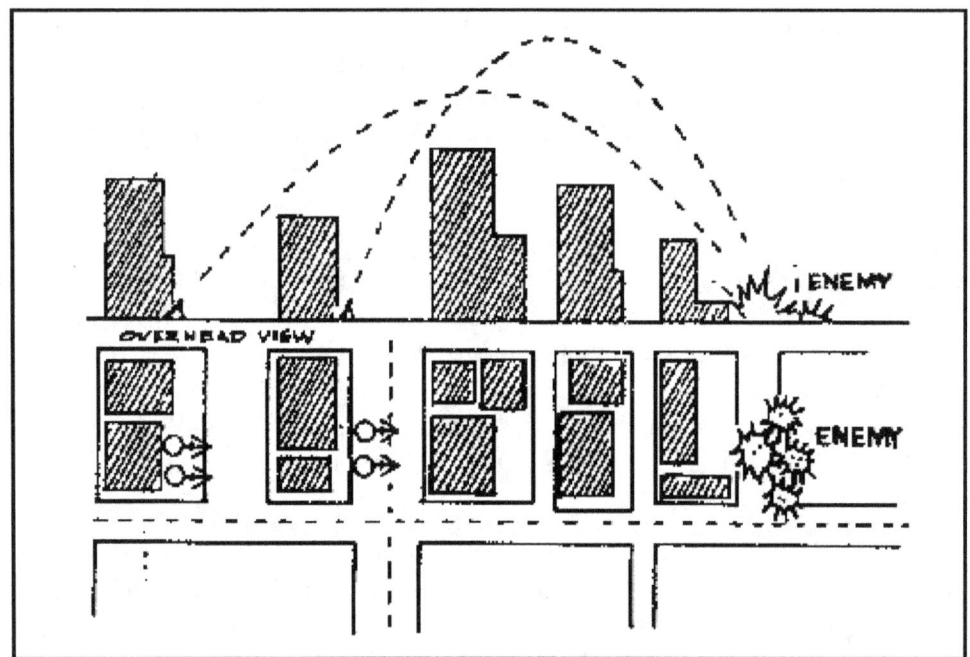

Figure 2-74. Split-section mortar operations on adjacent streets

(5) Because the artificial roughness of urban terrain reduces wind speed and increases atmosphere mixing, mortar smoke tends to persist longer and give greater coverage in built-up areas than in open terrain.

(6) Urban masking impacts on the use of illumination. In built-up areas it

168

is often necessary to plan illumination behind friendly positions which places friendly troops in shadows and enemy troops in the light. Illumination rounds are difficult to adjust and are often of limited use because of the deep-canyon nature of the urban area. Rapidly shifting wind currents in built-up areas also affect mortar illumination making it less effective.

b. Effects of Mortar Fire. The multi-option fuze on newer U.S. mortar rounds makes them effective weapons on urban terrain. Delay settings can increase penetration slightly, and proximity bursts can increase the lethal area covered by fragments. Tall buildings can cause proximity-fuzed mortar rounds to detonate prematurely if they pass too closely.

(1) Sixty-mm Mortar. The 60-mm mortar round cannot penetrate most rooftops, even with a delay setting. Small explosive rounds are effective however in suppressing snipers on rooftops and preventing roofs from being used by enemy observers. The 60-mm WP round is not normally a good screening round due to its small area of coverage. In combat in built-up areas however, the tendency of smoke to linger and the small areas to be screened, make it more effective. During the battle for Hue in South Vietnam, 60-mm WP rounds were used to create small short-term smoke screens to conceal movement across open areas such as parks, plazas, and bridges. Fragments from 60-mm HE rounds landing as close as 10 feet, cannot penetrate a single sandbag layer or a single-layer brick wall. The effect of a 60-mm mortar HE round making a direct hit on a bunker or fighting position is equivalent to one or two pounds of TNT. Normally the blast will not collapse a properly constructed bunker but can cause structural damage. The 60-mm mortar will not normally crater a hard-surfaced road.

(2) 81-mm Mortar. The 81-mm mortar has much the same effect against urban targets as the 60-mm mortar. It has a slightly greater lethal area and its smoke rounds (WP and RP [red phosphorus]) are more effective. A direct hit is equivalent to about four pounds of TNT. The 81-mm round cannot significantly crater a hard-surfaced road. With a delay setting the 81-mm round can penetrate the roofs of light buildings.

(3) 107-mm Mortar. The 107-mm mortar can affect moderately hard urban targets. It is more effective than the 81-mm mortar. Even when fired with a delay fuze setting, the round cannot penetrate deep into typical urban targets. The mortar's lethal fragment area is somewhat increased in built-up areas, because its blast picks up significant amounts of debris and throws it outward. The minimum range of the 107-mm mortar is the main constraint in its use during battle in a built-up area. Of all the United States mortars, the 107-mm is the least capable in reaching targets in deep defilade. The 107-mm mortar slightly craters a hard-surfaced road, but not enough to prevent vehicle traffic.

(4) 120-mm Mortar. The 120-mm mortar is large enough to have a major

effect on common urban targets. It can penetrate deep into a building, causing extensive damage because of its explosive power. A minimum of 18 inches of packed earth or sand is needed to stop the fragments from a 120-mm HE round impacting 10 feet away. The effect from a direct hit from a 120-mm round is equivalent to almost 10 pounds of TNT and can crush fortifications built with commonly available materials. The 120-mm mortar round can create a large but shallow crater in a road surface which is not deep or steep-sided enough to block vehicular movement. However, craters could be deep enough to damage or destroy storm-drain systems, water and gas pipes, and electrical or phone cables.

(5) Threat Munitions. The paragraphs above discuss the mortar rounds available to U.S. troops. The following two paragraphs address the Russian munitions U.S. troops could encounter in combat in built-up-areas around the world.

(a) 160-mm Mortar. The 160-mm mortar of the former Soviet can inflict massive damage to almost any urban structure. Only large buildings and deep cellars offer protection against this weapon. Even well-built bunkers can be crushed by near-misses. The effect from a direct hit by this weapon is equivalent to over 15 pounds of TNT. The 160-mm mortar creates significant craters in urban road surfaces. These craters are several meters wide and are deep enough to interfere with vehicular movement. The 160-mm mortar can destroy storm drainage systems, water mains, and underground power lines.

(b) 240-mm Mortar. The 2S4 240-mm self-propelled mortar of the former Soviet is designed to destroy heavy fortifications. Average buildings do not provide certain protection from this mortar. Its HE rounds weigh over 280 pounds. It has a concrete-piercing round for use in urban areas. The 2S4 can fire one round per minute. A round will do massive damage to urban road surfaces, breaking and heaving large slabs of road surface many yards from the point of impact. A towed 240-mm mortar was also in the inventory of Russia and the former Warsaw Pact countries.

10. 25-mm Automatic Gun.

The 25-mm automatic gun mounted on the M2/M3 Bradley fighting vehicle (BFV) and on the U.S. Marine Corps LAV-25 (light armored vehicle) offers infantrymen a new and effective weapon to aid them during combat in built-up areas. The primary roles of BFVs and LAV-25s during combat in built-up areas are to provide suppressive fire and to breach exterior walls and fortifications. (See paragraph B3 for the suppression effects and penetration of the 7.62-mm coaxial machine gun.) The wall and fortification breaching effects of the 25-mm automatic gun are major assets to infantrymen fighting in built-up areas.

a. Obliquity. The 25-mm gun produces its best urban target results when fired perpendicular to a hard surface (zero obliquity). In combat in built-up areas however, finding a covered firing position permitting low obliquity firing is unlikely unless the streets and gaps between buildings are wide. Most shots impact the target at an angle which normally reduces penetration. With the armor-piercing, discarding-sabot with tracer (APDS-T) round, an angle of obliquity of up to 20 degrees can actually improve breaching. The rounds tend to dislodge more wall material for each shot, but do not penetrate as deeply into the structure.

b. Target Types. The 25-mm gun has different effects when fired against different urban targets.

(1) Reinforced Concrete. Reinforced concrete walls which are 12 to 20 inches thick, present problems for the 25-mm gun when trying to create breach holes. It is relatively easy to penetrate, fracture, and clear away the concrete, but the reinforcing rods remain in place. These create a "jail window" effect by preventing entry, but allowing grenades or rifle fire to be placed behind the wall. Steel reinforcing rods are normally 3/4 inch thick and 6 to 8 inches apart -- there is no quick and easy way of cutting these rods. They can be cut with demolition charges, cutting torches, or special power saws. Firing with either APDS-T or high-explosive-incendiary with tracer (HEI-T) rounds from the 25-mm gun will not always cut these rods.

(2) Brick Walls. Brick walls are more easily defeated by the 25-mm gun regardless of their thickness and they produce the most spall.

(3) Bunker Walls. The 25-mm gun is devastating when fired against sandbag bunker walls. Obliquity has the least affect on the penetration of bunker walls. Bunkers with earth walls up to 36 inches thick are easily penetrated. At short ranges typical of combat in built-up areas, defeating a bunker should be easy, especially if the 25-mm gun can fire at an aperture.

c. Burst Fire. The 25-mm gun's impact on typical urban targets seem magnified if the firing is in short bursts. At close ranges the gunner might need to shift his point of aim in a spiral pattern to ensure the second and third bursts enlarge the hole. Even without burst fire, sustained 25-mm gun fire can defeat almost all urban targets.

d. Weapon Penetration. The penetration achieved by the two combat rounds (HEI-T and APDS-T) differ slightly -- both are eventually effective. However, the best target results are not achieved with either of the combat rounds. At close range against structural targets, the training round (TP-T) is significantly more effective. The TP-T round however has little utility when used against enemy armored vehicles. It will rarely, if ever, be carried into combat.

(1) APDS-T. The armor-piercing, discarding-sabot with tracer round penetrates urban targets by retaining its kinetic energy and blasting a small hole deep into the target. The APDS-T round gives the best effects behind the wall and the armor-piercing core (penetrator) often breaks into two or three fragments which can create multiple enemy casualties. The APDS-T needs as few as four rounds to achieve lethal results behind walls. The

table in Figure 2-75 shows the number of APDS-T rounds needed to create different-size holes in common urban walls.

TARGET	LOOPHOLE	BREACHHOLE
3-inch brick wall at 0-degree obliquity	22 rounds	75 rounds
3-inch brick wall at 45-degree obliquity	22 rounds	25+ rounds
5-inch brick wall at 0-degree obliquity	22 rounds	50+ rounds
8-inch reinforced concrete at 0-degree obliquity	22 rounds	75 rounds (Note: Reinforcing rods still in place)
8-inch reinforced concrete at 45-degrees obliquity	22 rounds	40+ rounds (Note: Reinforcing rods still in place)

*Obliquity and depth tend to increase the amount of wall material removed.

Figure 2-75. Breaching effects of 25-mm APDS-T rounds

(a) When firing single rounds, the APDS-T round provides the greatest capability for behind-the-wall incapacitation. The APDS-T round can penetrate over 16 inches of reinforced concrete with enough energy left to cause enemy casualties. It penetrates through both sides of a wood-frame or brick-veneer building. Field fortifications are easily penetrated by APDS-T rounds. The table on Figure 2-76 explains the number of APDS-T rounds needed to create different-size holes in commonly found bunkers.

(b) The APDS-T round creates a hazardous situation for exposed personnel because of the pieces of sabot thrown off the round. Personnel not under cover forward of the 25-mm gun's muzzle and within the danger zone, could be injured or killed by these sabots even though the penetrator passes overhead to hit the target. The danger zone extends at an angle of about 10 degrees below the muzzle level, out to at least 100 meters, and about 17 degrees left and right of the muzzle. Figure 2-77 shows the hazard area of the APDS-T round.

TYPE BUNKER	OBLIQUITY	PENE-TRATION	LOOP-HOLE	SMALL BREACHHOLE
36-inch sand/ timber	0 degree	1 round	25 rounds	40 rounds
36-inch sand/ 6-inch concrete	0 degree	6 rounds	6 rounds	20 rounds

Figure 2-76. Number of 25-mm APDS-T rounds needed to create different size holes in bunkers

Figure 2-77. APDS danger zone

(2) <u>HEI-T</u>. The high-explosive-incendiary with tracer round penetrates urban targets by blasting away chunks of material.

(a) The HEI-T round does not penetrate an urban target as well as the APDS-T, but it creates the effect of stripping away a greater amount of material for each round. The HEI-T does more damage to an urban target when fired in multiple short bursts because the accumulative impact of multiple rounds is greater than the sum of the individual rounds. The table shown in Figure 2-78 explains the number of HEI-T rounds needed to create different-size holes.

(b) The HEI-T round does not provide single-round perforation or incapacitating fragments on any external masonry structural walls. It can create first-round fragments behind wood-frame and brick-veneer walls. HEI-T rounds cannot penetrate a bunker as quickly as APDS-Ts, but they can create more damage inside the bunker once the external earth has been stripped away. Against a heavy bunker, about 40 rounds of HEI-T are needed to strip away the external earth shielding and breach the inner lining of concrete or timber.

TARGET	LOOPHOLE	BREACHHOLE
3-inch brick wall at 0-degree obliquity	10 rounds	20 rounds
3-inch brick wall at 45-degree obliquity	20 rounds	25 rounds
5-inch brick wall at 0-degree obliquity	30 rounds	60 rounds
8-inch reinforced concrete at 0-degree obliquity	15 rounds	25 rounds
8-inch reinforced concrete at 45-degree obliquity	15 rounds	30 rounds

Figure 2-78. Number of 25-mm HE-I rounds needed to create different size holes

11. Tank Cannon.

The powerful high-velocity cannon mounted on the M1, M1A1, M60, and M48 series tanks gives you a key requirement for victory in built-up areas -- heavy direct-fire support. Although the infantry assumes the lead role during combat in built-up areas, tanks and infantry work as a close team. Tanks move down streets protected by the infantry and in turn support the infantry with fire. The tank is one of the most effective weapons for heavy fire against structures. The primary role of the tank cannon during combat in built-up areas is to provide heavy direct-fire against buildings and strongpoints identified as targets by the infantry. The wall and fortification breaching effects of the 105-mm and 120-mm tank cannon are major assets to infantrymen fighting in built-up areas.

a. Obliquity. Tank cannons produce their best urban target effects when fired perpendicular to a hard surface (zero obliquity). During combat in built-up areas however, finding a covered firing position permitting low-obliquity firing is unlikely. Most shots strike the target at an angle that would normally reduce penetration. With tank cannon APDS rounds, obliquity angles up to 25 degrees have little affect, but angles greater than 45 degrees greatly reduce penetration. For example, a 105-mm APDS round cannot penetrate a two-inch reinforced concrete wall at an angle of obliquity greater than 45 degrees due to possible ricochet.

b. Ammunition. Armor-piercing, fin-stabilized, discarding-sabot (APFSDS) rounds are the most commonly carried tank ammunition. These rounds are best used against armored vehicles. Other, more effective types of ammunition can be carried for use against masonry targets. The 105-mm cannon has high-explosive antitank (HEAT) and WP rounds in addition to APDS. The 120-mm cannon has an effective high-explosive, antitank, multipurpose (HEAT-MP) round.

c. Characteristics. Both 105-mm and 120-mm tank cannons have two specific characteristics limiting their employment in built-up areas: limited elevation and depression, and short arming ranges. In addition the M1 and M1A1 tanks have another characteristic not involved with its cannon, but affecting infantrymen working with it -- extremely hot turbine exhaust.

(1) The M1 and M1A1 tank can elevate its cannon +20 degrees and depress it -10 degrees. The M60 and M48 series tanks have upper limits of +19 degrees and lower limits of -10 degrees. The lower depression limit creates a 35-foot (10.8-meter) ground-level dead space around a tank. On a 16-meter-wide street (common in Europe) this dead space extends to the buildings on each side (see Figure 2-79).

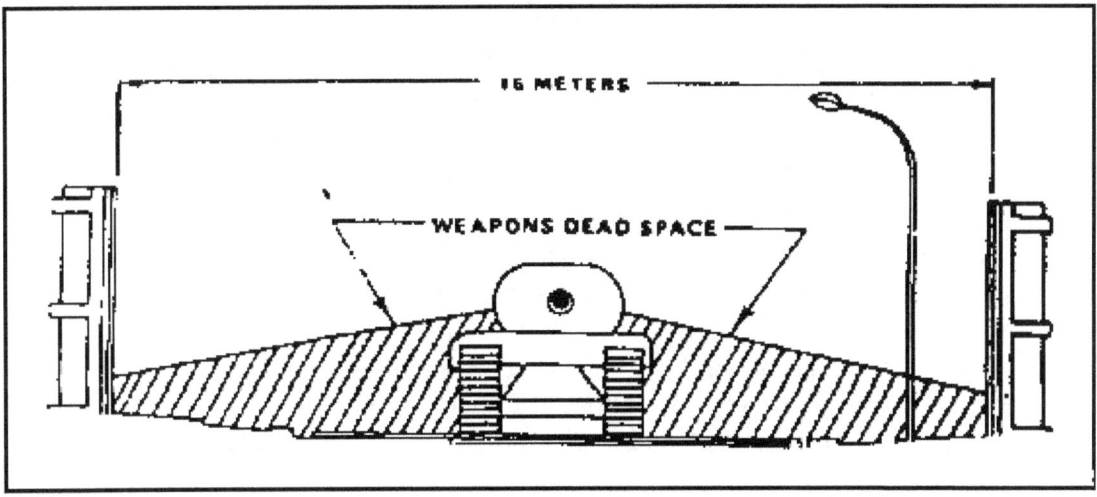

Figure 2-79. Tank cannon dead space at street level

Similarly, there is an overhead zone in which the tank cannot fire (see Figure 2-80). In the offensive, this dead space offers ideal locations for short-range antiarmor weapons and allows hidden enemy gunners to fire at the tank when the tank cannot fire back. It also exposes the tank's most vulnerable areas: the flanks, rear, and top. Infantrymen move ahead, alongside, and to the rear of tanks to provide close protection. The extreme heat produced immediately to the rear of the M1-series tanks prevents dismounted infantry from following closely, but protection from small-arms fire and fragments is still provided by the tank's bulk and armor. The M1-series tanks also have a blind spot caused by the 0-degree of depression available over part of the back deck. To engage any target in this area, the tank must pivot to convert the rear target to a flank target.

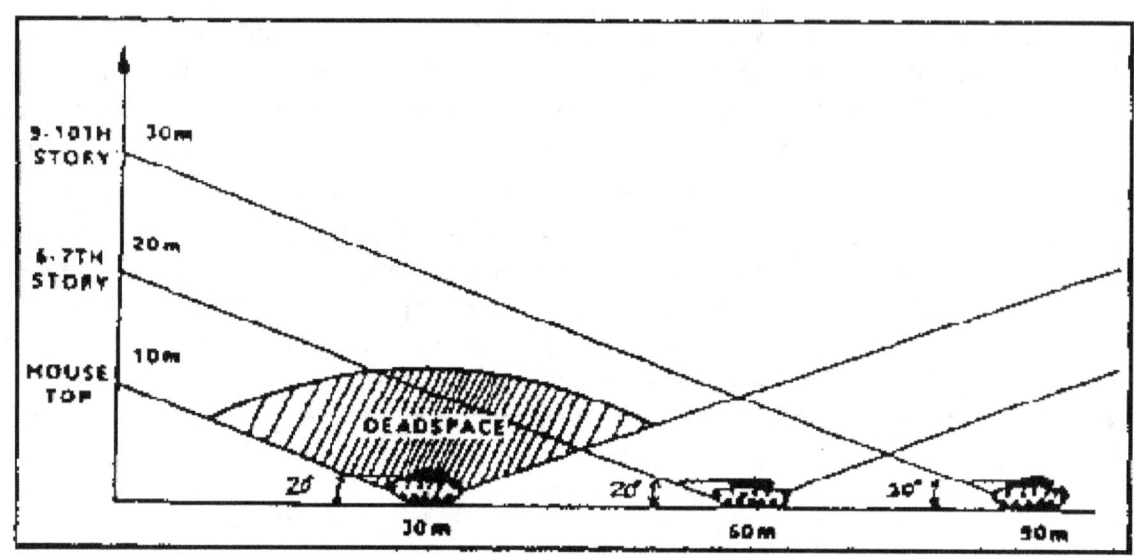

Figure 2-80. Tank cannon dead space above street level

(2) The 105-mm HEAT round arms within 25 to 30 feet and the 120-mm HEAT-MP round arms at about 36 feet. These arming distances allow the tank to engage targets from short ranges. The armor of the tank protects the crew from both the blowback effects of the round and enemy return fire. The APFSDS round does not need to arm, and can therefore be fired at almost any range. Just as discussed earlier with regard to the BFV's APDS-T rounds, the discarding portions of the tank's sabot round can be lethal to dismounted and exposed infantry forward of the tank.

d. <u>Target Effects</u>. High-explosives antitank rounds are most effective against masonry walls. The APFSDS round can penetrate deeply into a structure, but does not create a large hole or displace much spall behind the target. In contrast to lighter HEAT rounds (ATGMs), tank HEAT rounds are large enough to displace enough spall to inflict casualties inside a building. One HEAT round normally creates a breach hole in all but the thickest masonry construction -- brick-veneer and wood-frame construction are demolished by a single round. Even the 120-mm HEAT round cannot cut all the reinforcing rods, which are usually left in place and often hinder entry through the breach hole (see Figure 2-81). Both HEAT and APFSDS rounds are effective against all field fortifications. Only large earth berms and heavy mass construction buildings can provide protection against tank fire.

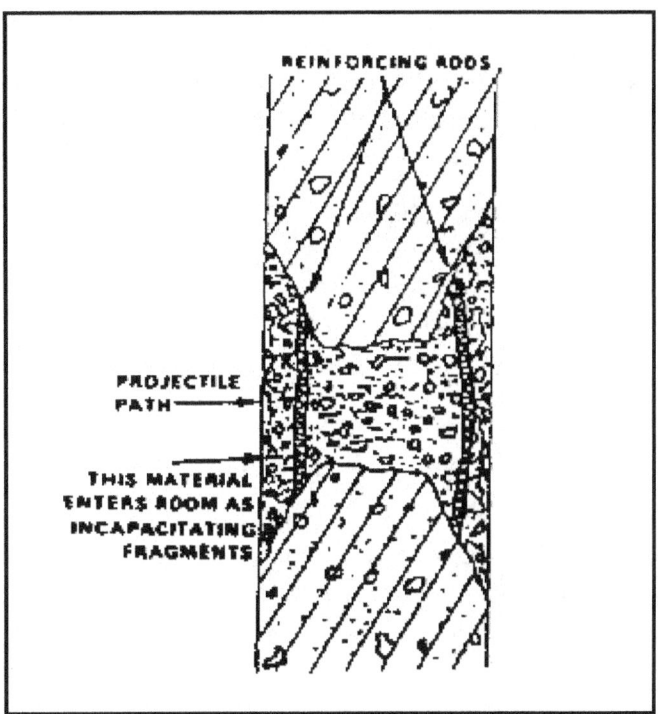

Figure 2-81. Tank HEAT round effects on reinforced-concrete walls

e. <u>Employment</u>. Tank-heavy forces by themselves could be at a severe disadvantage during combat in built-up areas, but a few tanks working with the infantry can be most effective, especially if they work well together at the small-unit level. Tanks, infantry, and engineer task forces are normally formed to attack a fortified area. Individual tanks or pairs of tanks can work together with rifle squads or platoons.

(1) Tanks need infantry on the ground to provide security in built-up areas and to designate targets. Against targets protected by structures, tanks are escorted forward to the most covered location providing a clear shot. On-the-spot instructions by the infantry unit leader ensures the tanks' fire is accurate and its exposure is limited. The tank commander may have to halt in a covered position dismount, and reconnoiter his route forward into a firing position.

(2) When the tank's main gun fires, it creates a large fireball and smoke cloud. In the confines of a built-up area, dirt and masonry dust are also picked up and added to this cloud. The target is further obscured by the smoke and dust of the explosion. Depending on local conditions, this obscuration could last as long as two or three minutes. Infantry can use this period to reposition or advance unseen by the enemy. Caution must be exercised however, because the enemy might also seize the opportunity to move.

(3) Tank cannon creates an overpressure and noise hazard to exposed infantrymen. All dismounted troops working near tanks should wear their Kevlar helmet and protective vest, as well as ballistic eye protection. If possible they should also wear earplugs and avoid the tank's frontal 60-

177

degree arc during firing.

(4) Tanks are equipped with powerful thermal sights used to detect enemy personnel and weapons hidden in shadows and behind openings. Dust, fires, and thick smoke significantly degrade these sights.

(5) Tanks have turret-mounted grenade launchers that project screening smoke grenades. The grenades use a bursting charge and burning red phosphorous particles to create this screen. Burning particles can easily start uncontrolled fires and are hazardous to dismounted infantry near the tank. The tank commander and the infantry small-unit leader must coordinate when, and under what conditions, these launchers are used. Grenade launchers are a useful feature to protect the tank, but they can cause significant problems if unwisely employed.

(6) The tank's size and armor can provide dismounted infantry with cover from direct-fire weapons and fragments. With coordination, tanks can provide moving cover for infantrymen as they advance across small open areas. However, enemy fire striking a tank but not penetrating, is a major threat to nearby infantry. Fragmentation generated by antitank rounds and ricochets off tank armor have historically been a prime cause of infantry casualties while working with tanks in built-up areas.

(7) Some tanks are equipped with dozer blades which can be used to remove rubble barriers under fire, breach obstacles, or seal exits.

12. Combat Engineer Vehicle Demolition Gun.

The combat engineer vehicle (CEV) is a special purpose engineer equipment tracked vehicle providing a heavy demolition capability. A 50-caliber machine gun is mounted in the commander's cupola. The main armament is provided by a 165-mm main gun with a 7.62-mm machine gun mounted coaxially. The main gun fires a high-explosive plastic (HEP) round of great power. The weapon's maximum range is 925 meters.

a. Target Effects. The HEP round is very effective against masonry and concrete targets. The pushing and heaving effects, caused by the HEP round's base detonating fuze and large amount of explosive, can demolish barriers and knock down walls. One round produces a one-foot diameter hole in a seven-inch thick reinforced concrete wall. The round's effects against bunkers and field fortifications are dramatic, often crushing or smashing entire walls.

b. Employment. The CEV is normally used for special engineer tasks in direct support of infantry battalions. You give it the same close infantry protection and target designation as tanks. Although the CEV consists of a tank hull and a short-barrelled turret, it is not a tank and cannot be used against enemy tanks. It is an excellent heavy assault support vehicle when used properly as part of a combined engineer-infantry team.

13. Artillery and Naval Gunfire.

A major source of fire support for infantry forces fighting in built-up areas is the fire of field artillery weapons. If the built-up area is near the coast, naval gunfire can be used.

Field artillery employment can be in either the indirect- or direct-fire mode.

a. Indirect Fire. Indirect artillery fire is not effective in attacking targets within walls and masonry structures. It tends to impact on roofs or upper stories rather than structurally critical wall areas or pillars.

(1) Weapons of at least 155-mm are necessary against thick reinforced concrete, stone, or brick walls. Even with heavy artillery, large expenditures of ammunition are required to knock down buildings of any size. Tall buildings also create areas of indirect-fire dead space which are areas unengageable by indirect fire due to a combination of building height and angle of fall of the projectile (see Figure 2-82). Usually the dead space for low-angle indirect fire is about five times the height of the highest building over which the rounds must pass.

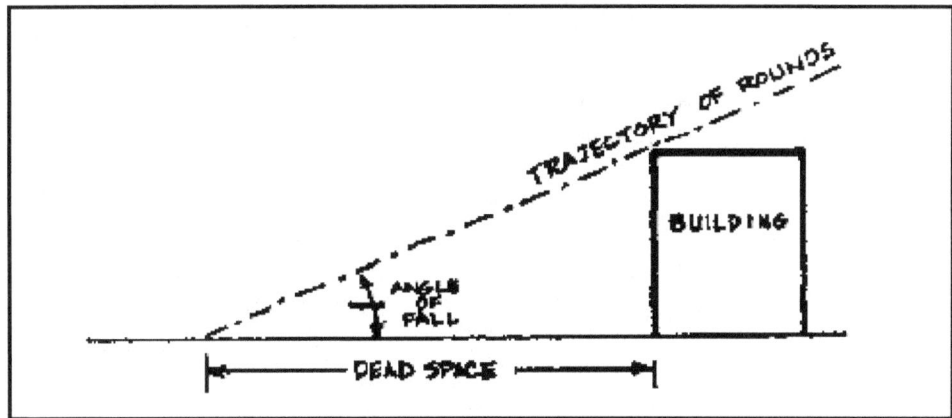

Figure 2-82. Indirect-fire dead space (low angle)

(2) Even when it is theoretically possible to hit a target in a street over a tall building, another problem arises because of range probable error (PE). Only 50 percent of the rounds fired on the same data can be expected to fall within one range PE of the target. This means that when firing indirect fire into built-up areas with tall buildings, it is necessary to double the normal ammunition expenditure to overcome the problem of a reduced target area and range PE. Also up to 25 percent of all HE rounds are duds due to glancing off hard surfaces.

(3) Naval gunfire, because of its flat trajectory, is even more affected by terrain masking. It is very difficult to adjust onto the target because the gun-target line is constantly changing.

b. Direct Fire. Self-propelled artillery pieces are not as heavily armored as tanks; but they can still be used during combat in built-up areas if adequately secured by infantry. The most likely use of U.S. artillery in an urban direct-fire role is to reinforce tank fires against tough or important urban targets. Because of their availability and habitual relationship with infantry, tanks remain a more common direct-fire support means than self-propelled artillery. Self-propelled artillery should be used in this role only after an analysis of the need for heavy direct fire and the tradeoff involved in the scattering of artillery firepower. SP artillery has the same need for close security and target designation as tanks.

179

c. Target Effects. Medium caliber (155-mm) and heavy caliber (203-mm) direct fire has a devastating affect against masonry construction and field fortifications. Smaller artillery pieces (105-mm) are normally towed, and therefore are difficult to employ in the direct-fire mode. Their target effects are much less destructive than the larger caliber weapons.

(1) 155-mm Howitzers. The 155-mm self-propelled howitzer offers its crew mobility and limited protection in built-up areas. It is effective due to its rate of fire and penetration. High-explosive rounds can penetrate up to 38 inches of brick and unreinforced concrete. Projectiles can penetrate up to 28 inches of reinforced concrete with considerable damage beyond the wall. HE rounds fuzed with concrete-piercing fuzes provide an excellent means of penetrating strong reinforced concrete structures. One round can penetrate up to 46 inches. Five rounds are needed to reliably create a 1.5-meter breach in a one-meter thick wall. About 10 rounds are needed to create a similar breach in a wall 1.5 meters thick. Superquick fuzing causes the rubble to be blown into the building, whereas delay fuzing tends to blow the rubble outward into the street.

(2) 203-mm Howitzers. The 203-mm howitzer is the most powerful direct-fire weapon available to the Army. It has a slow rate of fire, but its projectile has excellent penetration abilities. One round normally creates a breach hole in walls up to 56 inches thick. The howitzer crew is exposed to enemy fire. The vehicle only carries three rounds on board which limits its use.

(3) Naval Cannon. The most common naval cannon used to support ground troops is the 5-inch/54 caliber gun. In either single or double mounts, this weapon has a high rate of fire and is roughly equivalent to the 155-mm howitzer in target effect. The heaviest guns used to engage land targets are the 16-inch guns of the recently renovated Iowa-class battleships. When used singly or in salvo, these massive guns can penetrate any structure common to a built-up area. Their blast effect is destructive to buildings up to a block away from the point of impact. Battleship gunfire rarely, if ever, is used for close support of ground troops. Its long range and destructive power can be controlled and adjusted ahead of advancing forces by aerial observers, to clear or destroy enemy strongpoints and supporting artillery.

14. Aerial Weapons.

Both rotary and fixed-wing aircraft can quickly deliver large volumes of firepower over large built-up areas. Specific targets are hard to distinguish from the air. Successful application of aerial fire power demands good ground-to-air communications. Aviators historically tend to overestimate the effects of high-explosive ordnance on defenders. Modern large buildings are remarkably resistant to damage from bombs and rocket fire.

a. Rotary-Winged Aircraft. Armed attack helicopters can be used to engage targets in built-up areas. Enemy armored vehicles in small parks, boulevards, or other open areas are good targets for attack helicopters.

Note: The target effects of TOW missiles and 40-mm grenades carried by attack helicopters have already been discussed.

(1) The HELLFIRE missile has a larger warhead and greater range than the TOW, but it too is a shaped-charge warhead and is not specifically designed for use against masonry targets. Laser target designation for the HELLFIRE may not be possible due to laser reflections off glass and shiny metal surfaces. The use of attack helicopters to deliver ATGMs against targets in the upper stories of high buildings is sometimes desirable.

(2) The 2.75-inch folding-fin aerial rocket and the 20-mm cannon common to some attack helicopters are good area weapons to use against enemy forces in the open or under light cover. They are usually ineffective against a large masonry target. The 20-mm cannon produces many ricochets, especially if AP ammunition is fired into built-up areas.

(3) The 30-mm cannon carried by the Apache helicopter is an accurate weapon. It penetrates masonry better than the 20-mm cannon.

b. Fixed-Wing Aircraft. Close air support to ground forces fighting in built-up areas is a difficult mission for fixed-wing aircraft. Targets are hard to locate and identify, enemy and friendly forces could be intermingled, and enemy short-range air-defense weapons are hard to suppress.

(1) Because enemy and friendly forces can be separated by only one building, accurate delivery of ordnance is required. Marking panels, lights, electronic beacons, smoke, or some other positive identification of friendly forces is needed.

(2) General-purpose bombs from 500 to 2,000 pounds are moderately effective in creating casualties among enemy troops located in large buildings. High-dive-angle bomb runs increase accuracy and penetration but also increase the aircraft's exposure to antiaircraft weapons. Low-dive-angle bomb runs using high drag (retarded) bombs can be used to get bombs into upper stories. Penetration is not good with high-drag bombs. Sometimes aerial bombs pass completely through light-clad buildings and explode on the outside.

(3) Aerial rockets and cannons are only moderately effective against enemy soldiers in built-up areas since rockets lack the accuracy to concentrate their effects. The 20-mm cannon rounds penetrate only slightly better than the .50-caliber round, 20-mm AP rounds can ricochet badly, and tracers can start fires.

(4) The 30-mm cannon fired from the A-10 aircraft is an accurate weapon. It is moderately effective against targets in built-up areas penetrating masonry better than the 20-mm cannon.

(5) The AC-130 aircraft has weapons which are most effective during combat in built-up areas. This aircraft can deliver accurate fire from a 40-

mm Vulcan cannon, 40-mm rapid-fire cannon, and 105-mm howitzer. The 105-mm howitzer round is effective against the roof and upper floors of buildings. The AC-130 is accurate enough to concentrate its 40-mm cannon and 105-mm howitzer fire onto a single spot to create a rooftop breach which allows fire to be directed deep into the building.

(6) Laser and optically guided munitions can be effective against high-value targets. The USAF has developed special heavy laser-guided bombs to penetrate hardened weapons emplacements. These advanced weapons were used with success during Operation Desert Storm. Problems associated with dense smoke and dust clouds hanging over the built-up area and laser scatter can restrict their use. If the launching aircraft can achieve a successful laser designation and lock-on, these weapons have devastating effects, penetrating deep into reinforced concrete before exploding with great force. If launched without a lock-on or if the laser spot is lost, these weapons are unpredictable and can travel long distances before they impact.

15. Demolitions.

Combat in built-up areas requires the extensive use of demolitions. All soldiers, not just engineer troops, should be trained to employ demolitions.

a. Demolitions. Bulk demolitions come in two types, TNT and C4. Exposed soldiers must take cover or move at least 300 meters away from bulk explosives being used to breach walls.

(1) TNT comes in quarter- and one-pound blocks. About five pounds of TNT are needed to breach a nonreinforced concrete wall 12 inches thick if the explosives are laid next to the wall and are not tamped. If the explosives are tamped, about two pounds are sufficient.

(2) C4 comes in many different sized blocks. About 10 pounds of C4 placed between waist and chest high will blow a hole in the average masonry wall large enough for a man to walk through.

b. Shaped Charges. There are two sizes of U.S. Army shaped charges, a 15-pound M2A3 and a 40-pound M3A3. The M3A3 is the shaped charge most likely to be used in built-up areas. It can penetrate five feet of reinforced concrete. The hole tapers from five inches down to two inches. The amount of spall thrown behind the target wall is considerable. There is also a large safety hazard area for friendly soldiers.

c. Satchel Charges. There are two standard U.S. Army satchel charges: the M183 and the M37. Both come in their own carrying satchel with detonators and blasting cords. Each weighs 20 pounds. The M183 has 16 individual 1 1/4-pound blocks that can be used separately. When used untamped, a satchel breaches a three-foot thick concrete wall. Satchel charges are very powerful. Debris is thrown great distances. Friendly troops must move away and take cover before detonation.

d. Cratering Charges. The standard U.S. Army cratering charge is a 43-pound cylinder of ammonium nitrate. This explosive does not have the shattering effect of bulk TNT or C4. It is more useful in deliberate demolitions than in hasty ones.

PART C - MOUT TECHNIQUES

1. <u>Subterranean Operations</u>.

Knowledge of the nature and location of underground facilities is of great value to both the urban attacker and defender. To exploit the advantages of underground facilities, you need to take a thorough reconnaissance. This part of the lesson describes the techniques used to deny the enemy use of these features, the tactical value of subterranean passage techniques, and the psychological aspects of extended operations in subterranean passages.

    a. <u>Tactical Value</u>. In larger cities, subterranean features include sunken garages, underground passages, subway lines, utility tunnels (Figure 2-83), sewers, and storm drains. Most of these features allow the movement of many troops. Even in smaller European towns, sewers and storm drains permit soldiers to move beneath the fighting and surface behind the enemy.

        (1) Subterranean passages provide the attacker with covered and concealed routes into and through built-up areas. This enables the enemy to launch his attack along roads leading into the city while infiltrating a smaller force in the defender's rear. The objective of this attack is to quickly insert a unit into the defender's rear, thereby disrupting his defense and obstructing his avenues of withdrawal for his forward defense.

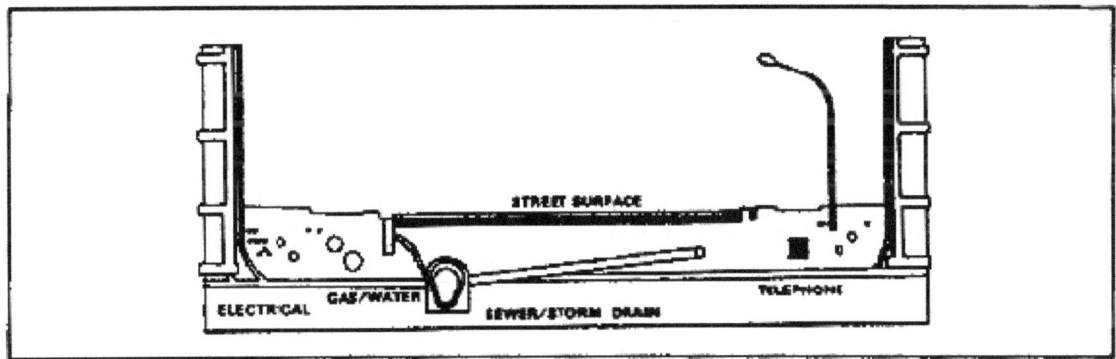

Figure 2-83. Tunnels

        (2) Depending upon the strength and depth of the defense, the attack along the subterranean avenue of approach could easily become the main attack. Even if the subterranean effort is not immediately successful, it forces the defender to fight on two levels and to extend his resources to more than just street-level fighting.

        (3) The existence of subterranean passages forces the defender to defend the built-up area above and below ground passages are more of a disadvantage to the defender than the attacker. However, subterranean

183

passages also offer some advantages. When thoroughly reconnoitered and controlled by the defender, subterranean passages provide excellent covered and concealed routes to move reinforcements or to launch counterattacks. They also provide ready-made lines of communication for the movement of supplies and evacuation of casualties and provide places to cache supplies for forward companies. Subterranean passages also offer the defender a ready-made conduit for communications wire which protects it from tracked vehicles and indirect fires.

b. Denial to the Enemy. Subterranean passages are useful to the defender only to the extent that the attacker can be denied their use. The defender has an advantage in that, given the confining dark environment of these passages, a small group of determined soldiers in a prepared position can defeat a numerically superior force.

(1) Tunnels afford the attacker little cover and concealment except for the darkness and any man-made barriers. The passageways provide tight fields of fire and amplify the effect of grenades. Obstacles at intersections in the tunnels set up excellent ambush sites and turn the subterranean passages into a deadly maze. These obstacles can be quickly created using chunks of rubble, furniture, and parts of abandoned vehicles interspersed with M18A1 Claymore mines.

(2) A thorough reconnaissance of the subterranean or sewer system must be made first. To be effective, obstacles must be located at critical intersections in the passage network so they trap attackers in a kill zone but allow defenders freedom of movement (Figure 2-84).

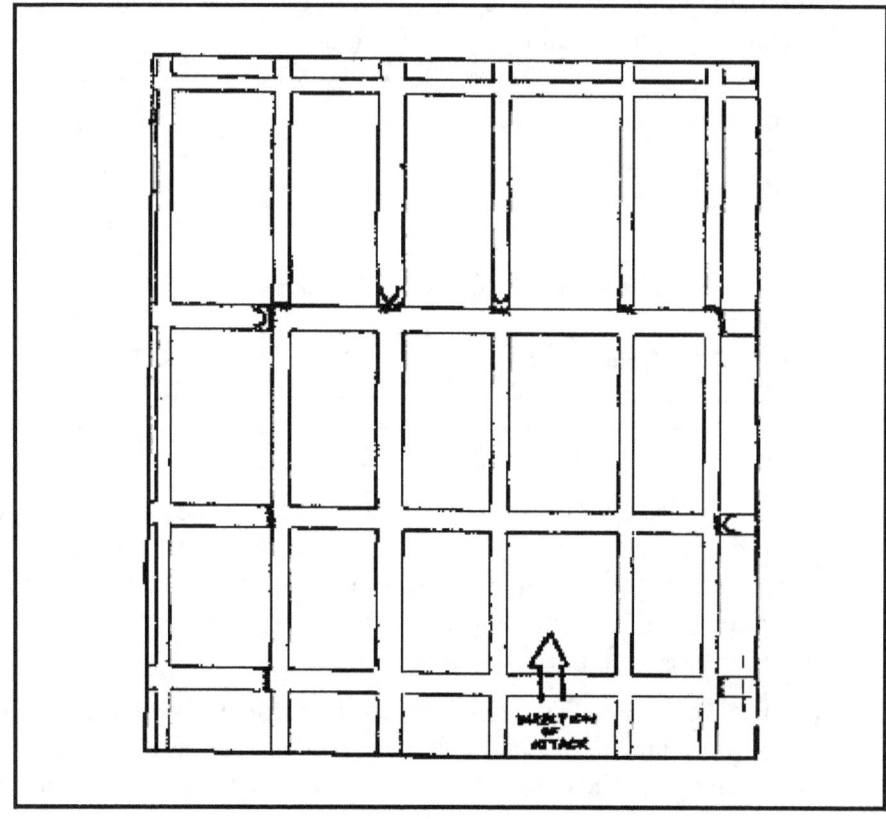

Figure 2-84. Defense of a sewer system

c. <u>Subterranean Reconnaissance Techniques</u>. The local reconnaissance mission (platoon/company area of responsibility) should be given to a squad-size element (six or seven personnel). Enough soldiers are in a squad to gather the required data without getting in each other's way in the confines of the tunnel. Only in extremely large subterranean features should the size of a patrol be increased.

(1) Your patrol leader should organize his patrol with two riflemen -- one tasked with security to the front (the point man) and one tasked with security to the rear (Figure 2-85). The patrol leader moves directly behind the point man and navigates and records data collected by the patrol. The grenadier follows the patrol leader and the demolitions man should follow the grenadier. Leave two riflemen as a security post at the point of entry. They are responsible for detecting any enemy who come upon the patrol unit's rear and for serving as the communications link between the patrol leader and his higher headquarters.

Figure 2-85. Organization of a patrol

(2) The patrol leader carries a map, compass, street plan, and notebook in which he has written the information he must gather for the platoon leader. The grenadier carries the tools needed to open manhole covers. If the patrol is to move more than 200 to 300 meters, or if the platoon leader directs, the grenadier should also carry a sound-powered telephone (TA-1) and wire dispenser (XM-306A) for communications. (Radios are unreliable in this environment). Equip the point man with night vision goggles to maintain surveillance within the sewer.

(3) All soldiers entering the sewer should carry a sketch of the sewer system to include magnetic north azimuths, distances, and manholes. They should also carry protective masks, flashlights, gloves, and chalk for marking features along the route. The patrol should also be equipped with a 120-foot safety rope to which each man is tied. To improve footing in slippery sewers and storm drains, the patrol could wrap chicken wire or screen wire around their boots.

185

(4) A constant concern to troops conducting a subterranean patrol is chemical defense. Enemy chemical agents used in tunnels are encountered in dense concentrations with no chance of dispersement. The M8 automatic chemical agent alarm system carried by the point man provides instant warning of the presence of chemical agents. M8 detector paper can also be used to detect chemical agents. At the first indication harmful gases are present, the patrol should mask up.

(5) In addition to enemy chemical agents, noxious gases from decomposing sewage can also pose a threat. These gases are not detected by the M8 chemical agent alarm system, nor are they completely filtered by the protective mask. Physical signs indicating their presence in harmful quantities are nausea and dizziness. The patrol leader should be constantly alert to these signs and know the shortest route to the surface for fresh air.

(6) Once the patrol is organized and equipped it moves to the entrance of the tunnel which is usually a manhole. With the manhole cover removed, the patrol waits 15 minutes before entry to allow any gases present in the tunnel to dissipate. Then the point man descends into the tunnel to determine whether the air is safe to breathe and if movement is restricted. The point man should remain in the tunnel for 10 minutes before the rest of the patrol follows. If he becomes ill or is exposed to danger, he can be pulled out by the safety rope.

(7) When the patrol is moving through the tunnel, the point man moves about 10 meters in front of the patrol leader. Other patrol members maintain 5-meter intervals. If the water in the tunnel is flowing faster than 2.5 meters per second or if the sewer contains slippery obstacles, those intervals should be increased to prevent all patrol members from falling if one man slips. All patrol members should stay tied into the safety rope so they can easily be retrieved from danger. The rear security man marks the route with chalk so other troops can find the patrol.

(8) The patrol leader should note the azimuth and pace count of each turn he takes in the tunnel. When he encounters a manhole to the surface, the point man opens it and determines the location, which the patrol leader then records. The use of recognition signals (Figure 2-86) prevents friendly troops from accidentally shooting the point man as he appears at a manhole.

(9) Once the patrol has returned and submitted its report, you must decide how to use the tunnel. In the offense, the tunnel could provide a covered route to move behind the enemy's defenses. In the defense, the tunnel could provide a covered passage between positions. In either case, the patrol members act as guides along the route.

(10) If the tunnel is to be blocked, the platoon should emplace concertina wire, early warning devices, and antipersonnel mines. A two-man position is established at the entrance of the sewer (Figure 2-87). It provides security against the enemy trying to approach the platoon's defense and is

abandoned should the water rise.

Figure 2-86. Recognition signals

Figure 2-87. Two-man position established at the entrance to a sewer

It should be equipped with command-detonated illumination flares. While listening for the enemy, soldiers manning this position should not wear earplugs (they should put them in their ears just before firing). The confined space amplifies sounds of weapons firing to a dangerous level. The overpressure from grenades, mines, and booby traps exploding in a sewer or tunnel can have adverse effects on friendly troops such as ruptured eardrums and wounds from flying debris. Also, gases found in sewers can be ignited by the blast effects of such munitions. For this reason, only small-arms weapons should be employed in tunnels and sewers. Friendly personnel should be out of the tunnel or out of range of the effects when mines or demolitions are detonated. Soldiers put on masks at the first sign of a chemical threat.

d. <u>Psychological Considerations</u>. Combat operations in subterranean passages are much like night combat operations. The psychological factors affecting soldiers during night operations reduce confidence, cause fears, and increase a feeling of isolation. This feeling of isolation is further magnified by the tight confines of the tunnels. The layout of tunnels could require greater dispersion between positions than is usual for operations in wooded terrain.

(1) You must enforce measures to dispel the feelings of fear and isolation experienced by soldiers in tunnels. These measures include leadership training, physical and mental fitness, sleep discipline, and stress management.

(2) Maintain communication with soldiers manning positions in the tunnels either by personal visits or by field telephone. Communications inform you of the tactical situation as well as the mental state of your soldiers. Soldiers manning positions below ground should be given as much information as possible on the organization of the tunnels and the importance of the mission. Brief them on contingency plans and alternate positions, should their primary positions become untenable.

(3) Physical and mental fitness can be maintained by periodically rotating soldiers out of tunnels so they can stand and walk in fresh air and sunlight. Stress management is also a factor of operations in tunnels. Historically, combat in built-up areas has been one of the most stressful forms of combat. Continuous darkness and restricted maneuver space cause more stress to soldiers than street fighting.

2. Fighting Positions.

A critical platoon- and squad-level defensive task in combat in built-up areas is the preparation of fighting positions. Fighting positions in built-up areas are usually constructed inside buildings. Their selection is based on an analysis of the area in which the building is located and the individual characteristics of the building.

a. Considerations. Consider the following factors when establishing fighting positions.

(1) Protection. Select buildings providing protection from direct and indirect fires. Reinforced concrete buildings with three or more floors provide suitable protection while buildings constructed of wood, paneling, or other light material must be reinforced to gain sufficient protection. One to two-story buildings without a strongly constructed cellar are vulnerable to indirect fires and require construction of overhead protection for each firing position.

(2) Dispersion. A position should not be established in a single building when it is possible to occupy two or more buildings permitting mutually supporting fires. A position in one building without mutual support is vulnerable to bypass, isolation, and subsequent destruction from any direction.

(3) Concealment. Don't select buildings that are obvious defensive positions (easily targeted by the enemy). Requirements for security and fields of fire could require the occupation of exposed buildings. Therefore,

reinforcements provide suitable protection within the building.

(4) <u>Fields of Fire</u>. To prevent isolation, positions should be mutually supporting and have fields of fire in all directions. Clearing fields of fire could require the destruction of adjacent buildings using explosives, engineer equipment, and field expedients.

(5) <u>Covered Routes</u>. Defensive positions should have at least one covered route for resupply, medical evacuation, reinforcement, or withdrawal from the building. The route can be established by one of the following:

- Through walls to adjacent buildings.

- Through underground systems.

- Through communications trenches.

- Behind protective buildings.

(6) <u>Observation</u>. The building should permit observation of enemy avenues of approach and adjacent defensive sectors.

(7) <u>Fire Hazard</u>. Avoid selecting positions in buildings which are fire hazards. If flammable structures must be occupied, the danger of fire can be reduced by wetting down the immediate environment, laying an inch of sand on the floors, and providing fire extinguishers and fire-fighting equipment. Also routes of escape must be prepared in case of fire.

(8) <u>Time</u>. Time available to prepare the defense can be the most critical factor. If enough time is not available, do not use buildings requiring extensive preparation. Conversely, buildings located in less desirable areas which require little improvement, could probably become the centers of defense.

b. <u>Preparation</u>. Preparation of fighting positions depends upon proper selection and construction.

(1) Selecting Positions (Figures 2-88 and 2-89). Assign each weapon a primary sector of fire to cover enemy approaches. Alternate positions overwatching the primary sector are also selected. These positions are usually located in an adjacent room on the same floor. Assign each weapon a supplementary position to engage attacks from other directions, and an FPL.

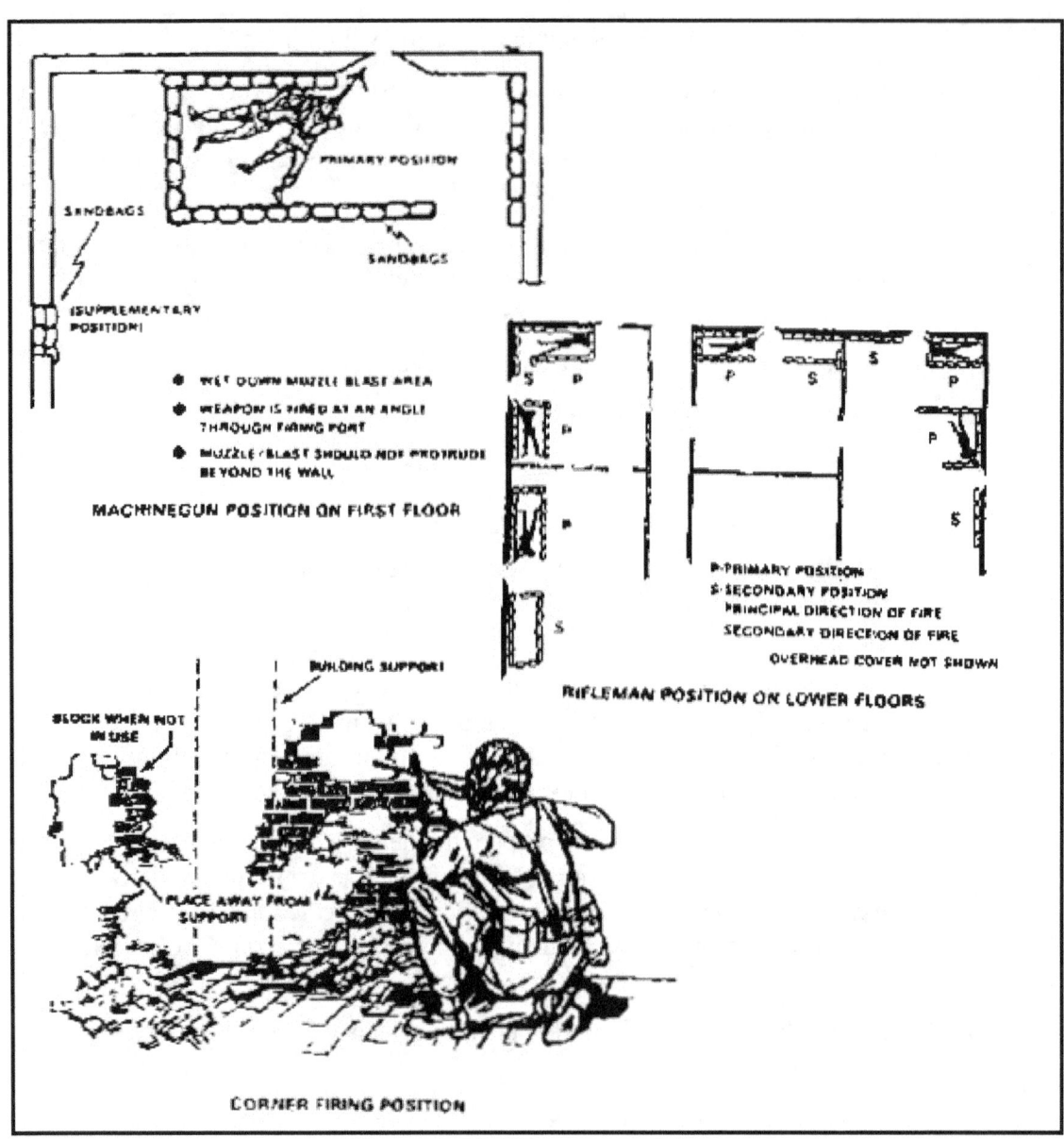

Figure 2-88. Weapon positions

190

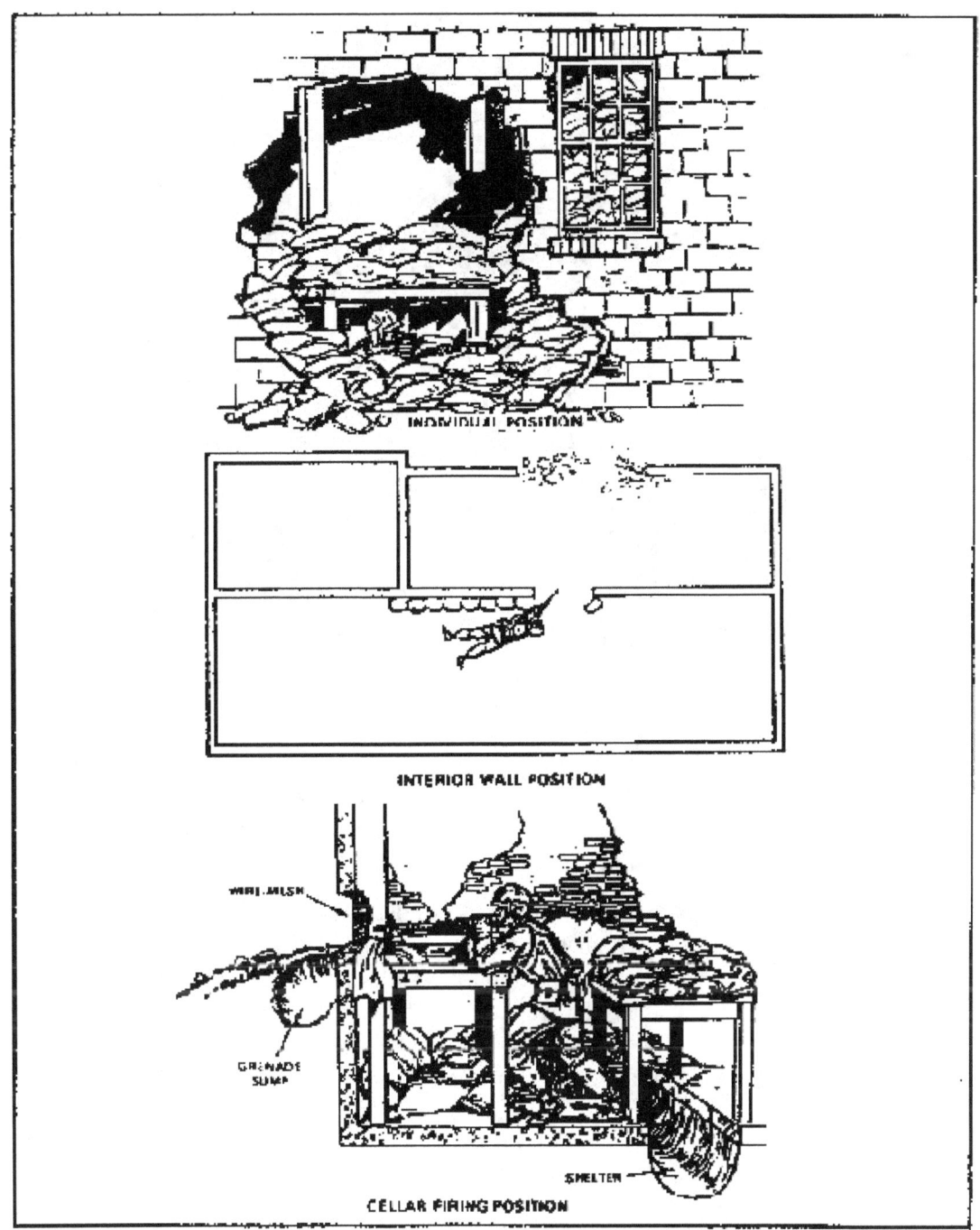

INDIVIDUAL POSITION

INTERIOR WALL POSITION

WIRE MESH

GRENADE SUMP

SHELTER

CELLAR FIRING POSITION

Figure 2-89. Weapon positions (continued)

(2) <u>Building Positions</u>. There are many ways to establish a fighting position in a building.

    (a) <u>Window position (Figure 2-90)</u>. Soldiers kneel or stand on either side of a window. To fire downward from upper floors, tables or similar objects can be placed against the wall to provide additional elevation, but they must be positioned to prevent the weapon from protruding through the window. Inspect the positions to determine the width of sector each position can engage.

Figure 2-90. Window position

(b) <u>Loopholes</u>. To avoid establishing a pattern of always firing from windows, have loopholes prepared in the walls. Soldiers should avoid firing directly through loopholes to enhance individual protection.

- Several loopholes are usually required for each weapon (primary, alternate, and supplementary positions). The number of loopholes should be carefully considered because they can weaken walls and reduce protection. Consult with the engineers before an excessive number of loopholes are made. Loopholes are made by punching or drilling holes in walls and should be placed where they are concealed. Blasting loopholes can result in a large hole easily seen by the enemy.

- Loopholes should be cone-shaped to obtain a wide arc of fire, to facilitate engagement of high and low targets, and to reduce the size of the exterior aperture (Figure 2-91).

  The edges of a loophole splinter when hit by bullets therefore protective linings such as an empty sandbag held in place by wire mesh will reduce spalling effects. When not in use loopholes should be covered with sandbags to prevent the enemy from firing into or observing through them.

192

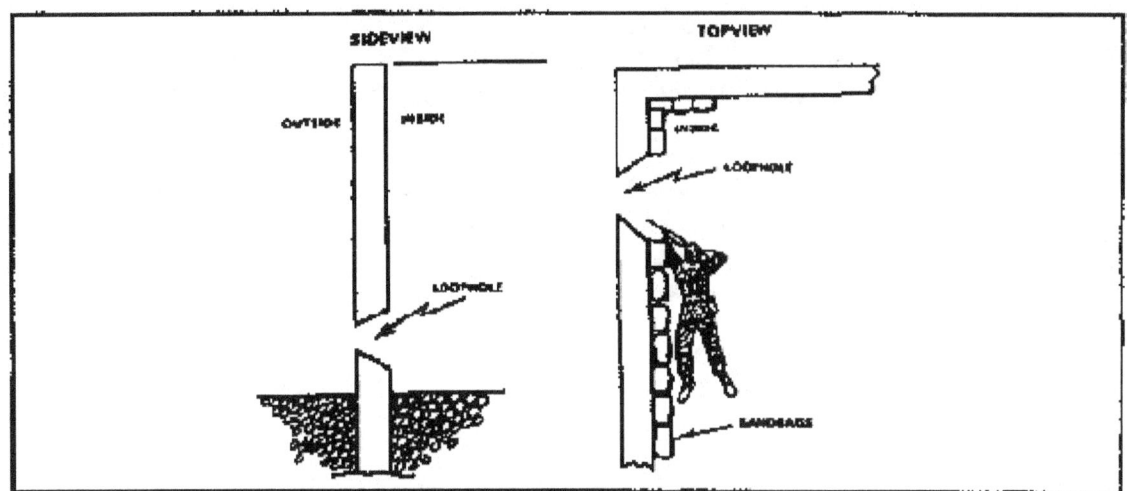

Figure 2-91. Cone-shaped loopholes

- Also have loopholes prepared in interior walls and ceilings of buildings to permit fighting within the position. Interior loopholes should overwatch stairs, halls, and unoccupied rooms and be concealed by pictures, drapes, or furniture. Loopholes in floors permit the defender to engage enemy personnel on lower floors with small-arms fire and grenades.

- Although walls provide some frontal protection, they should be reinforced with sandbags, furniture, filled with dirt, or other expedients. Each position should have overhead and all-round protection (Figure 2-92).

Figure 2-92. Position with overhead and all-round protection

(3) <u>Other Construction Tasks</u>. Other construction tasks in basements, on ground floors, and on upper floors will need to be performed.

193

(a) Basements and Ground Floors. Basements require preparation similar to that of the ground floor. Any underground system not used by the defender, providing the enemy access to the position must be blocked.

- Doors. Unused doors are locked, nailed shut, and blocked and reinforced with furniture, sandbags, or other field expedients. Outside doors can be booby trapped by engineers or other personnel.

- Hallways. If not required for your movement, hallways should be blocked with furniture and tactical wire (Figure 2-93). If authorized, use booby traps.

- Stairs. Block stairs not used by the defense with furniture and tactical wire (see Figure 2-93) or remove them. If possible all stairs should be blocked and ladders used to move from floor to floor and then removed when not being used. Booby traps should also be employed on stairs.

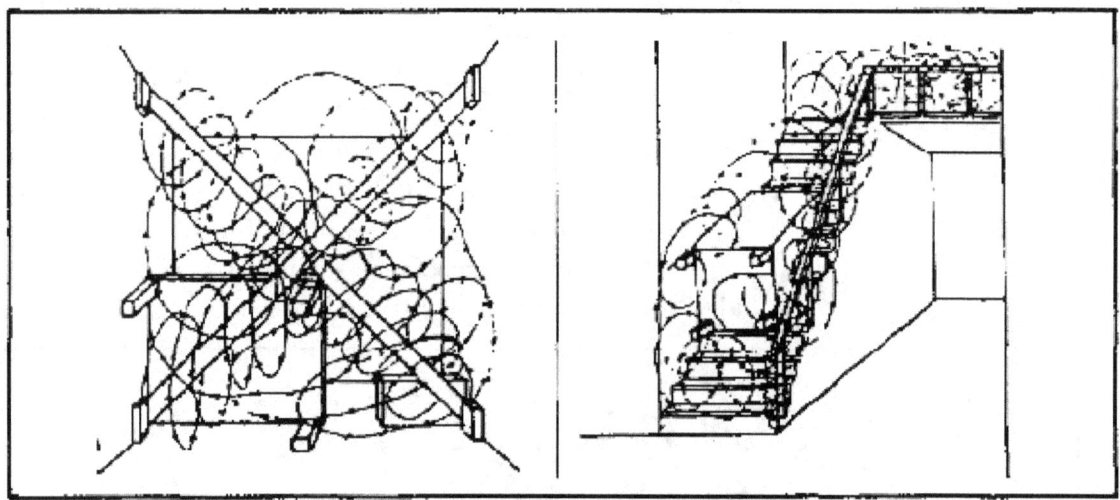

Figure 2-93. Blocking hallways and stairs

- Windows. All glass should be removed. Windows not used are blocked with boards or sandbags.

- Floors. Make fighting positions in floors. If there is no basement, fighting positions in the floors can give additional protection from heavy direct-fire weapons.

- Ceilings. Have support that can withstand the weight of rubble from upper floors placed under ceilings (Figure 2-94).

- Unoccupied Rooms. Rooms not required for defense are blocked with tactical wire or boobytrapped.

(b) Upper Floors. Upper floors require the same preparation as ground floors. Windows need not be blocked but they should be

194

covered with wire mesh which blocks grenades thrown from the outside. The wire should be loose at the bottom to permit defenders to drop grenades.

(c) <u>Interior Routes</u>. Routes are required that permit defending forces to move within the building to engage enemy forces from any direction. Plan and construct escape routes to permit rapid evacuation of a room or the building.

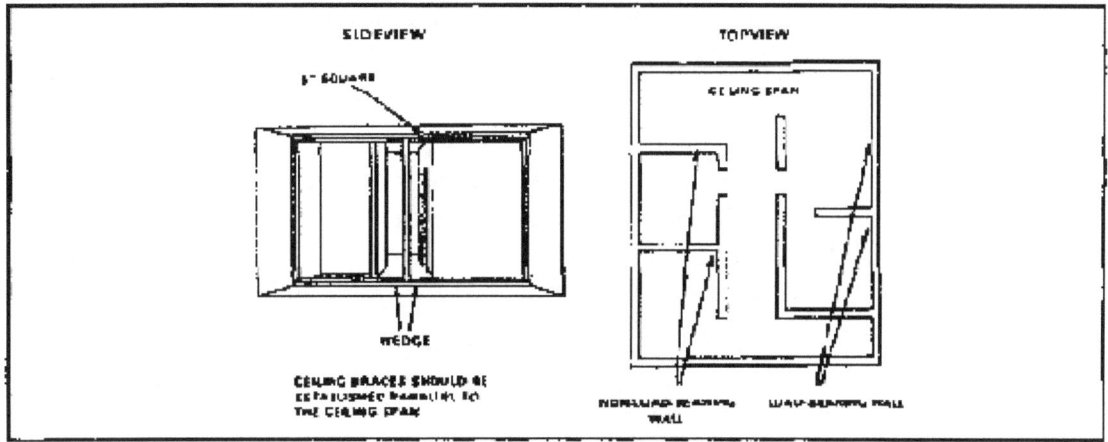

Figure 2-94. Ceiling reinforcement

Have small holes (called mouse holes) made through interior walls to permit movement between rooms. Once you have withdrawn to another level, such holes are clearly marked for both day and night identification. Brief all personnel as to where the various routes are located. Conduct rehearsals so everyone becomes familiar with the routes (Figure 2-95).

Figure 2-95. Movement between floors

195

(d) <u>Fire Prevention</u>. Buildings with wooden floors and raftered ceilings require extensive fire prevention measures. The attic and other wooden floors should be covered with about 1 inch of sand or dirt, and buckets of water should be positioned for immediate use. Have firefighting materials (dirt, sand, fire extinguishers, and blankets) placed on each floor for immediate use. Water basins and bathtubs should be filled as a reserve for firefighting. All electricity and gas is turned off. Fire breaks can be created by destroying buildings adjacent to the defensive position.

(e) <u>Communications</u>. Have telephone lines laid through adjacent buildings or underground systems, or buried in shallow trenches. Conceal your radio antennas by placing them among civilian television antennas, along the sides of chimneys and steeples, or out windows. Direct FM communications away from enemy early-warning sources and ground observation. Telephone lines within the building should be laid through walls and floors.

(f) <u>Rubbling</u>. Rubbling parts of the building provides additional cover and concealment for weapons emplacements and should be performed only by trained engineers.

(g) <u>Rooftops</u>. Positions in flat-roofed buildings require obstacles restricting helicopter landings. Rooftops accessible from adjacent structure should be covered with tactical wire or other expedients and must be guarded. Entrances to buildings from rooftops can be blocked if compatible with your overall defensive plan. Any structure on the outside of a building which could assist scaling the buildings to gain access to upper floors, or to the rooftop should be removed or blocked.

(h) <u>Obstacles</u>. Position obstacles adjacent to buildings to stop tanks and to delay infantry.

(i) <u>Fields of Fire</u>. Fields of fire should be improved around the defensive position. You can have selected buildings destroyed to enlarge fields of fire. Obstacles to antitank guided missiles, such as telephone wires should be cleared. Have dead space covered with mines and obstacles.

c. <u>Armored Vehicle Positions</u>. Fighting positions for tanks and infantry fighting vehicles are essential to a complete and effective defensive plan in built-up areas.

(1) <u>Armored Vehicle Positions</u>. Select and develop armored vehicle positions to obtain the best cover, concealment, observation, and fields of fire, while retaining the vehicle's ability to move.

(a) If fields of fire are restricted to streets, use hull-down positions to gain cover and to fire directly down streets (Figure 2-96). From these positions, tanks and BFVs are protected and can rapidly move to alternate positions. Buildings collapsing from enemy fires are a

196

minimal hazard to the armored vehicle and crew.

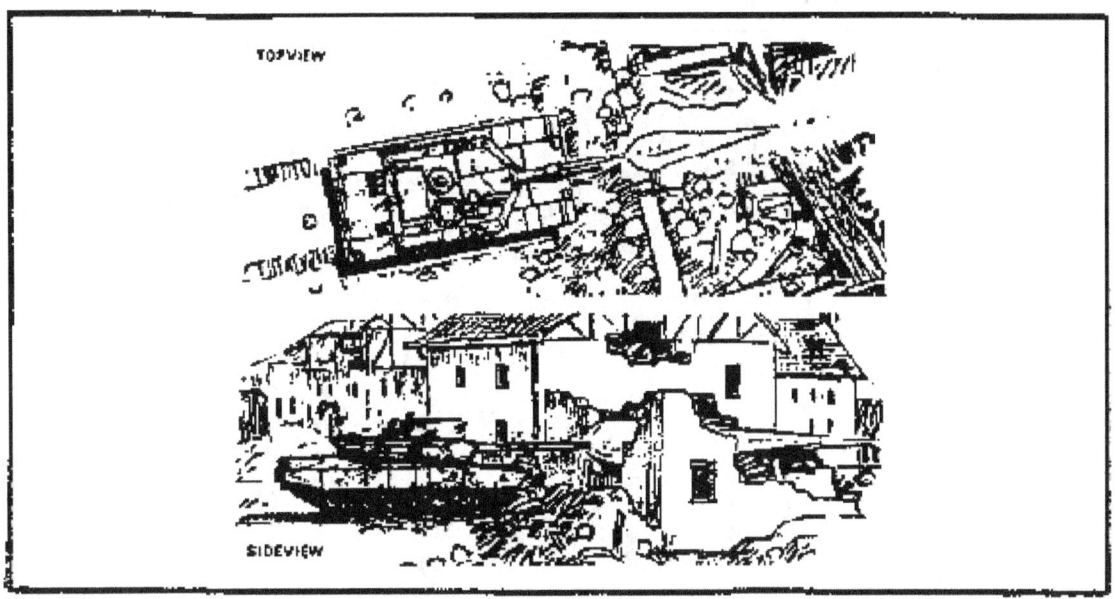

Figure 2-96. Hull-down position

(b) The hide position (Figure 2-97) covers and conceals the vehicle until time to move into position for engagement of targets. Since the crew will not be able to see advancing enemy forces, an observer from the vehicle or a nearby infantry unit is concealed in an adjacent building to alert the crew. The observer acquires the target and signals the armored vehicle to move to the firing position and to fire. After firing, the tank or BFV moves to an alternate position to avoid compromising the original location.

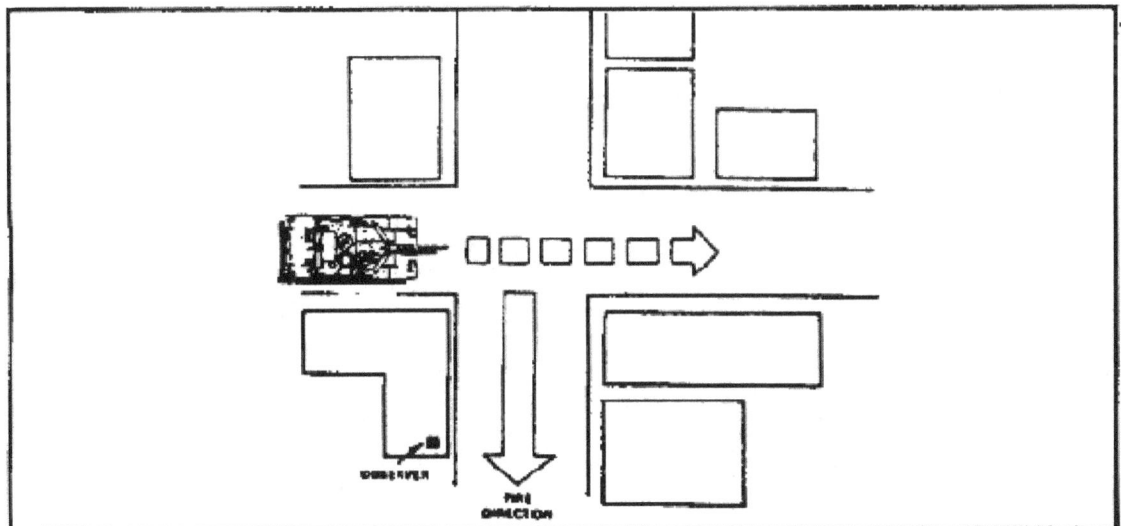

Figure 2-97. Hide position

(c) The building hide position (Figure 2-98) conceals the vehicle inside a building. If basement hide positions are inaccessible, have engineers evaluate the building's floor strength and prepare for the

197

vehicle. Once the position is detected it should be evacuated to avoid enemy fires.

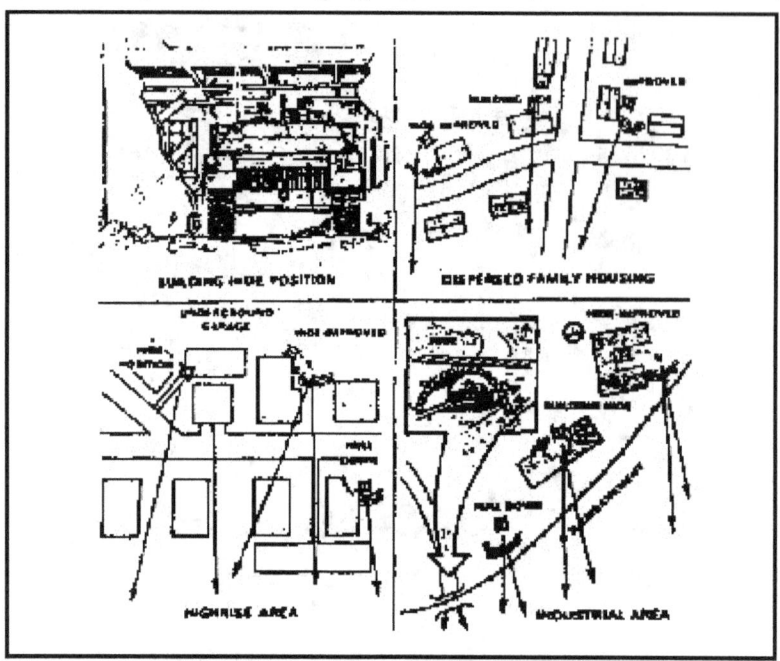

Figure 2-98. Building hide position

d. <u>Antitank Guided Missile Positions</u>. Employ your ATGMs in areas maximizing their capabilities in the built-up area. The lack of a protective transport could require the weapon to be fired from inside or behind a building or behind the cover of protective terrain (Figure 2-99).

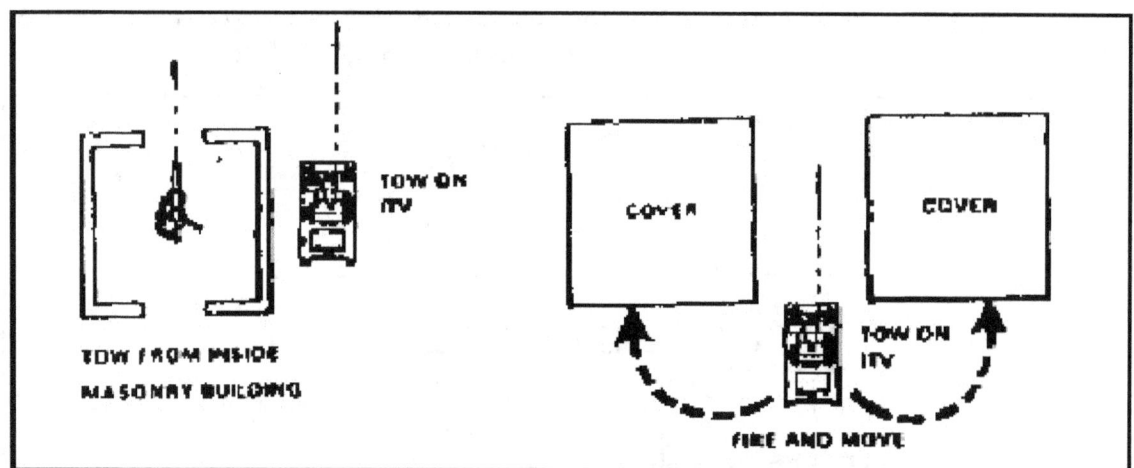

Figure 2-99. Antitank guided missile positions

(1) When ATGMs are fired from a vehicle or from street-level or bottom-floor fighting positions, rubble can interfere with missile flight. When firing down streets, missiles must have at least 30 inches of clearance over rubble. Other obstacles to missile flight include trees and brush, vehicles, television antennas, buildings, power lines and wires, walls and fences.

(2) A LAW is best suited for built-up areas because its 10-meter minimum

arming distance allows employment at close range. LAWs and other light and medium antitank weapons are not effective against the front of modern battle tanks. Because tanks have the least armor protection on the top and rear deck, and the tank presents a larger target when engaged from above, LAWs should fire down onto tanks.

e. Sniper Positions. Snipers contribute to combat in built-up areas by firing on selected enemy soldiers. An effective sniper organization can trouble the enemy far more than its cost in the number of friendly soldiers employed.

(1) General areas (a building or group of buildings) are designated as sniper positions (Figure 2-100), but the sniper selects the best position for engagement. Masonry buildings offering the best protection, long-range fields of fire and all-round observation are preferred. The sniper also selects several secondary and supplementary positions to cover his areas of responsibility.

Figure 2-100. Sniper positions

(2) Engagement priorities for snipers are determined by the relative importance of the targets to the effective operations of the enemy. Sniper targets usually include tank commanders, direct-fire support weapons' crewmen, crew-served weapons' crewmen, officers, forward observers, and radiotelephone operators.

(3) Built-up areas often limit snipers to firing down or across streets but open areas permit engagements at long ranges. Snipers can be employed to cover rooftops, obstacles, dead space, and gaps in the final protective fires (FPFs).

3. Attacking and Clearing Buildings.

199

At platoon and squad level, the major offensive tasks for combat in built-up areas are attacking and clearing buildings which involve the following:

- Suppressing defensive fires.

- Advancing infantry assault forces.

- Assaulting a building.

- Reorganizing the assault force.

a. <u>Requirements</u>. Regardless of a structure's characteristics or the type of built-up area, there are four interrelated requirements for attacking a defended building: fire support, movement, assault, and reorganization. Proper application and integration of these requirements reduce casualties and hasten accomplishment of the mission. The application is determined by the type of building to be attacked and the nature of the surrounding built-up area. For example, medium-size towns have numerous open spaces and larger cities have high-rise apartments and industrial and transportation areas, which are separated by parking areas or parks. In a large built-up area, you will need increased fire support to suppress and obscure enemy gunners covering the open terrain and spaces between buildings. Conversely, the centers of small- and medium-size towns with twisting alleys and country roads or adjoining buildings, provide numerous covered routes, decreasing your fire support requirements.

b. <u>Fire Support</u>. Fire support and other assistance to advance the assault force are provided by a support force. This assistance includes the following:

- Suppressing and obscuring enemy gunners within the objective building(s) and adjacent structures.

- Isolating the objective building(s) with direct or indirect fires to prevent enemy withdrawals, reinforcement, or counterattack.

- Breaching walls en route to, and in the objective structure.

- Destroying enemy positions with direct-fire weapons.

- Securing cleared portions of the objective.

- Providing replacements for the assault force.

- Providing resupply of ammunition and explosives.

- Evacuating casualties and prisoners.

(1) The size of the support force is determined by the type and size of the objective building(s), whether the adjacent terrain provides open or covered approaches, and the organization and strength of enemy defenses.

(2) The support force could consist of only one infantry fire team with M60 machine guns, M249 SAWs, M203 grenade launchers, and M202 multishot flame weapons. In the case of Bradley-equipped units, the BFV may provide support with the 25-mm gun as the rifle team assaults. In situations involving a larger assault force, a platoon or company reinforced

200

with tanks, engineers, and self-propelled artillery may be required to support movement and assault by an adjacent platoon or company.

(3) After seizing objective buildings, the assault force reorganizes and may be required to provide supporting fires for a subsequent assault. Assign each weapon a target or area to cover. Individual small-arms weapons place fires on likely enemy weapon positions -- loopholes, windows, roof areas. Snipers are best employed in placing accurate fire through loopholes or engaging long-range targets. Have the M202s and M203s direct their fires through windows or loopholes.

(4) Use LAWs to breach walls, doors, barricades, and window barriers on the ground level of structures. Tank main guns and BFV 25-mm guns engage first-floor targets and breach walls for attacking infantry. Tank machine guns engage suspected positions on upper floors and in adjacent structures. In addition to destroying or weakening structures, tank main gun projectiles cause casualties by explosive effects and by hurling debris throughout the interior of structures.

(5) Artillery and mortars use time fuzes to initially clear exposed personnel, weapons, observation posts, and radio sites from rooftops. They then use delayed-fuze action to cause casualties among the defenders inside the structure by high-explosive, shrapnel, and falling debris. Artillery can also be used in the direct-fire mode much like the tank and CEV.

c. Movement. The assault force (squad/platoon/company) minimizes enemy defensive fires during movement by taking the following actions:

- Using covered routes.

- Moving only after defensive fires have been suppressed or obscured.

- Moving at night or during other periods of reduced visibility.

- Selecting routes that will not mask friendly suppressive fires.

- Crossing open areas (streets, space between buildings) quickly under the concealment of smoke and suppression provided by support forces.

- Moving on rooftops not covered by enemy direct fires.

  (1) In lightly defended areas, the requirement for speed may dictate moving through the streets and alleys without clearing all buildings. Thus the maneuver element should employ infantry to lead the column, closely followed and supported by BFVs or tanks.

  (2) When dismounted, have rifle elements move along each side of the street with leading squads keeping almost abreast of the lead tanks. When not accompanied by tanks or BFVs, rifle elements can move single file along one side of the street under cover of fires from supporting weapons. They should be dispersed and move along quickly. Each man is detailed to observe and cover a certain area such as second-floor windows on the

201

opposite side of the street.

d. <u>Assault and Clearing</u>. The assault force, regardless of size, must quickly and violently execute its assault and subsequent clearing operations. Once momentum has been gained, it is maintained to prevent the enemy from organizing a more determined resistance on other floors or in other rooms. Keep your assault force moving, but do not allow the operation to become disorganized.

(1) An assault in a built-up area involves the elementary skills of close combat. Individual element leaders must have the following capabilities:

- Be trained in the required techniques to defeat the enemy in a face-to-face encounter.

- Keep themselves in excellent physical condition.

- Have confidence in their abilities.

(2) The composition of the assault force varies depending on the situation; however, the considerations for equipping the force remain the same. The assault force for a squad consists of three-man teams carrying only a fighting load of equipment and as much ammunition as possible, especially grenades (Figure 2-101). A three-man support team provides suppressive fire for the assault force. The assault teams use maneuver techniques to clear a building room by room.

(3) The M249 Machine Gun is normally employed with the support element but can also be used with the assault force to gain the advantages of its more powerful round. The Dragon might not be carried by the assault force due to its weight versus its expected effectiveness against the building being assaulted. The squad leader moves with the element from which he can best control the squad. If the squad is understrength or suffers casualties, priority is given to keeping the assault force up to strength at the expense of the support force (see the tables in Figures 2-102 and 2-103).

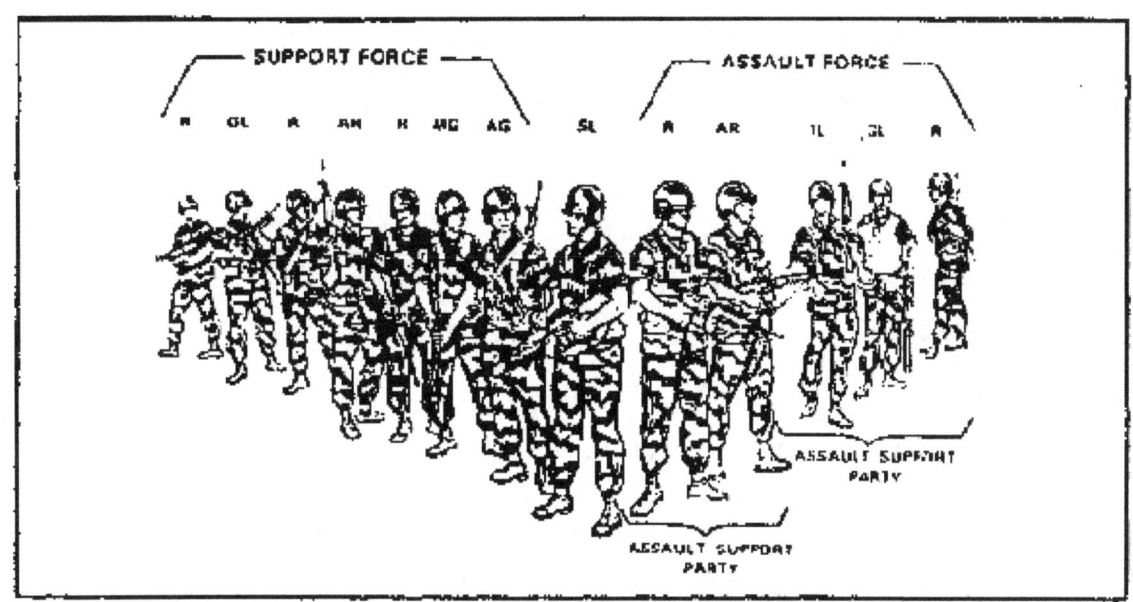

Figure 2-101. Rifle squad

SUPPORT FORCE	ASSAULT FORCE
3 - 7.62-mm (Coaxial)	(Each squad organized into two- or three-man assault/support parties)
2 - M249 SAWs	
1 - Dragon	2 - 7.62-mm (4 - M249)
1 - M202	* 2 - Dragons
LAWs	LAWs
4 - 25-mm guns	Hand grenades

* Dependent upon Dragon's effectiveness against building being attacked.

Figure 2-102. Bradley platoon

```
    SUPPORT FORCE                    ASSAULT FORCE

  2 - 7.62-mm                      LAWs

  2 - Dragons                      Hand grenades

  1 - M202                       * 1 - Dragon

  4 - M249s                        2 - M203s

  4 - M203s                        2 - M249s

  LAWs

  *  Dependent upon Dragon's effectiveness against building
being attacked.
```

Figure 2-103. Alternative with an infantry rifle platoon

(4) The criteria for the size of any party are the availability of equipment and personnel, and the tactical situation. Entry at the top and fighting downward is the preferred method of clearing a building (Figure 2-104). Clearing a building is easier from an upper story since gravity and building construction become assets to the assault force when throwing hand grenades and moving from floor to floor. This method is only feasible however, when access to an upper floor or rooftop can be gained from the windows or roofs of adjoining, secured buildings; or, when enemy air defense weapons can be suppressed and troops transported to the rooftops by helicopter.

Figure 2-104. Helicopter used to clear a building

Helicopters should land only on buildings having special heliports on the roofs or parking garages. Soldiers can rappel onto the roof or dismount as the helicopter hovers a few feet above the roof. Troops then breach the roof or common walls with explosives and use ropes to enter the lower floors. Stairs are guarded by friendly security elements when not used.

(5) Although the top-to-bottom method is preferred for clearing a building, assaulting the bottom floor and clearing upward is a common method in all areas except where buildings form continuous fronts. In this situation, the assault force attempts to close on the flank(s) or rear of the building. The assault team clears each room on the ground floor and then moving up, begins a systematic clearance of the remaining floors.

(6) Preferably, entry is gained through walls breached by explosives or gunfire. Assault teams avoid windows and doors since they are usually covered by fire or are boobytrapped. If tanks are attached to the company, they can breach the wall by using their main guns to fire at one entry point (Figure 2-105).

Figure 2-105. Main guns used to breach the exterior

(7) Just before the rush of the assault forces, suppressive fires on the objective should be increased by the support force and continued until masked by the advancing assault force. Once masked, fires are shifted to upper windows and continued until the assault force has entered the building. At that time, shift the fires to adjacent buildings to prevent enemy withdrawal or reinforcement.

(8) Have your assault parties close quickly on the building. Before entry through the breached wall, a hand grenade is cooked off (pin pulled, safety lever released, and held for two seconds before being thrown) and vigorously thrown inside. Immediately after the explosion, assault parties enter and spray the interior, using three-round bursts and concentrating on areas of the room that are possible enemy positions.

205

(9) Once inside the building, the priority tasks are to cover the staircase leading to upper floors and the basement and to seize rooms overlooking approaches to the building. These actions are required to isolate enemy forces within the building and to prevent reinforcement from the outside. The assault parties clear each ground floor room and then the basement.

(a) The assault team leader determines which room(s) to clear first.

(b) The support team provides suppressive fire while the assault team is systematically clearing the building. It also provides suppressive fire on adjacent buildings to prevent enemy reinforcements or withdrawal. The support team destroys any enemy trying to exit the building.

(c) After assault team 1 establishes a foothold in the building, a soldier from assault team 2 positions himself to provide security for the foothold. Assault team 1 proceeds to clear the first room.

- Soldier 1 throws a grenade into the room and yells "Frag out!" to alert friendly personnel a hand grenade has been thrown toward the enemy.

WARNING.

If walls and floor are thin, fragments from hand grenades can injure soldiers outside the room.

- After the grenade explodes, soldier 2 enters the room and positions himself to the left of the door, up against the wall, spraying the room with automatic fire and scanning the room from left to right. (Soldiers 1 and 3 provide outside room security.) Soldier 2 gives a voice command of "All clear" before soldier 3 enters the room.

- Soldier 3 shouts "Coming in" and enters the room. He positions himself to the right of the door, up against the wall and scans the room from right to left. (Soldier 2 provides inside room security and soldier 1 provides outside room security.).

- Soldier 1 positions himself up against the hall wall so he can provide security outside the room and can also observe into the room.

- Soldier 3 proceeds to clear the room while soldier 2 provides inside room security. Soldier 1 remains at his outside security position.

- After the room is cleared, the clearing team shouts "Coming

206

out" and proceeds to clear the next room(s). A soldier, from the second assault team positions himself to cover the cleared room. The cleared rooms are marked in accordance with (IAW) unit standing operating procedure (SOP).

- This procedure is continued until the entire floor is cleared.

(10) If the assault force is preparing to clear a building from the top floor down, they should gain entrance through a common wall or the roof of an adjoining building. Accompanied by the company's attached engineer squad, the force uses a demolition charge to breach the wall and to gain entrance to the top floor. Access to lower floors and rooms may be gained by breaching holes in the floor and having soldiers jump or slide down ropes to the lower floors. Stairs can be used if they are first cleared.

(11) When using the top-to-bottom method of clearing, security requirements remain the same as for other methods (Figure 2-106). After the floor is breached to gain access to a lower floor, a grenade is allowed to cook-off and is dropped to the lower room. A soldier then sprays the lower room with gunfire using three-round bursts and drops through the mousehole.

Figure 2-106. Upper floors secured

(12) Ensure your troops avoid clearing rooms the same way each time by having them vary techniques so the enemy cannot prepare for the assault (Figure 2-107). As rooms are cleared, doors should be left open and a predetermined mark (cloth, tape, spray paint) placed on the doorjamb or over the door.

207

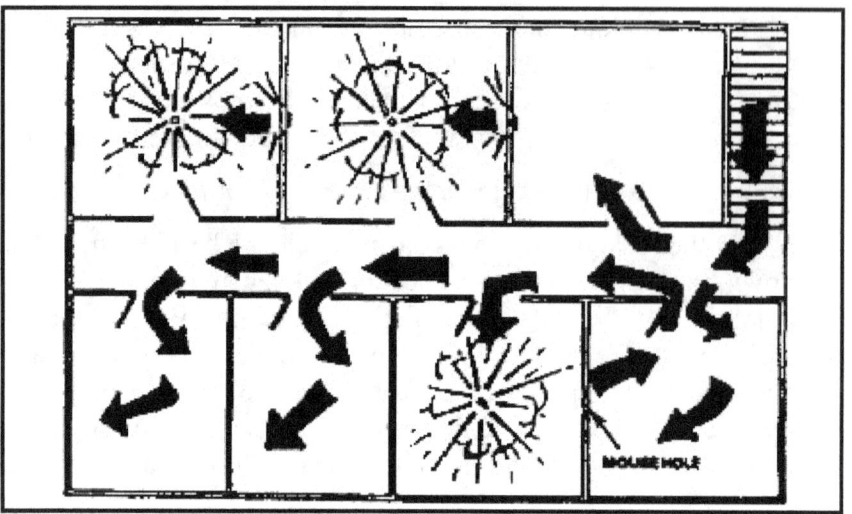

Figure 2-107. Varying techniques for clearing rooms

(13) If there is a basement, it should be cleared as soon as possible, preferably at the same time as the ground floor. The procedures for clearing a basement are the same as for any room or floor, but important differences do exist. Basements often contain entrances to tunnels such as sewers and communications cable tunnels. These should be cleared and secured to prevent the enemy from infiltrating back into cleared areas.

(14) The most common types of buildings encountered in clearing operations are brick buildings, brick houses, box-wall buildings, heavy-clad framed buildings, framed buildings, and light-clad framed buildings (Figure 2-108). The best way to enter a brick building is to blow a breaching hole in the side with a tank's main gun, firing HEAT ammunition. If tanks are not available, a door or window in the rear of the building usually provides better cover and concealment for entry than one in the front. If there is enough cover and concealment, the assault force can enter the rear of the building at an upper level using a fire escape or grappling hook.

Figure 2-108. Buildings being cleared

(a) To clear from building to building, the best method is to move from rooftop to rooftop, since the roofs of brick buildings are usually easy to breach. The walls between buildings are at least three bricks thick (a total of six bricks between buildings) and require large quantities of demolitions to breach. Walls are normally easier to breach on an upper floor than a lower floor since the walls are thinner on upper floors. If rooftops are covered by fire, and if there are not enough demolitions to breach walls between buildings, clearing from rear to rear of buildings is safer than clearing from front to front.

(b) The floor plans in brick buildings are different on ground floor levels than on upper levels (Figure 2-109).

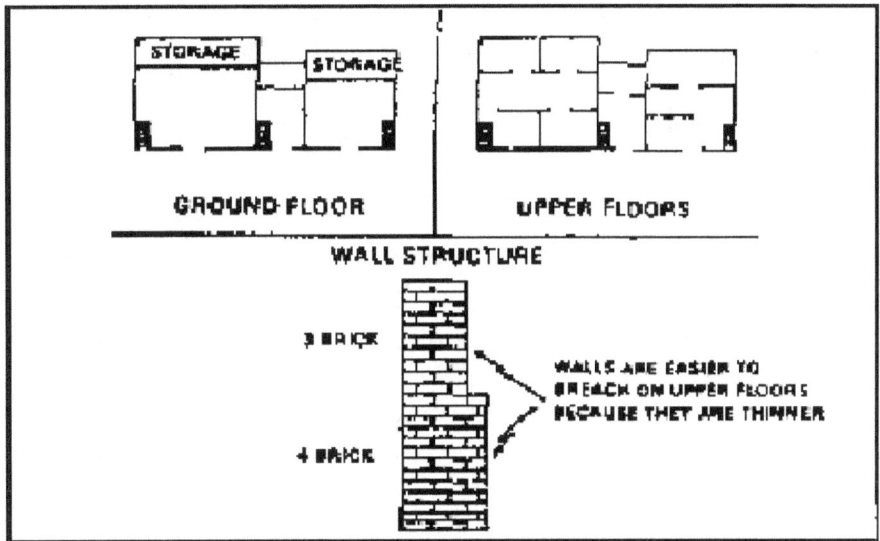

Figure 2-109. Floor plans of brick buildings

(15) Brick Houses. Brick houses have similar floor plans on each floor (Figure 2-110) therefore ground floors are cleared the same way as upper floors.

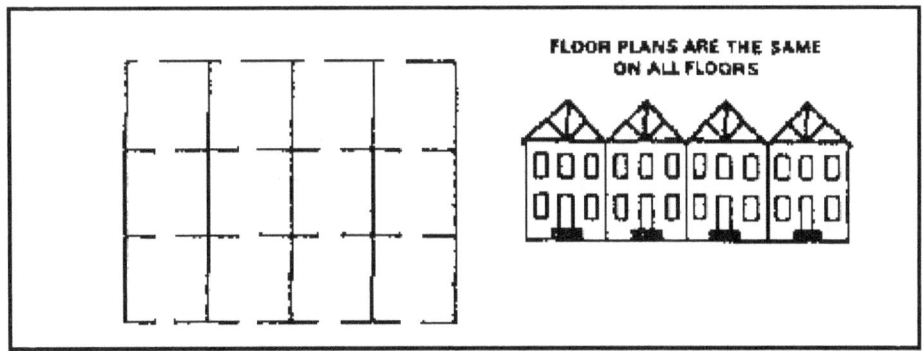

Figure 2-110. Similar floor plans

(16) Box-Wall Buildings. Box-wall buildings often have reinforced concrete walls (Figure 2-111), which are difficult to breach due to the

reinforcing bars. Therefore, the best way to enter is to blow down the door or to blow in one of the side windows. The floor plans of these buildings are predictable; clearing rooms is usually done from one main hallway. Interior walls are also constructed of reinforced concrete and are difficult to breach. The stairways at the ends of the building must be secured during clearing.

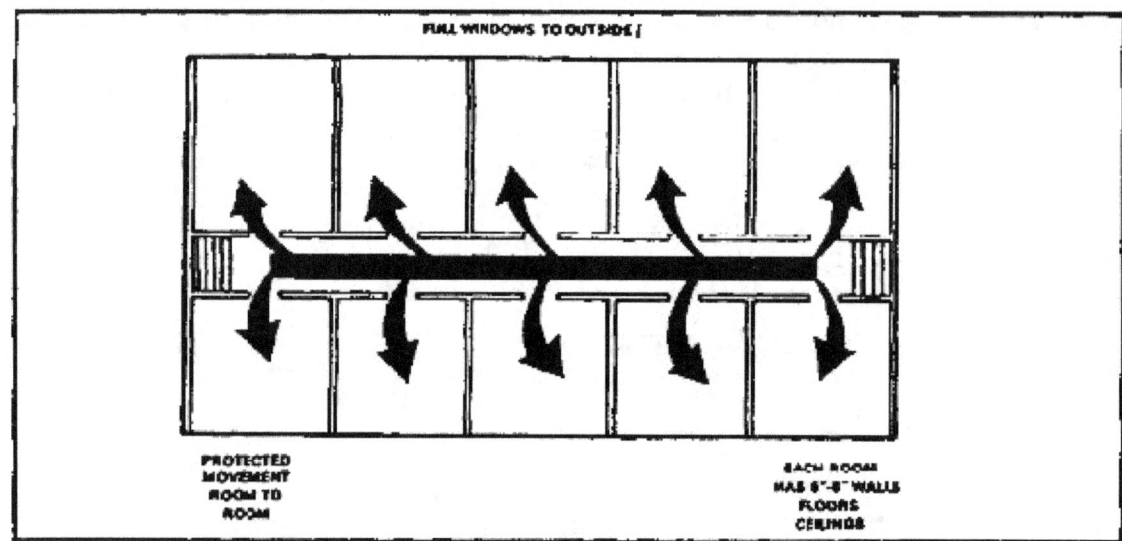

Figure 2-111. Box-wall principle buildings

(17) <u>Heavy-Clad Framed Buildings</u>. Heavy-clad framed buildings are relatively easy to breach, because a tank can breach a hole in the cladding (Figure 2-112). Their floor plans are oriented around a stairway or elevator, which must be secured during clearing. The interior walls of these buildings can be breached, although they may require use of demolitions.

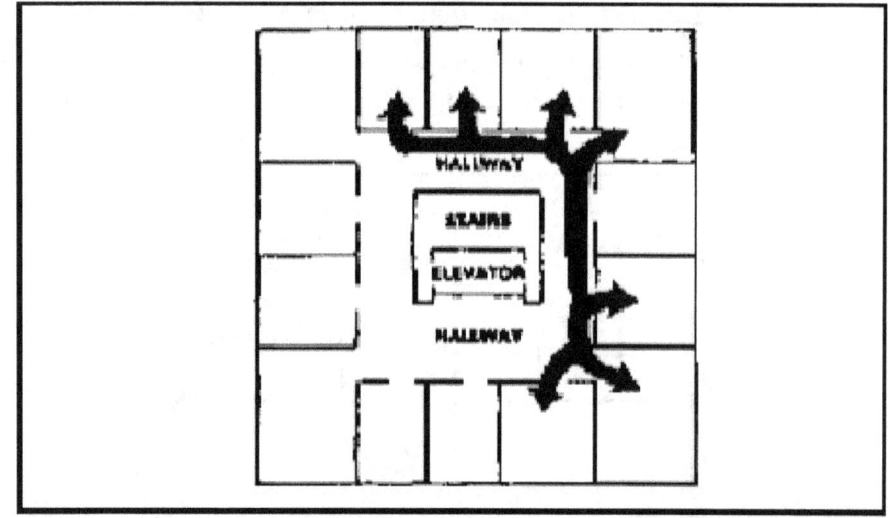

Figure 2-112. Heavy-clad framed buildings

(18) <u>Light-Clad Framed Buildings</u>. On light-clad framed buildings (Figure 2-113) the clearing tasks are usually the same: secure the central stairway

210

and clear in a circular pattern. Walls are easier to breach since they are usually thin enough to be breached with an axe.

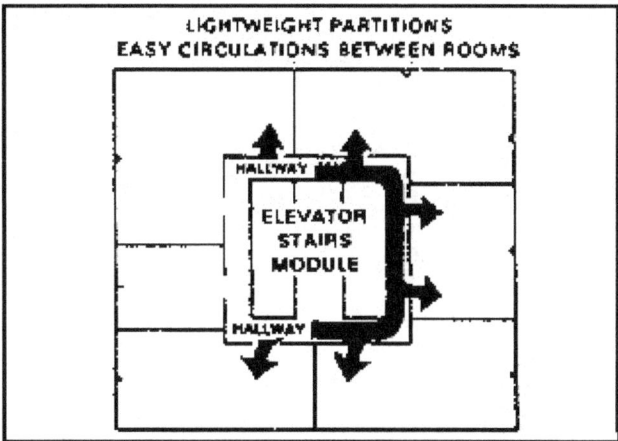

Figure 2-113. Light-clad framed building

e. <u>Reorganization</u>. Reorganization of the assault force in a cleared building must be quick to repel enemy counterattacks and to prevent the enemy from infiltrating back into the cleared building. After securing a floor (bottom, middle, or top), selected members of the assault force are assigned to cover potential enemy counterattack routes to the building. Those sentinels alert the assault force and place a heavy volume of fire on enemy forces approaching the building. They guard the following:

- Enemy mouseholes between adjacent buildings.
- Covered routes to the building.
- Underground routes into the basement.
- Approaches over adjoining roofs.

As the remainder of the assault force complete search requirements, assign them defensive positions. After the building has been cleared, the following actions are taken:

- Resupply and redistribute ammunition.
- Mark the building to indicate to friendly forces the building has been cleared.
- Assume an overwatch mission and support an assault on another building.
- Treat and evacuate wounded personnel.
- Develop a defensive position if the building is to be occupied for any period.